BA

THE MINI ROUGH GUIDE

There are more than one hundred Rough Guide travel,
phrasebook, and music titles, covering destinations
from Amsterdam to Zimbabwe, languages from Czech
to Thai, and musics from World to Opera and Jazz

Forthcoming titles include

Indonesia • New England • St Lucia • Toronto

Rough Guides on the Internet

www.roughguides.com

Rough Guide Credits

Text editor: Chris Schüler. Series editor: Mark Ellingham
Typesetting: James Morris
Cartography: Maxine Burke

Publishing Information

This first edition published January 1999 by
Rough Guides Ltd, 62–70 Shorts Gardens, London, WC2H 9AB

Distributed by the Penguin Group:

Penguin Books Ltd, 27 Wrights Lane, London W8 5TZ
Penguin Books USA Inc., 375 Hudson Street, New York 10014, USA
Penguin Books Australia Ltd, 487 Maroondah Highway,
PO Box 257, Ringwood, Victoria 3134, Australia
Penguin Books Canada Ltd, 10 Alcorn Avenue,
Toronto, Ontario, Canada M4V 1E4
Penguin Books (NZ) Ltd, 182–190 Wairau Road,
Auckland 10, New Zealand

Typeset in Bembo and Helvetica to an original design by Henry Iles.
Printed in Spain by Graphy Cems.

BANGKOK

THE MINI ROUGH GUIDE

by Paul Gray and Lucy Ridout

We set out to do something different when the first Rough Guide was published in 1982. Mark Ellingham, just out of university, was travelling in Greece. He brought along the popular guides of the day, but found they were all lacking in some way. They were either strong on ruins and museums but went on for pages without mentioning a beach or taverna. Or they were so conscious of the need to save money that they lost sight of Greece's cultural and historical significance. Also, none of the books told him anything about Greece's contemporary life – its politics, its culture, its people, and how they lived.

So with no job in prospect, Mark decided to write his own guidebook, one which aimed to provide practical information that was second to none, detailing the best beaches and the hottest clubs and restaurants, while also giving hard-hitting accounts of every sight, both famous and obscure, and providing up-to-the-minute information on contemporary culture. It was a guide that encouraged independent travellers to find the best of Greece, and was a great success, getting shortlisted for the Thomas Cook travel guide award, and encouraging Mark, along with three friends, to expand the series.

The Rough Guide list grew rapidly and the letters flooded in, indicating a much broader readership than had been anticipated, but one which uniformly appreciated the Rough Guide mix of practical detail and humour, irreverence and enthusiasm. Things haven't changed. The same four friends who began the series are still the caretakers of the Rough Guide mission today: to provide the most reliable, up-to-date and entertaining information to independent-minded travellers of all ages, on all budgets.

We now publish more than 100 titles and have offices in London and New York. The travel guides are written and researched by a dedicated team of more than 100 authors, based in Britain, Europe, the USA and Australia. We have also created a unique series of phrasebooks to accompany the travel series, along with an acclaimed series of music guides, and a best-selling pocket guide to the Internet and World Wide Web. We also publish comprehensive travel information on our Web site: **www.roughguides.com**

Help Us Update

We've gone to a lot of effort to ensure that this first edition of *The Rough Guide to Bangkok* is as up to date and accurate as possible. However, suggestions, comments or corrections are much appreciated.

We'll credit all contributions, and send a copy of the next edition (or any other Rough Guide if you prefer) for the best letters. Please mark letters "Rough Guide Bangkok Update" and send to:

Rough Guides, 62–70 Shorts Gardens, London, WC2H 9AB, or
Rough Guides, 375 Hudson St, New York NY 10014.
Or send email to: mail@roughguides.co.uk

Online updates about this book can be found on Rough Guides' Web site (see opposite)

The Authors

Paul Gray has been a regular visitor to Thailand since 1987, when he taught English for a year in Chiang Mai. He now works as a managing editor at the Rough Guide office in London, and is co-author of the *Rough Guide to Thailand*.

Lucy Ridout has spent most of the last decade travelling in and writing about Asia. She is co-author of the *Rough Guide to Thailand* and the *Rough Guide to Bali and Lombok*, and has also written a handbook for first-time travellers to Asia, called *First-Time Asia: A Rough Guide Special*.

Acknowledgements

The authors would like to thank the following people:

Apple and Noi in Kanchanaburi; Sumonta Nakornthab and Terri Yamaka at London TAT; Khun Satit, Khun Nongnit, Khun Apichai and Khun Supachai at Bangkok TAT; PJ Holt from Cambridge. Special thanks also to Margo Daly; Phil Cornwel-Smith; Paul Bateman; Jeff Cranmer and Steve Martin; and Chris Schüler for editing, James Morris for typesetting, Rosemary Morlin for proofreading and Maxine Burke for the cartography.

CONTENTS

Contents 259

Introduction

The headlong pace and flawed modernity of **Bangkok** match few people's visions of the capital of exotic Siam. Spiked with scores of high-rise buildings of concrete and glass, it's a vast flatness which holds a population of at least seven million, and feels even bigger. But under the shadow of the skyscrapers you'll find a heady mix of chaos and refinement, of frenetic markets and hushed golden temples, of early-morning almsgiving ceremonies and ultra hip designer boutiques.

Bangkok is a relatively young capital, established in 1782 after the Burmese sacked Ayutthaya, the former capital. A temporary base was set up on the western bank of the Chao Phraya River, in what is now Thonburi, before work started on the more defensible east bank, where the first king of the new dynasty, Rama I, built his fabulously ornate palace within a defensive ring of canals. He named this "royal island" **Ratanakosin**, and it remains the city's spiritual heart, not to mention its culturally most rewarding quarter. No visit to the capital would be complete without seeing Ratanakosin's four star attractions – if necessary, the **Grand Palace**, **Wat Phra Kaeo**, **Wat Po** and the **National Museum** can all be crammed into a single action-packed day.

Around the temples and palaces of the royal island spread an amphibious city of shops and houses built on bamboo rafts moored on the river and canals. Even though many of the canals have since been built over, one of the great pleasures of the city is a ride on its remaining waterways; the majestic **Chao Phraya River** is served by frequent ferries and longtail boats, and is the backbone of a network of canals and floating markets that remains fundamentally intact in the west-bank **Thonburi** district. Inevitably the waterways have earned Bangkok the title of "Venice of the East", a tag that seems all too apt when you're wading through flooded streets in the rainy season.

Bangkok began to assume its modern guise at the end of the nineteenth century, when the forward-looking Rama V relocated the royal family to a neighbourhood north of Ratanakosin called **Dusit**, constructing grand European-style boulevards, a new palace (still in use today), and a fine temple, Wat Benjamabophit (the "Marble Temple"). Since then, Bangkok has attracted mass migration from all over Thailand, pushing the city's boundaries ever eastwards in an explosion of modernization that has blown away earlier attempts at orderly planning and left the city without an obvious centre.

The capital now sprawls over 330 square kilometres and is far and away the country's most dominant city. Bangkokians own four-fifths of the nation's cars and the population is forty times that of the second city, Chiang Mai. London's *New Statesman* recently reported that Bangkok has the worst transport problems of any world city, and it boasts just 0.4 square metres of public parkland per inhabitant, the lowest figure in the world, compared, for example, to London's 30.4 square metres per person. Modern Bangkok is not without its beauty however, the sleek glass towers and cool marble malls lending an air of energy and big-city drama to the eastern districts of **Silom**, **Siam Square** and **Sukhumvit**.

North and west of the city, the unwieldy urban mass of Greater Bangkok peters out into the vast, well-watered central plains, a region that for centuries has grown the bulk of the nation's food. The atmospheric ruins of Thailand's fourteenth-century capital **Ayutthaya** lie here, ninety minutes' train ride from Bangkok and, together with the ornate palace at nearby **Bang Pa-In** make a rewarding excursion from the modern metropolis. Further west, the massive stupa at **Nakhon Pathom** and the traditional floating markets of **Damnoen Saduak** are also easily manageable as a day-trip, and combine well with an overnight stay at the town of **Kanchanaburi**, impressively sited on the River Kwai and location of several moving **World War II sites**, including the notorious Death Railway.

City of Angels

When Rama I was crowned in 1782, he gave his new capital a grand 43-syllable name to match his ambitious plans for the building of the city. Since then 21 more syllables have been added. Krungthepmahanakhornbowornrattanakosinmahintarayutthayamahadilokpopnopparatratchathaniburiromudomratchaniwetmahasathanamornpimanavatarnsathitsakkath-attiyavisnukarprasit is Guinness-certified as the longest place name in the world and roughly translates as "Great city of angels, the supreme repository of divine jewels, the great land unconquerable, the grand and prominent realm, the royal and delightful capital city full of nine noble gems, the highest royal dwelling and grand palace, the divine shelter and living place of the reincarnated spirits". Fortunately, all Thais refer to the city simply as Krung Thep, though plenty can recite the full name at the drop of a hat. Bangkok – "Village of the Plum Olive" – was the name of the original village on the Thonburi side; with remarkable persistence, it has remained in use by foreigners since the 1660s, when the French built a short-lived garrison fort in the area.

When to visit

Bangkok's climate is governed by three seasons. The **cool season**, which runs from November through February is the pleasantest time to visit; days are invariably bright and clear, and temperatures average a manageable 27°C (though they can still reach a broiling 31°C at midday). Not surprisingly this is peak season for the tourist industry, so it's well worth booking accommodation and flights in advance during this period; prices for hotel rooms are at their highest during this time, rising to a climax over Christmas and New Year. March sees the beginning of the **hot season**, when temperatures can rise to 36°C, and continue to do so beyond the end of April. During these sweltering months you'll probably be glad of an air-conditioned hotel room, and may find yourself spending more money than anticipated, simply because it's more comfortable to travel across the city in an air-conditioned taxi rather than sweat it out on foot (though air-con buses are a good compromise option). The daily downpours that characterize the **rainy season** can come as a welcome relief, though being hot and wet is a sensation that doesn't appeal to everyone. The rainy season varies in length and intensity from year to year, but usually starts with a bang in May, gathers force between June and August, and comes to a peak in September and October, when whole districts of the capital are flooded. Rain rarely lasts all day however, so as long as you're armed with an umbrella, there's no reason to reschedule your trip – and you'll get more for your money, too, as many hotels and airlines drop their prices right down at this time of year.

Bangkok's climate

	°F Average daily		°C Average daily		Rainfall Average monthly	
	MAX	MIN	MAX	MIN	IN	MM
Jan	83	70	28	21	2.6	66
Feb	83	69	28	21	1.1	28
March	85	70	29	21	1.3	33
April	86	72	30	22	1.4	36
May	87	73	31	23	2.3	58
June	87	74	31	23	4.4	112
July	86	74	30	23	5.8	147
Aug	87	74	31	23	5.8	147
Sept	87	74	31	23	6.7	170
Oct	86	73	30	23	7.0	178
Nov	85	73	29	23	8.1	206
Dec	83	71	28	22	3.8	97

BASICS

Getting there from Britain and Ireland

The fastest and most comfortable way of reaching Bangkok from the UK is to fly non-stop from **London** with either Qantas, British Airways, EVA Airways or Thai International – a journey time of about twelve hours. Many scheduled airlines operate indirect flights (ie flights with one or more connections), which usually take up to four hours longer, but work out significantly cheaper, particularly if you go with Lauda Air via Vienna, Kuwait Airways via Kuwait or Finnair via Helsinki. There are no non-stop flights from **Glasgow, Manchester, Dublin** or **Belfast**, only flights via other European cities, and fares generally work out about the same as for indirect flights from London.

Fares

The most expensive times to fly are July, August and December – you may have to book two to three months in advance for cheaper tickets during these peak periods. Discounted non-stop London–Bangkok return **fares** start at around £426 low season, rising to £670 during peak periods. Balkan Bulgarian usually comes out among the cheapest of the indirect flights, at £350 low season, £420 high season, but this involves a wait of four to six hours in Sofia; Aeroflot, Qatar Airways and Uzbekistan Airways prices are comparable. Kuwait Airlines via Kuwait range from about £418 to £523, and Finnair via Helsinki start from £459 in low season. Some agents offer special discounts (down to £405 return) with the more reputable airlines for full-time students and/or under-26s.

··

The Tourism Authority of Thailand (TAT) has offices at 49 Albemarle St, London W1, ©0839/300800. TAT's Web site is at *www.tat.or.th/*

··

Stopovers and RTW tickets

To make extra use of all that flying time and **stopover** on the way there or back, you'll probably have to go with the associated national airline – for example Air India for stops in Delhi or Bombay. This is an option which most airlines offer at the same price as their direct flights.

If you're planning a long trip with several stops in Asia or elsewhere, buying a **round–the–world** (RTW) **ticket** makes a lot of sense: a sample one-year open ticket, costing from £971, would depart and return to London, taking in two stops in Asia, one in Australia, two in the Pacific, and one in the US, perhaps leaving you to cover the Singapore–Bangkok and LA–New York legs overland.

AIRLINES AND DISCOUNT FLIGHT AGENTS

Airlines

Aeroflot ©0171/355 2233. Via Moscow.
Balkan Bulgarian Airways ©0171/637 7637. Via Sofia.
British Airways ©0345/222111. Daily non-stop flights.
EVA Airways ©0171/380 8300. Three non-stop flights a week.
Finnair ©0171/408 1222. Via Helsinki.

Kuwait Airways ✆0171/412 0007. Via Kuwait.
Lauda Air ✆0171/630 5924. Via Vienna.
Qantas ✆0345/747767. Daily non-stop flights.
Thai International ✆0171/499 9113. Daily non-stop flights.

Discount flight agents

UK

Apple Air ✆0181/741 7993. Balkan Bulgarian Airways flights.
Bridge the World ✆0171/911 0900.
Campus Travel London ✆0171/730 8111; and branches all over Britain.
Council Travel ✆0171/437 7767.
STA Travel London ✆0171/361 6262; Bristol ✆0117/929 4399; Cambridge ✆01223/366966; Manchester ✆0161/834 0668; Leeds ✆0113/244 9212; Oxford ✆01865/792800. Discount fares for students and under-26s.
Trailfinders London ✆0171/938 3939; branches in Birmingham, Bristol, Glasgow and Manchester.
Travel Bug Manchester ✆0161/721 4000.
Travel Cuts ✆0171/255 2082.
UniqueTravel ✆0171/495 4848. Cheap Aeroflot, Balkan Bulgarian, Qatar and Uzbekistan Airways flights.

IRELAND

Joe Walsh Tours Dublin ✆01/678 9555.
USIT Dublin ✆01/677 8117, 602 1777 or 678 9555; Cork ✆021/270900; and Belfast BT1 ✆01232/324073.
Trailfinders Dublin ✆01/677 7888.

GETTING THERE FROM BRITAIN AND IRELAND

Getting there from North America

There are no non-stop flights from North America to Bangkok, but plenty of airlines run daily flights from major east- and west-coast cities with only one stop. Excluding layovers, the actual **flying time** from LA via Asia is approximately eighteen hours, and from New York via Europe it's around nineteen hours. From Canada, travelling via Japan, you can expect to spend about sixteen hours in the air from Vancouver or 21 hours from Toronto.

Fares

Fares depend on the season, and are highest in December and January and from June through August. Expect to find regular, high-season published fares at $1110–1320 from the west coast and $1230–1410 from the east coast or the Midwest. Low-season fares go for $800–1050 from the west coast and $900–1150 from the east coast or Midwest. A discount travel agent, however, should be able to dig up a high-season fare from LA for around $1040, and special limited-offer promotional fares can bring low season fares down to as little as $735 from the west coast or $895 from the east coast.

Air Canada has the most convenient service to Bangkok from the largest number of **Canadian cities**, with stops in

Vancouver and Osaka. Expect to pay around CAN$1645 (low season) – CAN$1975 (high season) from Vancouver, and CAN$2045 – 2375 from Toronto.

The Tourism Authority of Thailand (TAT) has offices at 303 E Wacker Drive, Suite 400, Chicago, IL 60601 (✆312/819-3990); 3440 Wilshire Blvd, Suite 1100, Los Angeles, CA 90010 (✆213/382-2353); 5 World Trade Center, Suite 3443, New York, NY 10048 (✆212/432-0433); 55 University Ave #1208, Toronto, Ontario M5J 2H7 (✆416-364-3363); and 2840 West 6th Ave, Vancouver, BC V6K 1X1 (✆604-733-4540).
TAT's Web site is at *www.tat.or.th/*

Stopovers and RTW tickets

Circle Pacific deals allow you to make a certain number of **stopovers** and are generally valid for one year. Thai Airways' Asian Circle fare is offered as an add-on: for $360–$510 you can take in two to six extra Asian countries en route. Booking a Circle Pacific ticket through a discount travel agent, you're looking at around $2610 for Los Angeles round trip via Tokyo, Hong Kong, Bangkok, Singapore, Jakarta, Bali, Cairns, Sydney and LA, or as little as $1440 for New York return via Hong Kong, Bangkok, Jakarta, Bali and LA.

Typical off-the-shelf **round-the-world (RTW) tickets** include San Francisco round-trip via Hong Kong, Bangkok, Delhi, Bombay and London for $1480; and New York round-trip via Tokyo, Hong Kong, Bangkok, Singapore, Jakarta, Bali, Darwin, Sydney, Kuala Lumpur and Amsterdam for $2700.

GETTING THERE FROM NORTH AMERICA |

AIRLINES, DISCOUNT AGENTS AND CONSOLIDATORS

Airlines

Aeroflot ✆1-888/340-6400; Canada ✆514/288-2125.

Air Canada ✆1-800/776-3000. Daily via Osaka.

Air France ✆1-800/237-2747 or 212/247-0100; Canada ✆1-800/667-2747. Daily via Paris.

Canadian Airlines Canada ✆1-800/665-1177; US ✆1-800/426-7000.

Cathay Pacific ✆1-800/233-2742. Daily from New York and LA via Hong Kong.

China Air Lines ✆1-800/227-5118. Via Taipei from Los Angeles, San Francisco, New York and Anchorage.

Delta ✆1-800/241-4141. Daily via Seoul or Tokyo.

Finnair ✆1-800/950-5000; Canada ✆416/927-7400. From New York and Toronto via Helsinki.

Japan Air Lines ✆1-800/525-3663. Daily via Tokyo.

Malaysia Airlines ✆1-800/552-9264. Via Kuala Lumpur.

Northwest/KLM ✆1-800/374-7747; Canada ✆1-800/361-5073. Daily via Japan.

Singapore Airlines ✆1-800/742-3333. Daily via Singapore.

Swissair ✆1-800/221-4750; Canada ✆1-800/267-9477. Daily from Montréal, New York and Toronto via Zurich.

Thai Airways International ✆1-800/426-5204; Canada ✆1-800/668-8103. Daily from Los Angeles via Osaka.

United Airlines ✆1-800/538-2929. Daily via Tokyo.

Discount agents and consolidators

Air Brokers International ✆1-800/883-3273 or 415/397-1383; *www.airbrokers.com*

Air Courier Association ✆1-800/282-1202 or 303/215-0900;

www.aircourier.org Courier flight broker.

Airtech ✆1-800/575-8324 or 212/219-7000; *www.airtech.com* Standby seat broker, consolidator fares and courier flights.

Council Travel New York ✆1-800/226-8624, 888/COUNCIL or 212/822-2700; San Francisco ✆415/421-3473; Los Angeles ✆310/208-3551; Boulder ✆303/447-8101; Washington, DC ✆202/337-6464; Chicago ✆312/951-0585; Boston ✆617/266-1926.

Educational Travel Center ✆1-800/747-5551. Student/youth discount agent.

High Adventure Travel ✆1-800/350-0612 or 415/912-5600; *www.highadv.com*

STA Travel New York ✆1-800/777-0112 or 212/627-3111; Los Angeles ✆213/934-8722; San Francisco ✆415/391-8407; Boston ✆617/266-6014; Chicago ✆312/786-9050; Philadelphia ✆215/382-2928; Minneapolis ✆612/615-1800.

Travel Cuts US ✆1-888/238-2887; Toronto ✆1-800/667-2887 or 416/979-2406; Calgary ✆403/282-7687; Edmonton ✆403/488-8487; Montréal ✆514/843-8511; Vancouver ✆1-888/ FLY CUTS or 604/822-6890; Winnipeg ✆204/269-9530. Canadian student travel organization.

GETTING THERE FROM NORTH AMERICA

Getting there from Australia and New Zealand

There is no shortage of scheduled flights to Bangkok from Australia and New Zealand, with direct services being offered by Thai Airways, Qantas and Air New Zealand. Flight times are around 9 hours from Perth and Sydney, or around 11 hours from Auckland. In addition many Asian airlines can take you there via their home cities, which often works out cheaper than a direct flight.

Fares

Fares are structured according to season. High-season fares apply from mid-November to mid-January and May to the end of August, and cost about A/NZ$100–300 more than at other times. Direct flights **from Sydney** cost from A$1159 (low season) and A$1399 (high season) on Air New Zealand, Thai Airways or Qantas. Cheaper indirect flights start at A$920 – A$1199 on Royal Brunei, Garuda, Philippine Airlines, or Malaysia Airlines. Fares from **Perth** and **Darwin** work out about A$200 cheaper. Thai Airways offers the best direct fares from **Auckland**, for NZ$1299–

1499; indirect flights, with Garuda or Malaysia Airlines, start at NZ$1299. Expect to pay NZ$150–300 more from **Christchurch** and **Wellington**.

RTW tickets

There are a variety of **round-the-world** (RTW) combinations that include Bangkok. Qantas-Air France allows three free stops in each direction for around A$1699/NZ$2099, and Malaysia Airlines and Thai Airways offer routes via Bangkok and Kuala Lumpur for A$2399/NZ$2599. Cathay Pacific-UA's "Globetrotter", Air New Zealand-KLM-Northwest's "World Navigator" and Qantas-BA's "Global Explorer" all offer six free stopovers worldwide for A$2699–3299/NZ$3189–3799.

Travel via Indonesia

Australia's proximity to **Indonesia** makes this country the obvious starting point for overlanding through Asia, and the cheapest fares are from Darwin to Kupang in Timor with either Garuda or Merpati Airlines (A$198 single/A$330 return). From Kupang, you can island-hop all the way west to Malaysia and then on into Thailand: see Overland routes, p.14, for details.

Alternatively, you could fly from Australia to **Singapore** or **Malaysia** and then continue overland to Thailand. You can fly with Malaysian Airlines to Kuala Lumpur for

AIRLINES AND DISCOUNT TRAVEL AGENTS

Airlines

Air New Zealand Australia ✆13 2476; NZ ✆09/357 3000. From Auckland, Christchurch, Brisbane and Sydney.

Garuda Australia ✆02/9334 9944 & 1800/800 873; NZ ✆09/366 1855. Via Denpasar or Jakarta.

Malaysia Airlines Australia ✆13 2476; NZ ✆09/357 3000. Via Kuala Lumpur from Brisbane, Sydney, Melbourne, Perth and Auckland.

Qantas Australia ✆13 1211; NZ ✆09/357 8900 & 0800/808 767.

Royal Brunei Airlines Australia ✆02/9223 1566. Via Bandar Seri Begawan from Brisbane, Darwin and Sydney.

Singapore Airlines Australia ✆02/9350 0100 & 13 1011; NZ ✆09/379 3209. Daily from Sydney, Melbourne, Perth and Auckland, less frequently from Cairns, Brisbane, Christchurch and Darwin.

Thai Airways Australia ✆13 1960; New Zealand ✆1300/651960. Direct flights from Sydney, Brisbane, Melbourne, Perth and Auckland.

Discount travel agents

Anywhere Travel Sydney ✆02/9663 0411.

Brisbane Discount Travel Brisbane ✆07/3229 9211.

Budget Travel Auckland ✆09/366 0061 & 0800/808 040.

Destinations Unlimited Auckland ✆09/373 4033.

Discount Travel Specialists Perth ✆09/221 1400.

Flight Centres Australia ✆13 1600; NZ ✆09/309 6171.

Northern Gateway Darwin ✆08/8941 1394.

STA Travel www.statravelaus.com.au Australia ✆13 1776; New Zealand ✆09/309 0458.

Trailfinders Sydney ✆02/9247 7666.

Tymtro Travel Sydney ✆02/9223 2211 & 1300 652 969.

A\$950–1299; Royal Brunei Airlines and Garuda to Singapore or Kuala Lumpur for A\$899–1199; and Singapore Airlines to Singapore for A\$1099–1499.

Overland routes from southeast Asia

Thailand has land borders with Burma, Laos, Cambodia and Malaysia and works well as part of many overland itineraries, both across Asia and between Europe and Australia. Most passport holders should be able to get an on-the-spot thirty-day Thai transit **visa** at any of the land borders described below; see p.17 for details.

Malaysia and Singapore

It is possible to take a **train** all the way from **Singapore**, via **Malaysia** to Bangkok (1943km). The journey involves several changes, but the overall **Singapore–Bangkok** trip can be done in around 34 hours at a cost of about £60/US$90; trains leave at least once a day from both ends.

Plenty of **buses** also cross the Thai-Malaysian border every day. The southern Thai town of Hat Yai is the major transport hub for international bus connections, including Singapore (18hr; £8/US$12), Kuala Lumpur (12hr; £6/US$9), and Penang (6hr; £5/US$8); Hat Yai is 14–16hr from Bangkok by frequent buses and trains. You'll also find long-distance buses and minibuses to Bangkok, from Kuala Lumpur, Penang and Singapore, as well as in the reverse direction. **Ferries** connect Kuala Perlis and Langkawi in Malaysia with Satun in south Thailand.

Laos

There are currently five points along the **Laotian border** where it's permissible for tourists to cross into Thailand: Huay Xai to Chiang Kong; Vientiane to Nong Khai; Tha Khaek to Nakhon Phanom; Savannakhet to Mukdahan; and Pakse to Chong Mek. All these places have good rail and/or bus connections with Bangkok.

Details on how to obtain visas for southeast Asian countries in Bangkok are given on p.226.

Cambodia

Due to the serious possibility of being kidnapped, shot or robbed at gunpoint, most authorities are currently advising tourists against road or rail travel in **Cambodia**, which obviously makes overland routes in and out of Thailand seem dangerous too. However, at the time of writing, there are two legal **border crossings** between Cambodia and Thailand, but be sure to check with other travellers before opting for either crossing. The most commonly used crossing is at Poipet, which lies just across the border from the Thai town of Aranyaprathet and has reasonable transport connections with Sisophon, Siem Reap (for Angkor Wat) and Phnom Penh; buses and trains run between Aranyaprathet and Bangkok. At the time of writing, a new border crossing from Ko Kong Island to Thailand's Trat province had just been made legal. The safer alternative is to make use of the daily **flights** operated by Bangkok Airways between Phnom Penh and Bangkok and Siem Reap and Bangkok.

OVERLAND ROUTES FROM SOUTHEAST ASIA

Burma

At the time of writing, Western tourists are not allowed to cross between **Burma** and Thailand at Three Pagodas Pass near Kanchanaburi, at Myawaddy near Mae Sot, or at Mae Sai (except for a day-trip). However, foreign nationals may be able to cross in and out of Burma via Victoria Point and Ranong on the Andaman Coast.

Red tape and visas

There are three basic visa categories for entering Thailand. For stays of up to thirty days, most foreign passport holders automatically get a free non-extendable transit visa when passing through immigration at Don Muang Airport, at the Malaysian border or at the Laos border, but must show proof of onward travel arrangements: unless you have a confirmed bus, train or air ticket out of Thailand, you may well be put back on the next plane or sent back to get a sixty-day tourist visa from the Thai Embassy in Kuala Lumpur.

Thirty-day transit visas cannot be extended under any but the most exceptional circumstances. If you think you may want to stay longer, then from the outset you should apply for a **sixty-day tourist visa** from a Thai embassy or consulate, accompanying your application with your passport and two photos. The sixty-day visa costs £8 (UK), $15 (US) CAN$16.50 (Canada), A$18 (Australia). Because of a reciprocal arrangement with Thai immigration, New Zealanders (and nationals of South Korea, Sweden, Denmark, Norway and Finland) with a valid onward ticket get a free ninety-day visa.

Thai embassies will also accept applications for the slightly more expensive **ninety-day non-immigrant visas** (£15 in the UK) as long as you produce a letter of recommendation from an official Thai source (an employer or school principal for example) that explains why you need to be in the country for three months.

All sixty-day tourist visas can be extended for a further thirty days, at the discretion of officials; **extensions** cost B500 and are issued over the counter at immigration offices (*kaan khao muang*) across Thailand. For details of Bangkok's immigration office, see p.224. You'll need two extra photos, plus two photocopies of the first four pages and latest Thai visa page of your passport. If you use up the three-month quota, the quickest way of extending your stay is to head down to Malaysia and apply for another tourist visa at the embassy in Kuala Lumpur.

Immigration offices also issue **re-entry permits** (B500) if you want to leave the country and come back again within sixty days. If you **overstay** your visa limits, expect to be fined B100 per extra day when you depart Don Muang Airport, though an overstay of a month or more could land you in trouble with immigration officials.

THAI EMBASSIES AND CONSULATES ABROAD

Australia Optus Centre, Moore Street, Canberra ACT 2600 (✆02/6230 4200); plus consulates in Sydney, Adelaide, Brisbane, Melbourne, and Perth.

Canada 180 Island Park Drive, Ottawa, Ontario K1Y OA2 (✆613/722-4444); plus consulates in Vancouver, Montréal, Calgary and Toronto.

Malaysia 206 Jalan Ampang, 50450 Kuala Lumpur (✆03/248 8333); plus consulates in Kelantan and Penang.

New Zealand 2 Cook St, PO Box 17–226, Karori, Wellington (✆04/476 8619).

UK 29 Queens Gate, London SW7 (✆0891/600150 or 0171/589 2944); plus consulates in Birmingham, Cardiff, Glasgow, Hull and Liverpool.

US 1024 Wisconsin Ave, NW Washington, DC 20007 (✆202/944-3600 or 3608); plus consulates in Chicago, New York and Los Angeles.

Health

Thailand's climate, wildlife and cuisine present Western travellers with fewer health worries than in many Asian destinations. Bangkok **pharmacies** (*raan khai yaa*; daily 8.30am–8pm) are run by highly trained English-speaking pharmacists and are well stocked with local and international branded medicines. **Hospital** (*rong phayaabahn*) cleanliness and efficiency vary, but generally hygiene and health-care standards are good, and doctors usually speak English. In the event of a major health crisis, get someone to contact your embassy (see p.18) or insurance company – it may be best to get yourself flown home.

Inoculations

There are no compulsory **inoculation** requirements for people travelling to Thailand from the West, but it makes sense to ensure your polio and tetanus boosters are up to date (they last ten years); most doctors also strongly advise vaccinations against typhoid and hepatitis A.

For inoculation advice in the **UK** call up the pre-recorded 24-hour Travellers Health Line (℗0891/224100). In the **us**, contact the Travelers Medical Center, 31 Washington Square, New York, NY 10011 (℗212/982-1600); in **Canada** contact the International Association for Medical Assistance to Travellers, 40 Regal Rd, Guelph, Ontario N1K 1B5 (℗519/836-0102). In **Australia** and **New Zealand**, contact your nearest vaccination centre.

Mosquito-borne diseases

Only certain regions of Thailand are now considered to be malarial and **Bangkok is malaria-free**, so if you are restricting yourself to the capital you will not have to take malaria prophylactics. If you're going to other parts of the country, check with official sources first. Bangkok does however have it's fair share of **mosquitoes**, so you will probably want to take mosquito repellent with you (or buy it there from any supermarket or pharmacy); nearly all the city's hotels and guesthouses have screened windows.

A further reason to protect yourself from mosquitoes is the (remote) possibility of contracting **dengue fever**, a disease spread, unlike malaria, by mosquitoes that bite during daylight hours. There are occasional outbreaks of dengue fever in Bangkok, but there's no inoculation against it, and the only real cure for this viral disease is bed rest and non-asprin based painkillers. Symptoms often develop three weeks after visiting an area of infestation and include fever, a rash, headaches, and severe joint pain; it's rarely fatal.

HOSPITALS AND CLINICS IN BANGKOK

Bangkok Adventist Hospital 430 Phitsanulok Rd, ©281 1422.

Bangkok Christian Hospital 124 Silom Rd, ©233 6981.

Bangkok Nursing Home 9 Convent Rd, ©233 2610-9.

Clinic Banglamphu 187 Chakrabongse Rd, ©282 7479.

Dental Polyclinic 211–3 New Phetchaburi Rd, ©314 5070.

Pirom Pesuj Eye Hospital 117/1 Phaya Thai Rd, ©252 4141.

Travellers' Medical and Vaccination Centre 8th floor, Alma Link Building, 25 Soi Chitlom, Ploenchit Road, ©655 1024-5; fax 655 1026. General clinic, plus vaccinations and malaria advice.

HEALTH

Digestive problems

Digestive troubles are often caused by contaminated food and water, or sometimes just by an overdose of unfamiliar foodstuffs. Break your system in gently by avoiding excessively spicy curries and too much raw fruit in the first few days, and then use your common sense about choosing where and what to eat: any crowded restaurant or popular noodle stall should be perfectly safe. Stick to **bottled water**, which is sold everywhere, or else opt for boiled water or tea.

Stomach trouble usually manifests itself as diarrhoea, which is best combated by drinking lots of fluids. If this doesn't work, you're in danger of getting **dehydrated** and should take some kind of rehydration solution, either a commercial sachet sold in all Thai pharmacies or a do-it-yourself version which can be made by adding a handful of sugar and a pinch of salt to every litre of boiled or bottled water (soft drinks are *not* a viable alternative).

Rabies

Between four and seven percent of dogs in Bangkok are reported to be rabid, so steer clear of them whenever possible as **rabies** is transmitted by bites and scratches; cats and monkeys also carry rabies. If you are bitten or scratched, clean and disinfect the wound, preferably with alcohol, and if you suspect the animal might be infected you should seek medical advice right away.

HEALTH

Money, banks and costs

Thailand's unit of currency is the baht (abbreviated to "B"), which is divided into 100 satang. Notes come in B10, B20, B50, B100, B500 and B1000 denominations, and coins in 25 satang, 50 satang, B1, B5 and B10 denominations.

Following the drastic decline in the value of the Thai baht in 1997, the currency has been volatile, but at the time of writing the **exchange rate** was averaging B42 to US\$1 and B69.5 to £1.

Banking hours are Monday to Friday 8.30am–3.30pm, but exchange kiosks in the main tourist centres are always open till at least 5pm, sometimes 10pm, and upmarket hotels will change money 24 hours a day. The **Don Muang airport exchange counters** also operate 24 hours.

Travellers' cheques and credit cards

The safest way to carry your money is in sterling or dollar **travellers' cheques**, which are accepted at banks, exchange booths and many upmarket hotels across the city. All issuers give you a list of numbers to call in the case of **lost or stolen cheques** and will refund if you can produce the original receipts and a note of your cheque numbers, usually within 24 hours.

American Express, Visa, Mastercard and Diners Club **credit cards** and **charge cards** are accepted at top hotels as well as in some posh restaurants, department stores, tourist shops and travel agents, but surcharging of up to five percent is rife, and theft and forgery are major industries – always demand the carbon copies and destroy them immediately, and never leave cards in baggage storage. If you have a PIN number for your card, you should also be able to **withdraw cash** from the city's 24-hour ATMs ("automatic teller machines" or cashpoints) – call the issuing bank or credit company to find out which Thai bank's ATMs accept it. There's usually a handling fee of 1.5 percent on every withdrawal.

Costs

In a country where the daily minimum wage is under B150 a day, it's hardly surprising that Western tourists find Thailand an extremely inexpensive place to travel. At the bottom of the scale, you could manage on a **daily budget** of about B300–400 if you're willing to opt for basic accommodation and eat, drink and travel as the locals do. With extras like air conditioning, taxis, and a meal and a couple of beers in a more touristy restaurant, a day's outlay will rise to a minimum of B800. Staying in expensive hotels and eating in the more exclusive restaurants, you should be able to live in extreme comfort for around B2000 a day.

The economic crisis of late 1997 has wrought havoc on the cost of living in Thailand and, at the time of writing, prices are in a state of flux, so you may find that some of the **prices in this guide** have since risen quite considerably. Some tourist-oriented businesses have already started quoting their prices in dollars, particularly luxury hotels. **Bargaining** is expected practice for a lot of commercial transactions, particularly at markets and when hiring tuk-tuks and taxis. It's a delicate art that requires humour, tact, patience – and practice. If your price is way out of line, the vendor's vehement refusal should be enough to make you increase your offer.

MONEY, BANKS AND COSTS

Opening hours and festivals

Most shops open at least Monday to Saturday from about 8am to 8pm, and department stores operate daily from around 10am to 9pm. Usual office hours are Monday to Friday 8am–5pm and Saturday 8am–noon, though in tourist areas these hours are longer, with no break at weekends. Government offices work Monday to Friday 8.30am–noon and 1pm–4.30pm.

Nearly all Thai **festivals** have some kind of religious aspect. The most theatrical are generally **Brahmin** in origin, honouring elemental spirits with ancient rites and ceremonial parades. **Buddhist** celebrations usually revolve round the local temple (wat) and a light-hearted atmosphere prevails, as the wat grounds are swamped with food- and trinket-vendors and makeshift stages are set up to show *likay* folk theatre. Few of the **dates** for religious festivals are fixed (see box), so check with TAT for specifics.

Thais use both the Western Gregorian calendar and a **Buddhist calendar** – the Buddha is said to have died in the year 543 BC, so Thai dates start from that point: thus 1999 AD becomes 2542 BE (Buddhist Era).

NATIONAL HOLIDAYS AND FESTIVALS

Festivals marked with an asterisk are national holidays, when banks and offices close for the duration.

* **January 1** Western New Year's Day.
* **February Full Moon Day** *Maha Puja.* A day of merit-making marks the occasion when 1250 disciples gathered spontaneously to hear the Buddha preach. Best experienced at Wat Benjamabophit, where the festival culminates with a candlelit procession round the temple.
* **late February to mid-April** Frequent kite fights and kite-flying contests in Sanam Luang. Kites are judged both for their beauty, and for their fighting prowess as one team tries to ensnare the other team's kite in mid-air.
* **April 6** Chakri Day. The founding of the Chakri dynasty.
* **April, usually 13–15** *Songkhran,* Thai New Year. The most exuberant of the national festivals welcomes the Thai New Year with massive public waterfights in the streets of the capital (and across the country) and big parades.
* **May 5** Coronation Day.
* **early May** *Raek Na,* Royal Ploughing Ceremony. The royal ploughing ceremony marks the beginning of the rice-planting season. Ceremonially clad Brahmin priests parade sacred oxen and the royal plough across Sanam Luang and forecast the year's rice yield.
* **May Full Moon Day** *Visakha Puja.* The holiest day of the Buddhist year, commemorating the birth, enlightenment and death of the Buddha all in one go. The most public and photogenic part is the candlelit evening procession around Wat Benjamabophit.
* **July Full Moon Day** *Asanha Puja.* Commemorates the Buddha's first sermon.
* **July, the day after** *Asanha Puja Khao Pansa.* The start of the annual three-month Buddhist rains retreat, when new monks are ordained.

OPENING HOURS AND FESTIVALS

* **August 12** Queen's birthday.
* **October 23** Chulalongkorn Day. The anniversary of Rama V's death.

October Full Moon Day *Tak Bat Devo*. Devotees at temples across the city make offerings to monks and there's general merrymaking to celebrate the end of the Buddhist retreat period.

late October or early November *Loy Krathong*. One of Thailand's most picturesque festivals, when banana-leaf baskets of flowers and lighted candles are floated on *khlongs*, ponds and rivers all over Thailand to honour water spirits and celebrate the end of the rainy season.

first week of November *Ngan Wat Saket*. Probably Thailand's biggest temple fair, held around Wat Saket (see p.83) and the Golden Mount with all the usual festival trappings.

* **December 5** King's birthday.
* **December 10** Constitution Day.
* **December 31** Western New Year's Eve.

Cultural hints

Tourist literature has so successfully marketed Thailand as the "Land of Smiles" that a lot of foreigners arrive in the country expecting to be forgiven any outrageous behaviour. This is just not the case: there are some things so universally sacred in Thailand that even a hint of disrespect will cause deep offence.

The monarchy

The worst thing you can possibly do is to bad-mouth the **royal family**. The monarchy might be a constitutional one, but almost every household displays a picture of King Bhumibol and Queen Sirikit, and respectful crowds amass whenever either of them makes a public appearance. You should also be prepared to stand when the **king's anthem** is played at the beginning of every cinema programme. A less obvious point: as the king's head features on all Thai currency, you should never step on a coin or banknote, which is tantamount to kicking the king in the face.

Religion

Buddhism plays an essential part in the lives of most Thais, and Buddhist monuments should be treated accordingly – which basically means wearing long trousers or knee-length skirts, covering your upper arms, and removing your shoes whenever you visit one. All **Buddha images** are sacred and should never be clambered over or treated in any manner that could be construed as disrespectful.

Monks come only just beneath the monarchy in the social hierarchy, and are treated with deference. Theoretically, monks are forbidden to have any close contact with **women**, which means, as a female, you mustn't sit or stand next to a monk, or even brush against his robes; if it's essential to pass him something, put the object down so that he can then pick it up – never hand it over directly. **Nuns**, however, get treated like women rather than like monks.

The body

The Western liberalism embraced by the Thai sex industry is very unrepresentative of the majority Thai attitude to the body. **Clothing** – or the lack of it – is what bothers Thais most about tourist behaviour. You should dress modestly in all public places (see p.27) and, stuffy and sweaty as it sounds, keep shorts and vests for the beach.

According to ancient Hindu belief the head is the most sacred part of the **body** and the feet the most unclean. This means that it's very rude to touch a Thai person's head or to point your feet either at a human being or at a sacred image – when sitting on a temple floor, for example, you should tuck your legs beneath you rather than stretch them out towards the Buddha.

On a more practical note, the **left hand** is used for washing after defecating, so Thais never use it to put food in their mouth, pass things or shake hands – as a foreigner though, you'll be assumed to have different customs, so left-handers shouldn't worry unduly.

Social conventions

In fact, Thais very rarely shake hands anyway, using the **wai** to greet and say goodbye and to acknowledge respect, gratitude or apology. A prayer-like gesture made with raised hands, the *wai* changes according to the relative status of the two people involved: Thais can instantaneously assess which *wai* to use when, but as a foreigner your safest bet is to go for the "stranger's" *wai*, which requires that your hands be raised close to your chest and your fingertips placed just below your chin. If someone makes a *wai* at you, you should definitely *wai* back, but it's generally wise not to initiate.

Public displays of **physical affection** in Thailand are much more acceptable between friends of the same sex than between lovers, whether hetero- or homosexual. Holding hands and hugging is as common among male friends as with females, so if you're given fairly intimate caresses by a Thai acquaintance of the same sex, don't assume you're being propositioned.

THE GUIDE

INTRODUCING
THE CITY

Bangkok is sprawling, chaotic and exhausting: to do it justice and to keep your sanity, you need time, boundless patience and a bus map. The place to start is **Ratanakosin**, the royal island on the east bank of the Chao Phraya, where the city's most important and extravagant sights are to be found. On the edges of this enclave, the area around the landmark **Democracy Monument** includes some interesting and quirky religious architecture, forming a strong contrast with neighbouring **Chinatown**, whose markets pulsate with the aggressive business of making money. Quieter and more European in ambience are the stately buildings of the new royal district of **Dusit**, 2km northeast of Democracy Monument. Very little of old Bangkok remains, but the back canals of **Thonburi**, across the river from Ratanakosin and Chinatown, retain a traditional feel quite at odds with the modern high-rise jungle of **downtown Bangkok**, which has evolved across on the eastern perimeter of the city and can take an hour to reach by bus from Ratanakosin. It's here that you'll find the best **shops**, **bars**, **restaurants** and **nightlife**, as well as a couple of worthwhile sights.

Greater Bangkok now covers an area some 30km in diameter and though unsightly urban development predominates, an expedition to the **outskirts** is made worthwhile by **Chatuchak**, the city's largest market, a couple of interesting outdoor museums, and the chance to visit a peaceful suburb on the river.

**The telephone code for Bangkok is ℡02.
Calling Bangkok from abroad, dial ℡00-66-2,
followed by the subscriber's number.**

Arrival

Getting to your guesthouse or hotel on arrival in gridlocked Bangkok is unlikely to put you in a good mood, and unless you arrive by train, you should be prepared for a long slog into the centre. For most travellers, however, their first sight of the city is **Don Muang Airport**, a slow 25km to the north.

By air

Once you're through immigration at either of Don Muang Airport's two interconnected international terminals – queues are often horrendous, owing to the availability of free short-stay visas on the spot – you'll find a panoply of facilities, including 24-hour exchange booths, a helpful TAT information desk (daily 8am–midnight; ℡523 8972), post office and international telephone facilities, a left-luggage depot (B40 per item per day), an emergency clinic and, on the fourth floor of newer Terminal 2 opposite *Pizza Hut*, an expensive cybercafé. Among a wide variety of **food and drink** outlets – particularly in Terminal 2, which boasts Chinese and Japanese restaurants, and a British pub that offers 24-hour breakfasts – the cheapest and most interesting options are two food centres serving simple Thai dishes, one on the walkway between Terminal 2 and the domestic terminal, the other on the fourth floor, accessible from Terminals 1 and 2. You can **rest** and clean up at the international terminals' day rooms ($35 for 1–4hr without bath, $45 with bath) or at the *Amari Airport Hotel* (ℭ566 1020, fax 566 1941) just across the road, which has very upmarket bedrooms available for three-hour periods (B780) from 8am to 6pm, as well, of course, as overnight.

Note that you'll have problems checking in at some of the smaller, more budget-oriented guesthouses after 10pm (nightwatchmen aren't usually authorized to admit new arrivals), so if you're arriving after about 8pm, either hole up in the *We-Train* guesthouse (ℭ929 2301-10, fax 929 2300) near the airport, or resign yourself to shelling out for a pricey hotel room for your first night: a round-the-clock Thai Hotels Association **accommodation desk** can help with bookings.

The domestic terminal at Don Muang is 500m away from Terminal 2, connected by an air-conditioned covered walkway and by a free shuttle bus (daily 5am–11pm; every 20min).

Getting into town from the airport

The most economical way of getting into the city is by **public bus**, but this can be excruciatingly slow and the invariably crowded vehicles are totally unsuitable for heavily laden travellers. The bus stop is on the main highway which runs north–south just outside the airport buildings: to find it, head straight out from the northern end of arrivals. Ordinary buses run all day and night, with a reduced service after 10pm; the slightly more expensive air-conditioned buses stop running around 8.30pm. See the box on p.44 for a rough sketch of the most useful routes – the TAT office in arrivals has further details.

Unless you're already counting your baht, you're better off getting into the city by air-conditioned **airport bus**. Three routes are covered, each with a departure every half-hour between about 5am and 11pm from outside Terminal 1, Terminal 2 and the domestic terminal (clearly signposted outside each building); the set fare of B70 is paid on the bus. Route A1 runs along to the west end of Silom Road, via Pratunam and Rajdamri Road; route A2 goes to Sanam Luang, via Victory Monument, Phrayathai Road, Phetchaburi Road, Lan Luang Road, Democracy Monument, Tanao Road (for Khao San Road), Phra Sumen Road and Phra Athit Road; route A3 runs along Sukhumvit Road to Soi Thonglor via the Eastern Bus Terminal.

The **train** to Hualamphong Station is the quickest way into town, and ideal if you want to stay in Chinatown, but services are irregular. To reach the station at Don Muang follow the signs from arrivals in Terminal 1 (if in doubt head towards the big *Amari Airport Hotel*, across the main highway, carry on through the hotel foyer and the station is in front of you). More than thirty trains a day make the fifty-minute trip to Hualamphong, with fares starting from B5 in third class (though express trains command surcharges of up to B50), but they're not evenly spaced, with concentrations around the early morning – at other times of the day you might have to wait over an hour.

Taxis to the centre are comfortable, air-conditioned and not too extravagantly priced, although the driving can be hairy. A wide variety is on offer, from pricey limousines, through licensed metered and unmetered cabs, down to cheap unlicensed vehicles – avoid the last-mentioned, as newly arrived travellers are seen as easy victims for robbery, and the cabs are untraceable. Licensed taxis, the best option, are operated from counters that are signposted clearly outside Terminal 1. You can choose either a pre-determined fare in an unmetered cab – B250 and up, depending on which side of town you're aiming for – or a metered cab, which unless the traffic's heavy is usually less expensive. That's not quite the end of the story: you'll also be expected to stump up B50 in tolls for the overhead expressways which cut up to an hour off your journey.

By train

Travelling to Bangkok by **train** from Malaysia and most parts of Thailand, you arrive at **Hualamphong Station**, which is centrally located and served by numerous **city buses** – the most useful being bus #53 (non-air-con), which stops on the east side (left-hand exit) of the station and runs to the budget accommodation in Banglamphu, and #25 and #40 (both non-air-con), which run to Sukhumvit Road. The station is also well placed for **long-tail boats** to Banglamphu, with a stop beside the bridge just 30m to the right of the main station entrance – the regular service will take you to the bridge in front of Banglamphu's New World department store or the terminus 100m further west in fifteen minutes (daily 6.15am–7pm; every 20min; B6).

Station **facilities** include an exchange booth by Platform 8 (open daily until 5pm) and cashpoint machines, a post office and a free accommodation-booking service offered by the State Railway's Pacto PC&C travel agent (daily 5am–8pm; ©226 5711) in Room 100, close by the news-

37

paper stands – service is friendly and efficient, they can do good deals on some mid-range hotels (not Banglamphu), and they sell train, plane and bus tickets. The left-luggage office (daily 4am–10.30pm) charges B40 per item per day and will keep baggage for several months at a time.

By bus

Long-distance **buses** to Bangkok come to a halt at a number of far-flung spots: services from Malaysia and the south use the Southern Terminal at the junction of Pinklao and Nakhon Chaisri roads in Thonburi; services from the north and northeast come in at the new Northern Terminal (Moh Chit 2) on Kamphaeng Phet 2 Road; and most buses from the east coast use the Eastern Terminal at Soi 40, Sukhumvit Road. All of these will leave you with a long bus, tuk-tuk or taxi ride into town; for the main city bus routes serving the regional bus terminals see the box on p.44.

Orientation

Bangkok can be a tricky place to get your bearings as it's vast and flat, with largely featureless modern buildings and no obvious centre. The boldest line on the map is the **Chao Phraya River**, which divides the city into Bangkok proper on the east bank, and **Thonburi**, recently incorporated into Greater Bangkok, on the west.

The historic core and site of the original royal palace is **Ratanakosin**, which nestles into a bend in the river. Three concentric canals radiate eastwards around Ratanakosin: the southern part of the area between the canals is the old-style trading enclave of **Chinatown** and Indian **Pahurat**, linked to the old palace by New Road; the northern part is characterized by old temples and the **Democracy Monument**.

Beyond the canals to the north, **Dusit** is the site of many government buildings and the nineteenth-century palace, which is linked to Ratanakosin by Rajdamnoen Road.

"New" Bangkok begins to the east of the canals and beyond the main rail line, and stretches as far as the eye can see to the east and north. The main business district and most of the embassies are south of **Rama IV Road**, with the port of Khlong Toey at the southern edge. The diverse area north of Rama IV Road includes the sprawling campus of Chulalongkorn University, huge shopping centres around **Siam Square** and a variety of other businesses. Due north of Siam Square stands the tallest building in Bangkok, the *Baiyoke Tower Hotel* – its distinctive rainbow colour scheme makes it a good point of reference. To the east lies the swish residential quarter off **Sukhumvit Road**.

BANGKOK ADDRESSES

Thai **addresses** can be confusing as property is often numbered twice, firstly to show which real estate lot it stands in, and then to distinguish where it is on that lot. Thus 154/7–10 Rajdamnoen Rd means the building is on lot 154 and occupies numbers 7–10.

A minor road running off a major road is often numbered as a **soi** ("lane" or "alley", though it may be a sizeable thoroughfare), rather than be given its own street name. Sukhumvit Road, for example, has minor roads numbered Soi 1 to Soi 103, with odd numbers on one side of the road and even on the other; so a Sukhumvit Road address could read something like 27/9–11 Soi 15 Sukhumvit Rd, which would mean the property occupies numbers 9–11 on lot 27 on minor road number 15 running off Sukhumvit Road.

ORIENTATION

Information and maps

As well as the booth in the airport arrivals concourse, the **Tourism Authority of Thailand** (**TAT**) maintains an information office within walking distance of Banglamphu, at 4 Rajdamnoen Nok (daily 8.30am–4.30pm; ©281 0422), a twenty-minute stroll from Khao San Road, or accessible by bus AC#3, AC#9 or AC or non-AC#15. TAT has plenty of handouts about Bangkok, as well as a guide to officially approved shops. Other useful sources of information, especially about what to avoid, are the travellers' **noticeboards** in many of the Banglamphu guesthouses.

If you're staying in Bangkok for more than a couple of days and want to get the most out of the city, it's worth getting hold of *Metro*, a monthly **listings magazine** available in bookstores, hotel shops and 7–11 shops. For B100, you get a mixed bag of lively articles and especially useful sections on restaurants, cinemas, nightlife and gay life. The two English-language dailies, the *Nation* and the *Bangkok Post*, also give limited information about what's on across the city and carry details of cinema showings. Thailand is fairly well represented on the Internet, and some of the most useful **Web sites** are listed in the box below.

BANGKOK ON THE INTERNET

General Thailand resources

Rough Guides *www.roughguides.com* Regularly updated travel site, with forums, features and plenty of links.

Siam Net *www.siam.net/guide/* Decent jumping-off point, with general background on Thailand and its main tourist centres, plus links to some hotels.

Tourism Authority of Thailand (TAT) *www.tat.or.th/* The official

TAT site has general background on Thailand, plus links to accommodation and other standard stuff.

Travellers' resources and bulletin boards

hello café *www.hellocafe.com/* Bangkok's best Internet café runs a good traveller-oriented site, which hosts a travellers' tips forum, a message board and handy links.

Internet Travel Information Service *www.itisnet.com* Specifically aimed at budget travellers, this fairly new site includes weekly reports from the road, so there's heaps of up-to-the-minute info on things like current air fares and visa requirements.

Rec. travel Asia *rec.travel.asia* A Usenet forum that deals exclusively with Asian travel.

Lonely Planet Thorn Tree *www.lonelyplanet.com/thorntree/ thorn.htm* Highly recommended travellers' bulletin boards, divided into regions (eg mainland Southeast Asia). Ideal for exchanging information with other travellers and for starting a debate.

Online publications

Bangkok Metro *bkkmetro.com* The online version of Bangkok's monthly listings magazine includes archives of features, restaurant and club listings, plus readers' letters.

Bangkok Post *www.bangkokpost.net* The day's main stories from Thailand's leading English-language daily, plus archive headlines for the last two months, and travel stories. Free access to all. Recommended.

The Nation *www.nationgroup.com/* Thailand's other major English language daily has a lively site that includes headline stories and message boards on hot topics such as the state of the Thai economy.

BANGKOK ON THE INTERNET

Maps

To get around Bangkok without spending much money, you'll need to buy a colour **bus map**. Two similar versions (produced by rival map companies) are widely available from Bangkok guesthouses and bookshops; both maps are designed on blue backgrounds and both show ordinary and air-conditioned routes, as well as the names of dozens of streets and sois (side roads). Street locations are not always reliable however, and it can be hard to decipher exact bus routings. *Litehart's Groovy Map and Guide* pride themselves on marking their bus routes much more clearly – they are nicely colour coded for ease of use – but only select routes are given, which is not much good if you find yourself stranded and wanting to know where a particular bus is heading. The most accurate map for locating small streets and places of interest in the city is *GeoCenter's Bangkok 1:15,000*, best bought before you leave home, but also available in some Bangkok bookshops. Serious shoppers might also want to buy a copy of *Nancy Chandler's* idiosyncratic map of Bangkok, available in most tourist areas.

City transport

There can be few cities in the world where **transport** is such a headache as it is in Bangkok. Bumper-to-bumper vehicles create fumes so bad that a recent spot check revealed forty percent of the city's traffic policemen to be in need of hospital treatment, and it's not unusual for residents to spend three hours getting to work – and these are people who know where they're going. Although several mass-transit systems have been under discussion for over thirty years – and the pillars and lines for a downtown overhead railway have even been erected – the economic crisis of 1997 has severely hampered real progress. For now, water-borne transport provides the least arduous means of hopping from one site to another, but you're best advised to have low expectations of how much can be done in a day, and to find accommodation in the areas where you want to spend most time.

The main form of transport in the city is **buses**, and once you've mastered the labyrinthine complexity of the route map you'll be able to get to any part of the city, albeit slowly. Catching the various kinds of **taxi** can make a dent in your budget, and you'll still get held up by the daytime traffic jams. **Boats** are obviously more limited in their range, but they're regular and as cheap as buses, and you'll save a lot of time by using them whenever possible – a journey between Banglamphu and the GPO, for instance, will take around thirty minutes by water, half what it would take on land. **Walking** might often be quicker than travelling by road, but the heat can be unbearable, distances are always further than they look on the map, and the engine fumes are stifling. **Renting a car** is possible (see p.221), but is best kept for out-of-town trips – city traffic jams are just too much to cope with, and parking is impossible. As there are some novel rules of the road, it would be better to get a car with driver from a travel agent or hotel for about B1000 a day.

For each sight in the city, we've given numbers of the most useful buses that run past, or at least within a fifteen-minute walk, and details of boat transport, if any. The routes of all the bus numbers mentioned are outlined in the box on p.44, but for the full, highly complex, picture you'll need to get hold of a bus map (see p.42).

Buses

Bangkok has three types of bus service, and it's not uncommon for one route to be served by the full trio. **Ordinary** (non-air-conditioned) buses come in a variety of colours and sizes, and fares for most journeys range from B2 to B3, though on some services you can pay as little as B1 or up to B5.50. The minimum fare on the blue, advertisement-carrying **air-conditioned** buses is B6; after the first 8km the fare rises in B2 stages to a maximum of B16, reflecting the distance travelled. As buses can only go as fast as the car in front, which at the moment is averaging 4kph, you'll probably be spending a long time on each journey, so you'd be well advised to pay the extra for cool air – and the air-conditioned buses are usually less crowded, too. Air-conditioned services stop at around 8.30pm, but most ordinary routes have a reduced service throughout the night. It's also possible to travel certain routes on flashy, air-conditioned **microbuses**, which were designed with the commuter in mind and offer the use of an on-board fax, telephone and newspapers, plus the certainty of a seat (no standing allowed) for a B15–30 fare (exact money only), which is dropped into a box beside the driver's seat; however, note that the microbus franchise-holder has recently been in financial trouble.

USEFUL BUS ROUTES

Because of various one-way systems and other idiosyncracies, some of the following bus routes may not be exactly the same in reverse. Check official bus maps to be sure.

#2 (air-con): Oriental Hotel–Silom Rd–Phrayathai Rd (for Siam Square)–Victory Monument–Chatuchak Weekend Market–Moh Chit 1 (old Northern Bus Terminal)–Lard Phrao–Minburi.

#3 (air-con): Moh Chit 1 (old Northern Bus

Terminal)–Chatuchak Weekend Market–Victory Monument–Sri
Ayutthaya Rd (for National Library and guesthouses)–Wat
Benjamabophit–Rajdamnoen Nok (for TAT and boxing
stadium)–Democracy Monument–Rajdamnoen Klang (for
Banglamphu guesthouses) Sanam Luang–Rajdamnoen Nai,
Southern Bus Terminal.

#4 (air-con): Airport–Rajaprarop Rd–Silom Rd–Thonburi.

#7 (air-con): Southern Bus Terminal–Sanam Luang (for
Banglamphu guesthouses)–Yaowarat Rd (for Chinatown and Wat
Traimit)–Hualamphong Station–Rama IV Rd–Sukhumvit Rd.

#8 (air-con): Samut Prakan (for Ancient City)–Eastern Bus
Terminal–Sukhumvit Rd–Siam Square–Charoen Krung–Grand
Palace–Wat Po.

#9 (air-con): Nonthaburi–Moh Chit 1 (old Northern Bus
Terminal)–Chatuchak Weekend Market–Rajdamnoen Nok (for
TAT and Thai boxing)–Democracy Monument–Rajdamnoen
Klang (for Banglamphu guesthouses)–Thonburi.

#10 (air-con): Airport–Moh Chit 1 (old Northern Bus
Terminal)–Chatuchak Weekend Market–Victory
Monument–Dusit Zoo–Rajwithi Rd (for National Library and
guesthouses)–Thonburi.

#11 (air-con): Samut Prakan (for Ancient City)–Eastern Bus
Terminal–Sukhumvit Rd–Democracy Monument–Rajdamnoen
Klang (for Banglamphu guesthouses)–Phra Pinklao–Southern
Bus Terminal.

#13 (air-con): Airport– Moh Chit 1 (old Northern Bus
Terminal)–Chatuchak Weekend Market–Victory
Monument–Rajaprarop Rd–Sukhumvit Rd–Eastern Bus
Terminal–Sukhumvit 62.

#15 (air-con and ordinary): Phra Athit Rd–National
Museum–Sanam Luang–Democracy Monument (for
Banglamphu guesthouses)–Phanfa (for TAT office)–Siam
Square–Rajdamri Rd–Silom Rd–Charoen Krung (New
Rd)–Krungthep Bridge.

#25 (ordinary): Samut Prakan (for Ancient City)–Eastern Bus

USEFUL BUS ROUTES

Terminal–Sukhumvit Rd–Rama I Rd (for Siam
Square)–Hualamphong Station–Yaowarat Rd (for
Chinatown)–Charoen Krung–Tha Thien (for Wat Po and the
Grand Palace)–Tha Chang.

#29 (air-con and ordinary): Airport– Moh Chit 1 (old Northern
Bus Terminal)–Victory Monument–Siam Square–Hualamphong
Station.

#38 (ordinary): Moh Chit 1 (old Northern Bus
Terminal)–Rajprarop Rd–Eastern Bus Terminal.

#39 (ordinary): Airport–Moh Chit 1 (old Northern Bus
Terminal)–Democracy Monument–Rajdamnoen Klang (for Khao
San Rd guesthouses)–Sanam Luang.

#40 (ordinary): Sukhumvit Rd–Rama I Rd (for Siam
Square)–Hualamphong Station–Yaowarat Rd (for
Chinatown)–Thonburi.

#53 (ordinary): Hualamphong Station–Krung Kasem
Rd–Samsen Rd and Phra Athit Rd (for Banglamphu
guesthouses)–Sanam Luang (for National Museum and Wat
Mahathat)–Thanon Mahathat (for Grand Palace and Wat
Po)–Pahurat–Yaowarat–Krung Kasem Rd.

#56 (ordinary): Chakraphet Rd (for Chinatown)–Mahachai
Rd–Democracy Monument–Tanao Rd (for Khao San Rd
guesthouses)–Pracha Thipatai Rd (for National Library
guesthouses)–Vimanmek Palace.

#59 (ordinary): Airport–Moh Chit 1 (old Northern Bus
Terminal)–Victory Monument–Phanfa–Democracy Monument
(for Banglamphu guesthouses)–Sanam Luang.

#62 (ordinary): Soi Suan Plu (for immigration office)–Sathorn
Rd–Witthayu Rd–Pratunam Market–Sri Ayutthaya Rd (for Suan
Pakkad)–Victory Monument.

#72 (ordinary): Tha Thewes–Sri Ayutthaya Rd (for Dusit and
Suan Pakkad)–Pratunam Market–New Phetchaburi Rd.

#124 and #127 (ordinary): Southern Bus Terminal–Tha Pinklao
(for ferry to Phra Athit and Banglamphu guesthouses).

USEFUL BUS ROUTES

Express boats

Two rival companies operate **express-boat** (*reua duan*) services, using large, numbered water buses to plough up and down the Chao Phraya River. The **Chao Phraya Express** is the longer-established service and probably the more useful for tourists, its clearly signed piers (*tha*) appearing on all Bangkok maps. Its usual route, ninety minutes in total, runs between Krung Thep Bridge in the south and Nonthaburi in the north. These **"daily standard"** boats set off every ten to fifteen minutes or so from 6am to 7pm (that is, the first and last boats leave their termini at these times, with the last boat in each direction flying a blue flag). Boats do not necessarily stop at every landing – they'll only pull in if people want to get on or off. During rush hours (Mon–Fri 6–9am & 4–7pm), certain **"special express"** boats operate limited-stop services on set routes, flying either a **yellow** (Nonthaburi to Bangna, far downriver beyond Krung Thep Bridge), **orange** (Nonthaburi to Sathorn, upriver of Krung Thep Bridge), **red** (Nonthaburi to Krung Thep Bridge) or a **green flag** (Pakkred, north of Nonthaburi, to Krung Thep Bridge); correspondingly coloured flags are painted on pier signboards to show which services stop there. The important central Chao Phraya Express stops are outlined in the box below and marked on Map 2.

The much less frequent and useful boats of **Laemthong** (which is in some financial difficulty and stopped operating for over a month in late 1997) travel a slightly more extended route, from Pakkred to Krung Thep Bridge; they run from around 6am to 7pm (departure times are from the termini), with the last boat in each direction flying a **gold** flag. Most piers serve both Chao Phraya and Laemthong boats, but note that the latter don't use Tha Phra Athit (you'd have to get off at Phra Pinklao Bridge and cross the river on a one-baht ferry). As well as its regular service (green flag),

EXPRESS BOATS

47

Laemthong runs rush-hour express boats (each with an orange and red flag), which call at Nonthaburi and, in the centre, Thewes, Wisut Kasat (afternoons only), Phra Pinklao, Wang Lang, Chang, Saphan Phut, Rachavongse, Si Phraya and Sathorn.

Tickets for both companies' services can be bought either at the pier or on board, and cost B4–10 according to distance travelled; the additional Nonthaburi–Pakkred leg offered on Chao Phraya green-flag boats incurs a B7 supplement. Don't discard your ticket until you're off the boat, as the staff at some piers (such as Phra Athit and Oriental) impose a B1 fine on anyone disembarking without one.

CENTRAL STOPS FOR THE CHAO PHRAYA EXPRESS BOAT

Numbers correspond to those on **Map 2**.

1 Thewes (all daily standard and special express boats) – for National Library and guesthouses.

2 Wisut Kasat (*Visutkrasat*; daily standard, red and green flags) – for Samsen Rd guesthouses.

3 Phra Athit (daily standard) – for Khao San Rd and Banglamphu guesthouses.

4 Phra Pinklao Bridge (special express) – for Thonburi shops and city buses to the Southern Bus Terminal.

5 Bangkok Noi (daily standard) – for trains to Kanchanaburi.

6 Wang Lang (or Prannok; all daily standard and special express boats) – for Siriraj Hospital.

7 Chang (daily standard, orange, red and green flags) – for the Grand Palace.

8 Thien (daily standard) – for Wat Po, and the cross-river ferry to Wat Arun.

9 Ratchini (*Rajinee*; daily standard, red and green flags) – for Pak Khlong Talad market.

10 Saphan Phut (Memorial Bridge; daily standard, red and green flags) – for Pahurat (and Wat Prayoon in Thonburi).

11 Rachavongse (*Rajawong*; all daily standard and special express boats) – for Chinatown.

12 Harbour Department (daily standard).

13 Si Phraya (all daily standard and special express boats) – for River City shopping complex.

14 Wat Muang Kae (daily standard) – for GPO.

15 Oriental (daily standard, red and green flags) – for Silom Rd.

16 Sathorn (all daily standard and special express boats) – for Sathorn Rd.

Cross-river ferries

Smaller than express boats are the slow **cross-river ferries** (*reua kham fak*), which shuttle back and forth between the same two points. They can be found at every express stop and plenty of other piers in between and are especially useful for connections to Chao Phraya special express boat stops during rush hours. Fares are B1–2, which you usually pay at the entrance to the pier.

Longtail boats

Longtail boats (*reua hang yao*) ply the khlongs (canals) of Thonburi like buses, stopping at designated shelters (fares are in line with those of express boats), and are also available for individual rental here and on the river (see p.97). On the Bangkok side, **Khlong Sen Seb** has been opened up to longtails, which run frequently from the Phanfa pier at the Golden Mount (handy for Banglamphu, Ratanakosin and

Chinatown), and head way out east to Wat Sribunruang, with useful stops at Phrayathai Road, Pratunam, Soi Chitlom, Witthayu (Wireless) Road, and Soi Nana Neua (Soi 3), Soi Asoke (Soi 21), Soi Thonglo (Soi 55) and Soi Ekkamai (Soi 63), all off Sukhumvit Road. This is your quickest and most interesting way of getting across town, if you can stand the stench of the canal. State your destination to the conductor when he collects your fare, which will be between B5 and B13.

Another very useful longtail service travels along **Khlong Krung Kasem** between Hualamphong train station and Banglamphu, depositing passengers near the New World department store before terminating at a tiny pier off Phra Athit Road (every 20–30min; 15min; B6). It's also possible to get a longtail from Hualamphong to Phanfa pier.

Taxis

Bangkok **taxis** come in three forms, and are so plentiful that you rarely have to wait more than a couple of minutes before spotting an empty one of any description. Not all of them have meters, so you should agree on a price before setting off, and expect to do a fair amount of haggling. Rates for all rise after midnight, and during rush hours when each journey takes far longer.

The most sedate option, Bangkok's metered, air-conditioned **taxi cabs**, is also the most expensive, but well worth the extra in the heat of the day. Fares start at B35, increasing in stages on a combined speed/distance formula. However, this relatively new phenomenon of metering cabs is still having teething problems, largely because the drivers feel that cab-leasing fees are too high compared to the fare scale they are obliged to implement. The result is that they will sometimes refuse long, slow, less profitable journeys across town (especially in the middle of the afternoon, when many cabs have to return to the depot for a change of drivers), and will sometimes engage in the kind of meter-fiddling that's found in big cities across the world. If a string of metered-cab drivers don't like the sound of your destination, you'll have to try to negotiate a flat fare with one of them, or with an unmetered-cab driver, in which case avoid unlicensed cabs (white and black plates): they're no more expensive than licensed ones (yellow and black plates) and tend to be less reputable – you've got no comeback in the event of an accident – although outright rip-offs are confined mainly to the airport run. If you strike it really unlucky, phone Call-Taxi (©319 9911 or 624 9999).

Slightly less stable but typically Thai, **tuk-tuks** can carry three passengers comfortably and are the standard way of making shortish journeys (Banglamphu to Patpong will cost at least B60). These noisy, three-wheeled, open-sided buggies fully expose you to the worst of Bangkok's pollution, but are the least frustrating type of city transport – they are a lot nippier than taxi cabs, and the drivers have no qualms about taking semi-legal measures to avoid gridlocks. Be aware, however, that tuk-tuk drivers tend to speak less English than taxi drivers – and there have been cases of robberies and attacks on women passengers late at night.

Least costly (a short trip, say from Banglamphu to Wat Po, should cost B20) and quickest of the trio are **motorbike taxis**, though these are rarely used by tourists as they carry only one passenger and are too dangerous to recommend for cross-city journeys on Bangkok's hectic roads. Still, if you've got nerves of steel, pick the riders out by their numbered, coloured vests or find their taxi rank, often at the entrance to a long soi. Crash helmets are now compulsory on all main thoroughfares in the capital and passengers should insist on wearing one (traffic police fine non-wearers on the spot), though the local press has reported complaints

TAXIS

from people who've caught headlice this way (they suggest wearing a headscarf under the helmet).

Ratanakosin

When Rama I developed **Ratanakosin** as his new capital in 1782, after the sacking of the former capital Ayutthaya by the Burmese and a temporary stay across the Chao Phraya River in Thonburi, he paid tribute to its precursor by imitating Ayutthaya's layout and architecture, even shipping the building materials downstream from the ruins of the old city. Like Ayutthaya, the new capital was sited for protection beside a river and turned into an artificial island by the construction of defensive canals, with a central **Grand Palace** and adjoining royal temple, **Wat Phra Kaeo**, fronted by a cremation field, **Sanam Luang**. The Wang Na (Palace of the Second King), now doing service as the **National Museum**, was also built at this time.

Ratanakosin's other major temple, **Wat Po**, is far older, though it was enlarged by Rama I when he incorporated it into his new capital. The temple was further embellished by his successors, who also consolidated Ratanakosin's pre-eminence by building **Wat Mahathat**, the most important centre of Buddhist learning in southeast Asia, the National Theatre, Thammasat University, and several grand European-style palaces which now house government institutions.

> There are no hotels in Ratanakosin, but it's only a stone's throw from the accommodation in Banglamphu (see p.136). The best spots for refreshment in Ratanakosin are Na Pralan Café (see p.168) and the evening riverside bar Boh (see p.186).

Bangkok has expanded eastwards away from the river, leaving the Grand Palace a good 5km from the city's commercial heart, and the royal family have long since moved their residence to Dusit, but Ratanakosin remains the religious and ceremonial centre of the whole kingdom – so much so that it feels as if it might sink into the boggy ground under the weight of its own mighty edifices. The heavy, stately feel is lightened by noisy **markets** along the riverside strip, and by the open space of Sanam Luang, still used for royal cremations and the king's Ploughing Ceremony, but also serving as a popular park and the hub of the city's bus system.

Ratanakosin is within easy walking distance of Banglamphu, but is best approached from the river, via the **express-boat piers** Chang (for the Grand Palace) or Thien (for Wat Po).

WAT PHRA KAEO AND THE GRAND PALACE

Map 4, D6. Express boat to Chang pier. Daily 8.30am–3.30pm; B125, including brochure with map, as well as admission to the Vimanmek Palace in Dusit; free tours in English at 10am, 10.30am, 11am, 1pm, 1.30pm & 2pm. Bus AC#8 or #25, plus dozens of others to Sanam Luang.

Hanging together in a precarious harmony of strangely beautiful colours and shapes, **Wat Phra Kaeo** is the apogee of Thai religious art and the holiest Buddhist site in the

SANAM CHAI ROAD

NA PHRA LAN ROAD

Sanam Luang

N

50 m

0

To Tha Chang

Wat Phra Kaeo

Inner Palace
(not open to the public)

Offices of the Royal Household
(not open to the public)

Grand Palace

MAHARAT ROAD

Gate of Glorious Victory	1	Royal Pantheon	11
Ticket office	2	Phra Mondop	12
Coins and Decorations Pavilion	3	Angkor Wat model	13
Entrance to Wat Phra Kaeo	4	Phra Si Ratana Chedi	14
Chapel of the Gandhara Buddha	5	Exit from Wat Phra Kaeo	15
The bot and Emerald Buddha	6	Phra Thinang Amarin Winichai	16
Royal mausoleum	7	Chakri Maha Prasat	17
Porcelain viharn	8	Dusit Maha Prasat	18
Library	9	Mount Krailas model	19
Prangs	10	Exit from Grand Palace	20

WAT PHRA KAEO & THE GRAND PALACE

WAT PHRA KAEO AND THE GRAND PALACE |

55

country, housing the most important image, the **Emerald Buddha**. Built as the private royal temple, Wat Phra Kaeo occupies the northeast corner of the huge **Grand Palace**, whose official opening in 1785 marked the founding of the new capital and the rebirth of the Thai nation after the Burmese invasion. Successive kings have all left their mark here, and the palace complex now covers nearly a quarter of a square kilometre, though very little apart from the wat is open to tourists. The only **entrance** to the complex in 2km of crenellated walls is the Gate of Glorious Victory in the middle of the north side, on Na Phra Lan Road. This brings you onto a driveway with a tantalizing view of the temple's glittering spires on the left and the dowdy buildings of the Offices of the Royal Household on the right – the powerhouse of the kingdom's ceremonial life, providing everything down to chairs and catering, and even lending an urn when someone of rank dies.

> **Visitors to Wat Phra Kaeo are required to dress smartly – no vests, shorts, see-through clothes, sarongs, mini-skirts, fisherman's trousers, slip-on sandals or flip-flops. Suitable clothes and shoes can be borrowed (free, socks B15) from the office to the right inside the Gate of Glorious Victory, if you leave some identification as surety.**

Wat Phra Kaeo

Entering the temple is like stepping onto a lavishly detailed stage set, from the immaculate flagstones right up to the gaudy roofs. Although it receives hundreds of foreign sight-seers and at least as many Thai pilgrims every day, the temple, which has no monks in residence, maintains an unnervingly sanitized look, as if it were built only yesterday.

Its jigsaw of structures can seem complicated at first, but the basic layout is straightforward: the turnstiles in the west wall open onto the back of the bot, the temple's main sanctuary, which contains the Emerald Buddha; to the left, the upper terrace runs parallel to the north side of the bot, while the whole temple compound is surrounded by arcaded walls, decorated with extraordinary murals of scenes from the *Ramayana*.

The approach to the bot

Immediately inside the turnstiles, you'll be confronted by six-metre tall *yaksha*, gaudy demons from the *Ramayana*, who watch over the Emerald Buddha from every gate of the temple and ward off evil spirits. Less threatening is the toothless ancient, cast in bronze and sitting on a plinth by the back wall of the bot, who represents a Hindu hermit credited with inventing yoga and herbal medicine.

Skirting around the bot, you'll reach its **main entrance** on the eastern side, in front of which stands a cluster of grey **statues**, which have a strong Chinese feel: next to Kuan Im, the Chinese Goddess of Mercy, are a sturdy pillar topped by a lotus flower, which Bangkok's Chinese community presented to Rama IV during his 27 years as a monk, and two handsome cows which commemorate Rama I's birth in the Year of the Cow. Worshippers make their offerings to the Emerald Buddha in among the statues, where they can look at the image through the open doors of the bot without messing up its pristine interior with candle wax and joss-stick ash.

Nearby in the southeastern corner of the temple precinct, look out for the beautiful country scenes painted in gold and blue on the doors of the **Chapel of the Gandhara Buddha**, a building which was crucial to the old royal rain-making ritual. Adorning the roof are thousands of nagas (serpents), symbolizing water; inside the locked chapel, among the paraphernalia used in the ritual, is kept the Gandhara Buddha, a bronze image in the gesture of calling down the rain with its right hand, while cupping the left to catch it. In times of drought the king would order this week-long ceremony to be conducted, during which he was bathed regularly and kept away from the opposite sex, while Buddhist monks and Hindu Brahmins chanted continuously. Traditional methods still have their place in Thai weather reading: 1991 was said to be a good wet year, with the rain measured at "five nagas".

The bot and the Emerald Buddha

The **bot**, the largest building of the temple, is one of the few original structures left at Wat Phra Kaeo, though it has been augmented so often it looks like the work of a wildly inspired child. Eight *sema* stones mark the boundary of the consecrated area around the bot, each sheltering in a psychedelic fairy castle, joined by a low wall decorated with Chinese porcelain tiles which depict delicate landscapes. The walls of the bot itself, sparkling with gilt and coloured glass, are supported by 112 golden *garudas* (birdmen) holding nagas – they represent the god Indra saving the world by slaying the serpent-cloud which had swallowed up all the water. The symbolism reflects the king's traditional role as a rainmaker.

Inside the bot, a nine-metre-high pedestal supports the tiny **Emerald Buddha**, a figure whose mystique draws pilgrims from all over Thailand – here especially you must act with respect, sitting with your feet pointing away from the Buddha. The sixty-centimetre jadeite image draws its spiritual power from its legendary past; reputedly created in Sri Lanka, it was discovered when lightning cracked open an ancient chedi in Chiang Rai in the early fifteenth century. The image was then moved around the north, dispensing miracles wherever it went, before being taken to

Laos for two hundred years. It was believed to bring great fortune to its possessor, and when the future Rama I captured Vientiane in 1779, he snatched back the figure and installed it at the heart of his new capital as a talisman for king and country.

To this day the king himself ceremonially changes the Buddha's costumes, of which there are three, one for each season: the crown and ornaments of an Ayutthayan king for the hot season; a gilt monastic robe dotted with blue enamel for the rainy season, when the monks retreat into the temples; and a full-length gold shawl to wrap up in the cool season. (The spare outfits are displayed in the Coins and Decorations Pavilion outside the turnstiles leading into the temple.) Among the paraphernalia in front of the pedestal is the tiny, black Victory Buddha, which Rama I always carried with him into war for luck. The two lowest Buddhas were both put there by Rama IX: the one on the left on his sixtieth birthday in 1987, the other when he became the longest-reigning Thai monarch in 1988.

The upper terrace

The eastern end of the **upper terrace** is taken up with the **Prasat Phra Thep Bidorn**, known as the **Royal Pantheon**, a splendid hash of styles. The pantheon has its roots in the Khmer concept of *devaraja*, or the divinity of kings: inside are bronze and gold statues, precisely life-size, of all the kings since Bangkok became the Thai capital. The building is open only on special occasions, such as Chakri Day (April 6), when the dynasty is commemorated.

From here you get the best view of the **royal mausoleum**, the **porcelain viharn** and the **library** to the north, all of which are closed to the public, and, running along the east side of the temple, a row of eight bullet-like **prangs**, each a different nasty colour, which Somerset Maugham described as "monstrous vegetables": these ceramic-covered towers represent, in turn, the Buddha, Buddhist scripture, the monkhood, the nunhood, the three Buddhas to come, and finally the king.

In the middle of the terrace, dressed in deep-green glass mosaics, the **Phra Mondop** was built by Rama I to house the Tripitaka, or Buddhist scripture. It's famous for the mother-of-pearl cabinet and solid-silver mats inside, but is never open. Four tiny memorials at each corner of the mondop show the symbols of each of the nine Chakri kings, from the ancient crown representing Rama I to the present king's sun symbol, while the bronze statues surrounding the memorials portray each king's lucky white elephants, labelled by name and pedigree. On the north side of the mondop is a **scale model of Angkor Wat** contributed by Rama IV – during his reign this prodigious Cambodian temple was under Thai rule. He also erected the **Phra Si Ratana Chedi,** a blaze of gold at the western end of the terrace, to enshrine a piece of the Buddha's breastbone.

The murals

Extending for over a kilometre in the arcades which run inside the wat walls, the **murals of the Ramayana** depict every blow of this ancient story of the triumph of good over evil, using the vibrant buildings of the temple itself as backdrops, and setting them off against the subdued colours of richly detailed landscapes. Because of the humidity, none of the original work of Rama I's time survives: maintenance is a never-ending process, so you'll always find an artist working on one of the scenes.

The story is told in 178 panels, labelled and numbered in Thai only, starting in the middle of the northern side: in the first episode, a hermit, while out ploughing, finds the baby Sita, the heroine, floating in a gold urn on a lotus leaf, and brings her to the city. Panel 109 shows the climax of the story, when Rama, the hero, kills the ten-headed demon Totsagan, and the ladies of the enemy city weep at the demon's death. Panel 110 depicts his elaborate funeral procession, and in 113 you can see the funeral fair, with acrobats, sword jugglers, and tightrope walkers. In between, Sita – Rama's wife – has to walk on fire to prove that she has been faithful during her fourteen years of imprisonment by Totsagan. If you haven't the stamina for the long walk round, you could sneak a look at the end of the story, to the left of the first panel, where Rama holds a victory parade and distributes thank-you gifts.

The palace buildings

The exit in the southwest corner of Wat Phra Kaeo brings you to the **palace** proper, a vast area of buildings and gardens, of which only the northern edge is on show to the public. Though the king now lives in the Chitrlada Palace in Dusit, the Grand Palace is still used for state receptions and official ceremonies, during which there is no public access to any part of the palace.

Phra Maha Monthien

Coming out of the temple compound, you'll first be confronted by a beautiful Chinese gate covered in innumerable tiny porcelain tiles. The **Phra Maha Monthien**, which extends in a straight line behind the gate, was the grand residential complex of earlier kings. Only the **Phra Thinang Amarin Winichai**, the main audience hall at the front of the complex, is open to the public. The supreme court in the era of the absolute monarchy, it nowadays serves as the venue for the king's birthday speech; dominating the hall is the *busbok*, an open-sided throne with a spired roof, floating on a boat-shaped base. The rear buildings are still used for

The Ramayana

The **Ramayana** is generally thought to have originated as an oral epic in India, where it appears in numerous dialects. The most famous version is that of the poet Valmiki, who as a tribute to his king drew together the collection of stories over two thousand years ago. From India, the *Ramayana* spread to all the Hindu-influenced countries of South Asia and was passed down through the Khmers to Thailand, where as the **Ramakien** it has become the national epic, acting as an affirmation of the Thai monarchy and its divine Hindu links. As a source of inspiration for literature, painting, sculpture and dance-drama, it has acquired the authority of holy writ, providing Thais with moral and practical lessons, while its appearance in the form of films and comic strips shows its huge popular appeal. The version current in Thailand was composed by a committee of poets sponsored by Rama I, and runs to three thousand pages.

The **central story** of the *Ramayana* concerns **Rama** (in Thai, Phra Ram), son of the king of Ayodhya, and his beautiful wife **Sita**, whose hand he wins by lifting and stringing a magic bow. The couple's adventures begin when they are exiled to the forest, along with Rama's good brother, **Lakshaman** (Phra Lak), by the hero's father under the influence of his evil stepmother. Meanwhile, in the city of Lanka (in Thai, Longka), the demon king **Totsagan** (also known as Ravana) has conceived a passionate desire for Sita and, disguised as a hermit, sets out to kidnap her. By transforming one of his subjects into a beautiful deer, which Rama and Lakshaman go off to hunt, Totsagan catches Sita alone and takes her back to Lanka. Rama then wages a long war against the demons of Lanka, into which are woven many battles, spy scenes and diversionary episodes, and eventually kills Totsagan and rescues Sita.

The Thai version shows some characteristic differences from the Indian. Hanuman, the loyal monkey king, is given a much more playful role in the *Ramakien*, with the addition of many episodes which display his cunning and talent for mischief, but the major alteration comes at the end of the story, when Rama doubts Sita's faithfulness after rescuing her from Totsagan. In the Indian story, this ends with Sita being swallowed up by the earth so that she doesn't have to suffer Rama's doubts any more; in the *Ramakien* the ending is a happy one, with Rama and Sita living together happily ever after.

the most important part of the elaborate coronation ceremony, and each new king is supposed to spend a night there to show solidarity with his forefathers.

Chakri Maha Prasat and the Inner Palace

Next door you can admire the facade – nothing else – of the "foreigner with a Thai hat", as the **Chakri Maha Prasat** is nicknamed. Rama V, whose portrait you can see over the entrance, employed an English architect to design a purely Neoclassical residence, but other members of the royal family prevailed on the king to add the three Thai spires. This used to be the site of the elephant stables: the large red tethering posts are still there and the bronze elephants were installed as a reminder. The building displays the emblem of the Chakri dynasty on its gable, which has a trident (*ri*) coming out of a *chak*, a discus with a sharpened rim.

The **Inner Palace**, which used to be the king's harem (closed to the public), lies behind the gate on the left-hand side of the Chakri Maha Prasat. The harem was a town in itself, with shops, law-courts and a police force for the huge all-female population: as well as the current queens, the minor wives and their servants, this was home to the daughters and consorts of former kings, and the daughters of the aristocracy who attended the harem's finishing school. Today, the Inner Palace houses a school of cooking, fruit-carving and other domestic sciences for well-bred young Thais.

Dusit Maha Prasat

On the western side of the courtyard, the delicately proportioned **Dusit Maha Prasat**, an audience hall built by Rama I, epitomizes traditional Thai architecture. Outside, the soaring tiers of its red, gold and green roof culminate in a gilded *mongkut*, a spire shaped like the king's crown which symbolizes the 33 Buddhist levels of perfection. Each tier of the roof bears a typical *chofa*, a slender, stylized bird's head, and several *hang hong* (swan's tails), which represent three-headed nagas. Inside, you can still see the original throne, the **Phra Ratcha Banlang Pradap Muk**, a masterpiece of mother-of-pearl inlaid work. When a senior member of the royal family dies, the hall is used for the lying-in-state: the body, embalmed and seated in a huge sealed urn, is placed in the west transept, waiting up to two years for an auspicious day to be cremated.

To the right and behind the Dusit Maha Prasat rises a strange model mountain, decorated with fabulous animals and topped by a castle and prang. It represents **Mount Krailas**, a version of Mount Meru, the centre of the Hindu universe, and was built as the site of the royal tonsure ceremony. In former times, Thai children had shaved heads except for a tuft on the crown which, between the age of five and eight, was cut in a Hindu initiation rite to welcome adolescence. For the royal children, the rite was an elaborate ceremony that sometimes lasted five days, culminating with the king's cutting of the hair knot. The child was then bathed at the model Krailas, in water representing the original river of the universe flowing down the central mountain.

WAT PO

Map 4, D9. Daily 8am–5pm; B20. Express boat to Thien pier. Bus AC#8 or #25, plus dozens of others to Sanam Luang.

Where Wat Phra Kaeo may seem too perfect and shrink-wrapped for some, **Wat Po** is lively and shambolic, a huge and complex arrangement of lavish structures which jostle with classrooms, basketball courts and a turtle pond. Busloads of tourists shuffle in and out of the **north entrance** stopping only to gawp at the colossal Reclining Buddha, but you can avoid the worst of the crowds by using the **main entrance** on Soi Chetuphon to explore the huge compound, where you'll more than likely be approached by friendly young monks wanting to practise their English.

Wat Po is the oldest temple in Bangkok, and older than the city itself, having been founded in the seventeenth century under the name Wat Potaram. Foreigners have stuck to the contraction of this old name, even though Rama I, after enlarging the temple, changed the name in 1801 to Wat Phra Chetuphon, which is how it is generally known to Thais. The temple had another major overhaul in 1832, when Rama III built the chapel of the Reclining Buddha, and turned the temple into a public centre of learning by decorating the walls and pillars with inscriptions and diagrams on subjects such as history, literature, animal husbandry and astrology.

Dubbed Thailand's first university, the wat is still an important centre for traditional medicine, notably Thai massage, which is used against all kinds of illnesses, from backaches to viruses. Thirty-hour training courses in English, held over either ten or fifteen days, cost B6000; alternatively you can simply turn up and suffer a massage yourself in the ramshackle buildings on the east side of the main compound, for B200 per hour (allow two hours for the full works and note that the massage school stays open until 6pm; ℗221 2974 or 225 4771).

WAT PO

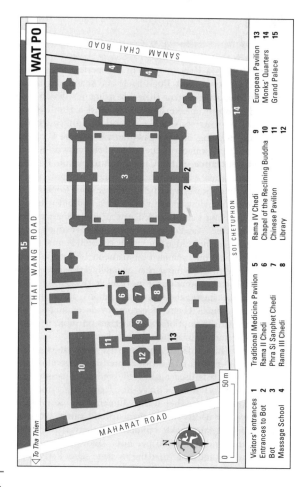

WAT PO

THAI WANG ROAD

SANAM CHAI ROAD

SOI CHETUPHON

MAHARAT ROAD

To Tha Thien

N

0   50 m

Visitors' entrances	1	Traditional Medicine Pavilion	5	Rama IV Chedi	9	European Pavilion	13
Entrances to Bot	2	Rama II Chedi	6	Chapel of the Reclining Buddha	10	Monks' Quarters	14
Bot	3	Phra Si Sanphet Chedi	7	Chinese Pavilion	11	Grand Palace	15
Massage School	4	Rama III Chedi	8	Library	12		

The eastern courtyard

The main entrance on Soi Chetuphon is one of a series of sixteen monumental gates around the main compound, each guarded by stone **giants**, many of them comic Westerners in wide-brimmed hats – ships which exported rice to China would bring these statues back as ballast.

The entrance brings you into the eastern half of the main complex, where a courtyard of structures radiates from the bot – the principal congregation and ordination hall – in a disorientating symmetry. To get to the bot at the centre, turn right and cut through the two surrounding cloisters, which are lined with 394 Buddha images, many of them covered with stucco to hide their bad state of repair – anyone can accrue some merit by taking one away and repairing it.

The elegant **bot** has beautiful teak doors decorated with mother-of-pearl, showing stories from the *Ramayana* in minute detail. Look out also for the stone bas reliefs around the base of the bot, which narrate a longer version of the *Ramayana* in 152 action-packed panels. The plush interior has a well-proportioned altar on which ten statues of disciples frame a graceful Buddha image containing the remains of Rama I, the founder of Bangkok. Rama IV placed them there so that the public could worship him at the same time as the Buddha.

Back outside the entrance to the double cloister, keep your eyes open for a miniature mountain covered in statues of naked men in tall hats who appear to be gesturing rudely: they are *rishis* (hermits), demonstrating various positions of healing massage. Skirting the southwestern corner of the cloisters, you'll come to a pavilion between the eastern and western courtyards, which displays plaques inscribed with the precepts of traditional medicine, as well as anatomical pictures showing the different pressure points and the illnesses that can be cured by massaging them.

THE EASTERN COURTYARD

The western courtyard

Amongst the 95 chedis strewn about the grounds, the four **great chedis** in the western courtyard stand out as much for their covering of garish tiles as for their size. The central chedi is the oldest, erected by Rama I to hold the remains of the most sacred Buddha image of Ayutthaya, the Phra Si Sanphet. (All chedis, or reliquary towers, are supposed to hold the ashes of the Buddha or some other important religious figure.) Later, Rama III built the chedi to the north for the ashes of Rama II and the chedi to the south to hold his own remains. Rama IV built the fourth, with bright blue tiles, for an uncertain purpose.

In the northwest corner of the courtyard stands the chapel of the **Reclining Buddha**, a 45-metre-long gilded statue of plaster-covered brick which depicts the Buddha entering Nirvana, a common motif in Buddhist iconography. The chapel is only slightly bigger than the statue – you can't get far enough away to take in anything but a surreal close-up view of the beaming five-metre smile. As for the feet, the vast black soles are beautifully inlaid with delicate mother-of-pearl showing the 108 *lakshanas* or auspicious signs which distinguish the true Buddha. Along one side of the statue are 108 bowls which will bring you good luck and a long life if you put 25 satang in each.

LAK MUANG

Map 4, E5. Express boat to Chang pier. Bus AC#8 or #25, plus dozens of others to Sanam Luang.

At 6.54am on April 21, 1782 – the astrologically determined time for the auspicious founding of Bangkok – a pillar containing the city's horoscope was ceremonially driven into the ground opposite the northeast corner of the Grand Palace. This pillar, the **lak muang** – all Thai cities have one, to provide a home for their guardian spirits – was made from a four-metre tree trunk carved with a lotus-shaped crown, and is now sheltered in an elegant shrine surrounded by immaculate gardens. It shares the shrine with the taller *lak muang* of Thonburi, which was recently incorporated into Greater Bangkok.

Hundreds of worshippers come every day to pray and offer flowers, particularly childless couples seeking the gift of fertility. In one corner of the gardens you can often see short performances of **classical dancing**, paid for by well-off families when they have a piece of good fortune to celebrate.

SANAM LUANG

Map 4, E4. Express boat to Chang pier. Bus AC#8 or #25, plus dozens of others.

Sanam Luang, a bare field to the north of the Grand Palace, is one of the last open spaces left in Bangkok, where residents of the capital gather in the evening to meet, eat and play. The nearby pavements are the marketplace for some exotic spiritual salesmen: on the eastern side sit astrologers and palm readers, and sellers of bizarre virility potions and contraptions; on the western side and spreading around Thammasat University and Wat Mahathat, scores of small-time hawkers sell amulets. In the early part of the year, the sky is filled with kites, which every afternoon are flown in kite-fighting contests.

As it's in front of the Grand Palace, the field is also the venue for national ceremonies, such as the **Ploughing Ceremony**, held every May at a time selected by astrologers to bring good fortune to the rice harvest. The elaborate Brahmin ceremony is led by an official from the Ministry of Agriculture, who stands in for the king in case the royal power were to be reduced by any failure in the ritual. At the designated time, the official cuts a series of circular furrows with a plough driven by two oxen, and scatters rice which has been sprinkled with lustral water by the Brahmin priests of the court. When the ritual is over, spectators rush in to grab handfuls of the rice, which they then plant in their own paddies for good luck.

Kite flying

Flying intricate and colourful **kites** is now done mostly for fun in Thailand, but it has its roots in more serious activities. Filled with gunpowder and fitted with long fuses, kites were deployed in the first Thai kingdom at Sukhothai (1240–1438) as machines of war. In the same era, special *ngao* kites, with heads in the shape of bamboo bows, were used in Brahmin rituals: the string of the bow would vibrate in the wind and make a noise to frighten away evil spirits (nowadays noisy kites are still used, but only by farmers, to scare the birds). By the height of the Ayutthayan period (1351–1767) kites had become largely decorative: royal ceremonies were enhanced by fantastically shaped kites, adorned with jingling bells and ornamental lamps.

In the nineteenth century Rama V, by his enthusiastic lead, popularized kite flying as a clean-cut and fashionable recreation. **Contests** are now held all over the country between February and April, when winds are strong and farmers have free time after harvesting the rice. These contests fall into two broad categories: those involving manoeuvrable flat kites, often in the shapes of animals; and those in which the beauty of static display kites is judged. The most popular contest of all, which comes under the first category, matches two teams, one flying star-shaped *chula*s, two-metre-high "male" kites, the other flying the smaller, more agile *pakpao*s, diamond-shaped "females". Each team uses its skill and teamwork to ensnare the other's kites and drag them back across a dividing line.

In a tiny park by the hectic bus stops at the northeast corner of Sanam Luang stands the abundant but rather neglected figure of **Mae Toranee**, the earth goddess, wringing the water from her ponytail. Originally part of a fountain built here by Rama V's queen, Saowaba, to provide Bangkokians with fresh drinking water, the statue illustrates a Buddhist legend featured in the murals of many temples. While the Buddha was sitting in meditation at a crucial stage of his enlightenment, Mara, the force of evil, sent a host of earthly temptations and demons to try to divert him from his path. The Buddha remained cross-legged and pointed his right hand towards the ground – the most popular pose of Buddha statues in Thailand – to call the earth goddess to bear witness to his countless meritorious deeds, which had earned him an ocean of water stored in the earth. Mae Toranee obliged by wringing her hair and engulfing Mara's demons in the deluge.

WAT MAHATHAT

Map 4, C4. Daily 9am–5pm; free. Express boat to Chang pier. Buses AC#8 or #25, plus dozens of others to Sanam Luang.

On Sanam Luang's western side, with its main entrance on Maharat Road, **Wat Mahathat**, founded in the eighteenth century, provides a welcome respite from the surrounding tourist hype, and a chance to engage with the eager monks studying at **Mahachulalongkorn Buddhist University** here. As the nation's centre for the Mahanikai monastic sect, and housing one of the two Buddhist universities in Bangkok, the temple buzzes with purpose. It's this activity, and the chance of interaction and participation, rather than any special architectural features, which make a visit so rewarding. The many university-attending monks at the wat are friendly and keen to practise their English, and are more than likely to approach you: diverting topics might range from the poetry of Dylan Thomas to English football results gleaned from the BBC World Service.

Every day the grounds host an interesting **herbal medicine market**, and outside, along the pavements of Maharat and surrounding roads, vendors set up stalls to sell some of the city's most reasonably priced amulets (though the range and quality are not as good as at the main market at Wat Rajnadda), taking advantage of the spiritually auspicious location.

Situated in Section Five of the wat is its **International Buddhist Meditation Centre** where meditation practice is available in English; regular English-language sessions are held on the second Saturday of the month between 4 and 6pm, or you are welcome to make an appointment for any time that suits on ℂ02/222 6011 (the phone is more likely to be answered in the evening).

THE NATIONAL MUSEUM

Map 4, E3. Wed–Sun 9am–4pm; B40 including free leaflet and map. Express boat to Chang pier. Bus AC#8 or #25, plus dozens of others to Sanam Luang.

The **National Museum** houses a colossal hoard of Thailand's chief artistic riches, ranging from sculptural treasures in the north and south wings, through bizarre decorative objects in the older buildings, to outlandish funeral chariots and the exquisite Buddhaisawan Chapel, as well as occasionally staging worthwhile temporary exhibitions (details on ℂ224 1396). The free **guided tours in English** (Wed & Thurs 9.30am) are worth making time for: they're generally entertaining and their explication of the choicest exhibits provides a good introduction to Thai religion and culture. Should you linger longer than anticipated – and most people do – the **cafeteria** there serves good, inexpensive Thai food.

History and prehistory

The building which houses the information office and bookshop provides a quick whirl through the **history** of Thailand, a display in which are hidden a couple of gems. The first is a black stone inscription, credited to King Ramkhamhaeng of Sukhothai, which became the first capital of the Thai nation in the thirteenth century. Discovered in 1833 by the future Rama IV, it's the oldest extant inscription using the Thai alphabet. This, combined with the description it records of prosperity and piety in Sukhothai's Golden Age, has made the stone a symbol of Thai nationhood. Further on is a four-foot-tall carved *kinnari*, a graceful half-human, half-bird creature said to live in one of the Himalayan heavens. This delicate masterpiece is from the best period of Thai woodcarving, the seventeenth and early eighteenth centuries, before the fall of Ayutthaya.

The **prehistory** room is entered through a separate door at the back end of the building. Prominent here are bronze artefacts from Ban Chiang in the northeast of Thailand, one of the earliest Bronze Age cultures ever discovered, including the world's oldest socketed tool, an axe head set in a sandstone mould (3600–2300 BC).

The main collection: southern building

At the back of the compound, two large modern buildings, flanking an old converted palace, house the museum's **main collection**, kicking off on the ground floor of the **southern building**. Look out here for some historic sculptures from the rest of Asia, including one of the earliest representations of the Buddha, from Gandhara in northwest India. Alexander the Great left a garrison at Gandhara, which explains why the image is in the style of Classical Greek sculpture: for example, the *ushnisha*, the supernatural bump on the top of the head, which symbolizes the Buddha's intellectual and spiritual power, is rationalized into a bun of thick, wavy hair.

Upstairs, in the **Dvaravati** rooms (sixth to eleventh centuries), the pick of the stone and terracotta Buddhas is a small head in smooth, pink clay, whose downcast eyes and faintly smiling full lips typify the serene look of this era. You can't miss a voluptuous Javanese statue of elephant-headed Ganesh, Hindu god of wisdom and the arts, which, being the symbol of the Fine Arts Department who run the museum, is always freshly garlanded. As Ganesh is known as the clearer of obstacles, Hindus always worship him before other gods, so by tradition he has grown fat through getting first choice of the offerings – witness his trunk jammed into a bowl of food in this sculpture.

Room 9 contains the most famous piece of **Srivijaya** art (seventh to thirteenth centuries), a bronze Bodhisattva Avalokitesvara found at Chaiya – according to the Mahayana school of Buddhism, which still holds sway in most of East Asia, a bodhisattva is a saint who has postponed his passage into Nirvana to help ordinary believers gain enlightenment. With its pouting face and sinuous torso, this image has become the ubiquitous emblem of southern Thailand.

The rough chronological order of the collection continues back downstairs with an exhibition of **Khmer** and **Lopburi sculpture** (seventh to fourteenth centuries), most notably some dynamic bronze statuettes and stone lintels. Look out for an elaborate lintel which depicts Vishnu reclining on a dragon in the sea of eternity, dreaming up a new universe after the old one has been annihilated in the Hindu cycle of creation and destruction. Out of his navel comes a lotus, and out of this emerges four-headed Brahma, who will put the dream into practice. Nearby, a smooth, muscular stone statue with a sweet smile and downcast eyes shows the twelfth-century king Jayavarman VII, last of the great Khmer emperors. Such royal statues are very rare and the features borrowed from Buddha images suggest that Jayavarman believed that he was close to Buddhahood himself.

The main collection: northern building

The second half of the survey, in the northern building, begins upstairs with the **Sukhothai** collection (thirteenth to fifteenth centuries), which is short on Buddha images but has some chunky bronzes of Hindu gods and a wide range of ceramics. The **Lanna** room (thirteenth to sixteenth centuries) includes a miniature set of golden regalia, including tiny umbrellas and a cute pair of filigree flip-flops, which would have been enshrined in a chedi.

An ungainly but serene Buddha head, carved from grainy, pink sandstone, represents the **Ayutthaya** style of sculpture (fourteenth to eighteenth centuries): the faintest incision of a moustache above the lips betrays the Khmer influences which came to Ayutthaya after its conquest of Angkor. A sumptuous scripture cabinet, showing a cityscape of old Ayutthaya, is a more unusual piece, one of a surviving handful of such carved and painted items of furniture.

Downstairs in the **Bangkok** rooms (eighteenth century onwards), a stiffly realistic standing bronze brings you full circle: in his zeal for Western naturalism, Rama V had the statue made in the Gandhara style of the earliest Buddha image displayed in the first room of the museum.

The funeral chariots

To the east of the northern building, beyond the café on the left, stands a large garage where the fantastically elaborate **funeral chariots** of the royal family are stored. Pre-eminent among these is the Vejayant Rajarot, built by Rama I in

1785 for carrying the urn at his own funeral. The ten-metre-high structure symbolizes heaven on Mount Meru, while the dragons and divinities around the sides – piled in five golden tiers to suggest the flames of the cremation – represent the mythological inhabitants of the mountain's forests. Weighing forty tonnes and pulled by three hundred men, the teak chariot was used as recently as 1985 for the funeral of Queen Rambhai Bharni, wife of Rama VII.

Wang Na (Palace of the Second King)

The central building of the compound was originally part of the **Wang Na**, a huge palace stretching across Sanam Luang to Khlong Lod, which housed the "second king", appointed by the reigning monarch as his heir and deputy. When Rama V did away with the office in 1887, he turned the "Palace of the Second King" into a museum, which now contains a fascinating array of Thai *objets d'art*.

As you enter (room 5), the display of sumptuous rare gold pieces behind heavy iron bars includes a well-preserved armlet taken from the ruined prang of fifteenth-century Wat Ratburana in Ayutthaya. In adjacent room 6, an intricately carved ivory seat turns out, with gruesome irony, to be a *howdah*, for use on an elephant's back. Among the masks worn by *khon* actors next door (room 7), look out especially for a fierce Hanuman, the white monkey-warrior in the *Ramayana* epic, gleaming with mother-of-pearl.

The huge and varied ceramic collection in room 8 includes some sophisticated pieces from Sukhothai, while the room above (9) holds a riot of mother-of-pearl items, whose flaming rainbow of colours comes from the shell of the turbo snail from the Gulf of Thailand. It's also worth seeking out the display of richly decorated musical instruments in room 15, where you can hear tapes of the unfamiliar sounds they produce.

The Buddhaisawan Chapel

The second holiest image in Thailand, after the Emerald Buddha, is housed in the **Buddhaisawan Chapel**, the vast hall in front of the eastern entrance to the Wang Na. Inside, the fine proportions of the hall, with its ornate coffered ceiling and lacquered window shutters, are enhanced by painted rows of divinities and converted demons, all turned to face the chubby, glowing **Phra Sihing Buddha**, which according to legend was magically created in Sri Lanka and sent to Sukhothai in the thirteenth century. Like the Emerald Buddha, the image was believed to bring good luck to its owner and was frequently snatched from one northern town to another, until Rama I brought it down from Chiang Mai in 1795 and installed it here in the second king's private chapel. Two other images (in Nakhon Si Thammarat and Chiang Mai) now claim to be the authentic Phra Sihing Buddha, but all three are in fact derived from a lost original – this one is in a fifteenth-century Sukhothai style. It's still much loved by ordinary people and at Thai New Year is carried out onto Sanam Luang, where worshippers sprinkle it with water as a merit-making gesture.

The careful detail and rich, soothing colours of the surrounding 200-year-old **murals** are surprisingly well-preserved; the bottom row between the windows narrates the life of the Buddha, beginning in the far right-hand corner with his parents' wedding.

Tamnak Daeng

On the south side of the Buddhaisawan Chapel, the sumptuous **Tamnak Daeng** (Red House) stands out, a large, airy Ayutthaya-style house made of rare golden teak, surmounted by a multi-tiered roof decorated with carved foliage and swan's tail finials. Originally part of the private quarters of

Princess Sri Sudarak, elder sister of Rama I, it was moved from the Grand Palace to the old palace in Thonburi for Queen Sri Suriyen, wife of Rama II; when her son became second king to Rama IV, he dismantled the edifice again and shipped it here to the Wang Na compound. Inside, it's furnished in the style of the early Bangkok period, with some of the beautiful objects that once belonged to Sri Suriyen, a huge, ornately carved box bed, and the uncommon luxury of an indoor toilet and bathroom.

THE NATIONAL GALLERY

Map 4, F2. Wed–Sun 9am–4pm; B30. Express boat to Phra Athit pier. Bus AC#3, AC#7, AC#15, #15, #39, #53 or #59.

Thailand's **National Gallery**, across the hectic Phra Pinklao Road from Sanam Luang, accommodates a permanent collection of largely uninspiring and derivative twentieth-century Thai art, but its temporary exhibitions can be pretty good – see *Bangkok Metro* magazine for details. The fine old wooden building that houses the gallery is also worth more than a cursory glance – it used to be the Royal Mint, and is constructed in typical early twentieth-century style, around a central courtyard.

Around Democracy Monument

E ast of the canal that defines the royal island of Ratanakosin lies a handful of important and fairly interesting temples, which can all be reached on foot from the **Democracy Monument**, and from the guesthouses of Banglamphu and the Grand Palace. The huge stone Democracy Monument forms the centrepiece of an enormous roundabout that siphons traffic from the major Rajdamnoen Klang artery, and it's only once you've escaped the roar and fumes of this multi-laned road that you can enjoy the more peaceful neighbourhoods that adjoin it.

Most of these areas retain a traditional flavour, and there is as yet hardly any high-rise architecture. The string of temple-supply shops around **Wat Suthat** and **Sao Ching Cha** make this a rewarding area to explore, and the amulet market in the grounds of **Loh Prasat** is also well worth seeking out. Even the backpackers' ghetto of **Banglamphu**, just ten minutes' walk west of Democracy Monument, still boasts a good number of wooden shophouses and narrow alleyways alongside the purpose-built guesthouses, travel agents and jewellery shops.

> **There are plenty of accommodation and eating options within walking distance of Democracy Monument, most of them located in the backpackers' district of Banglamphu (see p.136).**

Democracy Monument is served by dozens of **buses** from all parts of the city. As a landmark, it's hard to miss, and if you're coming from eastern or northern parts of the city (such as Hulamaphong Station, Siam Square or Sukhumvit), get off the bus as soon as you see it – it's almost impossible to cross the road at the second (western-most) bus stop on Rajdamnoen Klang. You can also reach this district by **boat**. Close by the Golden Mount, five minutes' walk east of Democracy, Phanfa pier lies at the intersection of Khlong Banglamphu and Khlong Sen Seb, both of them served by frequent longtail boats (see p.49). The easiest access to Banglamphu and Wat Indraviharn is by Chao Phraya Express boat.

DEMOCRACY MONUMENT

Map 3, G9. Longtail boat to Phanfa pier. Bus AC#3, AC#9, AC#11, AC#15, #15, #39, #56, or #59.

Begun in 1939, the **Democracy Monument** was conceived as a testament to the ideals that fuelled the 1932 revolution and the changeover to a constitutional monarchy, hence its symbolic positioning between the royal residences. Its **dimensions** are also significant: the four stone wings, set in a circle, tower to a height of 24m, the same as the radius of the monument – an allusion to June 24, the date the system was changed; the 75 cannons around the perimeter refer to the year, 2475 BE (1932 AD). The monument contains a copy of the constitution and is a focal point for public events and demonstrations – it was a rallying-point during the pro-democracy protests of May 1992 and, less traumatically, gets decked out with flowers every year on December 5, in honour of the king's birthday. If you're prepared to brave the traffic that streams round Democracy day and night, you can climb the steps at the base of the monument and inspect its facades at closer quarters. Each wing is carved with friezes showing heroic scenes from Thailand's history.

The monument was designed by **Corrado Feroci**, an Italian sculptor invited to Thailand by Rama VI in 1924 to encourage the pursuit of Western art. He changed his name to Silpa Bhirasi and stayed in Thailand until his death, producing many of Bangkok's statues and monuments – including the Rama I statue at Memorial Bridge and Victory Monument in the Phrayathai district – as well as founding the first Institute of Fine Arts.

LOH PRASAT AND THE AMULET MARKET

Map 2, D4. Longtail boat to Phanfa pier. Bus AC#3, AC#9, AC#11, AC#15, #15, #39, #56, or #59.

Five minutes' walk southeast of Democracy Monument, at the point where Rajdamnoen Klang meets Mahachai Road, stands the assortment of religious buildings known collectively as Wat Rajnadda. It's immediately recognizable by the dusky-pink, multi-tiered, castle-like structure called **Loh Prasat** or "Iron Monastery" – a reference to its numerous metal spires. The only structure of its kind in Bangkok, Loh Prasat is the dominant and most bizarre of Wat Rajnadda's components. Each tier is pierced by passageways running north–south and east–west (fifteen in each direction at

Amulets

To protect themselves from malevolent spirits and physical misfortune, Thais wear or carry at least one amulet at all times. The most popular **images** are copies of sacred statues, while others show holy men, kings, or a many-armed monk closing his eyes, ears and mouth to concentrate better on reaching Nirvana. On the reverse is often inscribed a *yantra*, a combination of letters and figures designed to ward off evil; these can be very specific, protecting your durian orchards from storms, for example, or your tuk-tuk from oncoming traffic.

Amulets can be made from bronze, clay, plaster or gold, and some have sacred ingredients added, such as the ashes of burned holy texts. But what really determines an amulet's efficacy is its history: where and by whom it was made, who or what it represents, and who consecrated it. Monks are often involved in making the images, and are always called upon to consecrate them – the more charismatic the monk, the more powerful the amulet. In return, the proceeds from the sale of amulets contributes to wat funds.

The **belief in amulets** probably originated in India, where tiny images were sold to pilgrims who visited the four holy sites associated with the Buddha. But not all amulets are Buddhist-related – there's a whole range of other enchanted objects, including tigers' teeth, tamarind seeds, coloured threads and miniature phalluses. The latter are of Hindu origin; worn around the waist, they are associated with fertility and provide protection for the genitals.

AMULETS

ground level), with small meditation cells at each point of intersection. The Sri Lankan monastery on which it is modelled contained a thousand cells; this one probably has half that number.

An adjoining compound contains Bangkok's biggest **amulet market**, where at least a hundred stalls open up daily to sell tiny Buddha images of all designs, materials and prices. Alongside these miniature charms are statues, dolls and carved wooden phalluses, also bought to placate or ward off disgruntled spirits.

....

Though the amulet market at Wat Rajnadda is probably the best in Bangkok, you should also check out the amulet flea market that sets up daily on the pavements in front of Wat Mahathat (Map 4, C4). Prices at these stalls start as low as B10 and rise into the thousands.

....

THE GOLDEN MOUNT

Map 2, D4. Longtail boat to Phanfa pier. Bus AC#3, AC#9, AC#11, AC#15, #15, #39, #56, or #59.

The dirty yellow hill crowned with a gleaming gold chedi just across the road from Loh Prasat is the grandiosely named Golden Mount, or Phu Khao Tong. It rises within the compound of **Wat Saket**, a dilapidated late eighteenth-century temple built by Rama I just outside his new city walls to serve as the capital's crematorium. During the following hundred years the temple became the dumping ground for some sixty thousand plague victims – the majority of them too poor to afford funeral pyres, and thus left to the vultures.

The **Golden Mount** was a late addition to the compound. Early in the nineteenth century, Rama III built a huge chedi here, but the ground proved too soft to support it, and the whole thing collapsed. Since Buddhist law states that a religious building can never be destroyed, however tumbledown, the hill of rubble was left in place; fifty years later Rama V topped it with a more sensibly sized chedi in which he placed a few relics, believed by some to be the Buddha's teeth.

To reach the base of the mount, follow the renovated crenellations of the old city wall, going past a small market selling caged birds, before veering left at the sign. Climbing to the top, you'll pass remnants of the collapsed chedi and plaques commemorating donors to the temple. The **terrace** surrounding the base of the new chedi is a good place for landmark-spotting: immediately to the west are the gleaming roofs of Wat Rajnadda and the salmon-pink Loh Prasat, and behind them you should be able to see the spires of the Grand Palace and, even further beyond, the beautifully proportioned prangs of Wat Arun on the other side of the river.

> **Wat Saket hosts an enormous annual temple fair in the first week of November, when the mount is illuminated with coloured lanterns and the whole compound seethes with funfair rides, food sellers and travelling performers.**

WAT SUTHAT AND SAO CHING CHA

Map 2, C4. Bus AC#7, AC#8, #25 or #56.

Located about 1km southwest of the Golden Mount, and a similar distance directly south of Democracy Monument along Thanon Dinso, **Wat Suthat** contains Bangkok's tallest **viharn**, built in the early nineteenth century to house the meditating figure of **Phra Sri Sakyamuni Buddha**. This eight-metre-high statue was brought all the way from Sukhothai by river, and now sits on a glittering mosaic dais surrounded with surreal **murals** that depict the last 24 lives of the Buddha rather than the more usual ten. The courtyard and galleries around the bot are full of **Chinese statues**, most of which were brought over from China during Rama I's reign, as ballast in rice boats: check out the gormless Western sailors and the pompous Chinese scholars. The viharn is often locked on weekdays, however, so you may not get the chance to see Phra Sri Sakyamuni.

The area just in front of Wat Suthat is dominated by the towering, red-painted teak posts of **Sao Ching Cha**, otherwise known as the **Giant Swing**, once the focal point of a Brahmin ceremony to honour Shiva's annual visit to earth. Teams of two or four young men would stand on the outsized seat (now missing) and swing up to a height of 25 metres, to grab between their teeth a bag of gold suspended on the end of a bamboo pole. The act of swinging probably symbolized the rising and setting of the sun, though legend also has it that Shiva and his consort Uma were banned from swinging in their heavenly abode because doing so caused cataclysmic floods on earth – prompting Shiva to demand that the practice be continued on earth as a rite to ensure moderate rains and bountiful harvests. The terrestrial version led to so many accidents that it was outlawed in the 1930s.

The streets leading up to Wat Suthat and Sao Ching Cha are renowned as the best place in the city to buy **religious paraphernalia**, and are well worth a browse. Thanon Bamruang in particular is lined with shops selling everything a good Buddhist could need, from household offertory tables to temple umbrellas and two-metre-high Buddha images. They also sell special alms packs for devotees to donate to monks; a typical pack is contained within a holy saffron-coloured plastic bucket (which can be used by the monk for washing his robes, or himself), and comprises such daily necessities as soap, toothpaste, soap powder, toilet roll, candles and incense.

WAT SUTHAT AND SAO CHING CHA

WAT RAJABOPHIT

Map 4, G7. Bus AC#7, AC#8 or #25.

On Rajabophit Road, midway between Wat Suthat and the Grand Palace, stands **Wat Rajabophit**, one of the city's prettiest temples and another example of Chinese influence. It was built by Rama V and is characteristic of this progressive king in its unusual design, with the rectangular bot and viharn connected by a circular cloister that encloses a chedi. Every external wall in the compound is covered in the pastel shades of Chinese *bencharong* ceramic tiles, creating a stunning overall effect, while the interior of the bot looks like a tiny banqueting hall, with gilded Gothic vaults and intricate mother-of-pearl doors.

Heading west from Wat Rajabophit towards the Grand Palace, you'll pass a gold statue of a pig as you cross the canal. It was erected in tribute to one of Rama V's wives, born in the Chinese Year of the Pig.

WAT INDRAVIHARN

Map 3, E3. Express boat to Wisut Kasat pier. Bus #53.

North of Democracy, at the edge of the Banglamphu district on Wisut Kasat Road, **Wat Indraviharn** (also known as Wat In) features on some tourist itineraries by virtue of the enormous standing Buddha that dominates its precincts. Commissioned by Rama IV in the mid-nineteenth century to enshrine a Buddha relic from Sri Lanka, the 32-metre-high image certainly doesn't rate as a work of art: its enormous, overly flattened features give it an ungainly aspect, while the gold mirror-mosaic surface only emphasizes its faintly kitsch effect. But the beautifully pedicured foot-long toenails peep out gracefully from beneath devotees' garlands of fragrant jasmine, and you can get reasonable views of the neighbourhood by climbing the stairways of the tower supporting the statue from behind; when unlocked, the doorways in the upper part of the tower give access to the interior of the hollow image, affording vistas from shoulder level. Elsewhere in the wat's compact grounds you'll find the usual amalgam of architectural and spiritual styles, including a Chinese shrine and statues of Ramas IV and V.

WAT INDRAVIHARN

Chinatown and Pahurat

When the newly crowned Rama I decided to move his capital across to the east bank of the river in 1782, the Chinese community living on the proposed site of his palace was given no choice but to relocate downriver, to the **Sampeng** area. Two hundred years on, **Chinatown** has grown into the country's largest Chinese district, a sprawl of narrow alleyways, temples and shophouses packed between Charoen Krung (also known as New Road) and the river, separated from Ratanakosin by the Indian area of **Pahurat** – famous for its cloth and dressmakers' trimmings – and bordered to the east by Hualamphong train station. Real estate in this part of the city is said to be the most valuable in the country, with land prices on the Charoen Krung and Yaowarat Road arteries reputed to fetch over a million baht per square metre; not surprisingly, there are almost a hundred gold shops in the Sampeng quarter.

For the tourist, Chinatown is chiefly interesting for its markets and shophouses, its open-fronted warehouses, and remnants of colonial-style architecture, though it also has a few noteworthy temples. The following account covers Chinatown's main attractions and most interesting neighbourhoods, sketching a meandering and quite lengthy route which could easily take a whole day to complete on foot.

For accommodation and eating options in Chinatown, see p.143 and p.170.

Easiest access is to take the *Chao Phraya Express* **boat** to Tha Rajavongse (Rajawong) at the southern end of Rajawong Road, which runs through the centre of Chinatown; or use the Banglamphu–Hualamphong longtail boat service (every 20–30min; 15min), getting off at the Hualamphong terminus and then walking for five minutes until you reach Chinatown. This part of the city is also well served by **buses** from downtown Bangkok, as well as from Banglamphu and Ratanakosin; your best bet is to take any Hualamphong-bound bus (see box on p.44) and then walk from the train station; the non-air-con bus #56 is also a useful link from Banglamphu, as it runs along Tanao Road at the end of Khao San Road and then goes all the way down Mahachai and Chakraphet roads in Chinatown – get off just after the Merry King Department Store for Sampeng Lane.

Orientation in Chinatown can be quite tricky: the alleys (known as trok rather than the more usual soi) are extremely narrow, their turn-offs and other road signs often obscured by the mounds of merchandise that clutter the sidewalks and the surrounding hordes of buyers and sellers.

WAT TRAIMIT AND THE GOLDEN BUDDHA

Map 5, G6. Daily 9am–5pm; B20. Longtail boat along Khlong Banglamphu to Hualamphong. Bus #25 or #53.

Given the confusing layout of the district, it's worth starting your explorations at the eastern edge of Chinatown,

The Chinese in Thailand

The **Chinese** have been a dominant force in the shaping of Thailand, and **commerce** is the foundation of their success. When the capital was moved from Ayutthaya to Bangkok in 1782 it was to an already flourishing Chinese trading post and, as the economy began to boom, both Rama I and Rama II encouraged Chinese immigration to boost the indigenous workforce. Thousands of migrants came, most of them young men eager to earn money that could be sent back to families impoverished by civil wars and persistently bad harvests.

By the close of the nineteenth century, the Chinese dominated Thailand's commercial and urban sector, while the Thais remained in firm control of the political domain. It was an arrangement that apparently satisfied both parties – as the old Chinese proverb goes, "We don't mind who holds the head of the cow, providing we can milk it" – and one that still holds true today.

Because so few Chinese women had emigrated, **intermarriage** between the two communities was common until the beginning of the twentieth century – indeed, there is some Chinese blood in almost every Thai citizen today, including the king. But in the early 1900s Chinese women started to arrive in Thailand, making Chinese society more self-sufficient and enclosed. **Anti-Chinese feelings** grew and discriminatory laws ensued, including the closing of some jobs to Chinese citizens, a movement that increased in fervour as communism began to be perceived as a threat. Since the 1970s, strict immigration controls have limited the number of new settlers to one hundred per nationality per year, a particularly harsh imposition on the Chinese.

just west of Hualamphong station, with the triangle of land occupied by **Wat Traimit**. Outwardly unprepossessing, the temple boasts a quite stunning interior feature.

The world's largest solid gold Buddha is housed here, fittingly for a community so closely linked with the gold trade, even if the image has nothing to do with China's spiritual heritage. Over three metres tall and weighing 5.5 tons, the **Golden Buddha** gleams as if coated in liquid metal, seated amid candles and surrounded with offerings of lotus buds and incense. A fine example of the curvaceous grace of Sukhothai art, the beautifully proportioned figure is best appreciated by comparing it with the much cruder Sukhothai Buddha in the next-door bot, to the east.

Cast in the thirteenth century, the image was brought to Bangkok by Rama III, completely encased in stucco – a common ruse to conceal valuable statues from would-be thieves. The disguise was so good that no one guessed what was underneath until 1955 when the image was accidentally knocked in the process of being moved to Wat Traimit, and the stucco cracked to reveal a patch of gold. The discovery launched a country-wide craze for tapping away at plaster Buddhas in search of hidden precious metals, but Wat Traimit's is still the most valuable – it's valued, by weight alone, at US$14 million. Sections of the stucco casing are now on display alongside the Golden Buddha.

SAMPENG LANE AND SOI ISSARANUPHAP

Map 5, F6 & E5. Express boat to Rajavongse (Rajawong) pier. Bus #25, #53 or #56.

Turn right outside Wat Traimit onto Yaowarat Road, then left onto Songsawat Road, to reach **Sampeng Lane** (also signposted as Soi Wanit 1), an area that used to thrive on opium dens, gambling houses and brothels, but now sticks to more reputable (if tacky) commerce. Stretching southeast–northwest for about a kilometre, Sampeng Lane is a fun place to browse and shop, unfurling itself like a ramshackle department store selling everything at bargain-basement rates. Among other things, this is the cheapest place in town to buy Chinese silk pyjama pants, electronic pets and other computer games, sarongs, alarm clocks, underwear and hair accessories. And, to complete this perfect shopping experience, there are food stalls every few steps to help keep up your energy.

For a rather more sensual experience, take a right about half way down Sampeng Lane, into **Soi Issaranuphap** (also signed in places as Soi 16). Packed with people from dawn till dusk, this long, dark alleyway, which also traverses Charoen Krung (New Road), is the place to come in search of ginseng roots (essential for good health), quivering fish heads, cubes of cockroach-killer chalk, and pungent piles of cinnamon sticks. Alleys branch off in all directions to gaudy Chinese temples and market squares. You'll see Chinese grandfathers discussing business in darkened shops, and ancient pharmacists concocting bizarre potions to order. Soi Issaranuphap finally ends at the Plaplachai Road intersection amid a flurry of shops specializing in paper **funeral art**. Believing that the deceased should be well provided for in their afterlife, Chinese buy miniature paper replicas of necessities to be burned with the body: especially popular are houses, cars, suits of clothing and, of course, money.

....

The only time you'll find Chinese-run shops, hotels and restaurants closed is over the annual three-day holiday at Chinese New Year. This is the community's most important festival, but is celebrated much more as a family affair than in the Chinatowns of other countries.

....

SAMPENG LANE AND SOI ISSARANUPHAP

WAT MANGKON KAMALAWAT

Map 5, F3. Bus AC#7, #25 or #53.

If Soi Issaranuphap epitomizes traditional Chinatown commerce, then **Wat Mangkon Kamalawat** (also known as Wat Leng Nee Yee, or "Dragon Flower Temple") stands as a superb example of the community's spiritual practices. Best approached via its dramatic multi-tiered gateway 10m northwest up Charoen Krung (New Road) from the Soi Issaranuphap junction, Wat Mangkon receives a constant stream of devotees, who come to leave offerings at one or more of the small altars inside this important Mahayana Buddhist temple. As with the Theravada Buddhism espoused by the Thais, Mahayana Buddhism (see Religion, p.278) fuses with other ancient religious beliefs, notably Confucianism and Taoism, and the statues and shrines within Wat Mangkon cover the whole spectrum. Passing through the secondary gateway, under the glazed ceramic gables topped with undulating Chinese dragons, you're greeted by a set of four outsized statues of bearded and rather forbidding sages, each clasping a symbolic object: a parasol, a pagoda, a snake's head and a mandolin. Beyond them, a series of Buddha images swathed in saffron netting occupies the next chamber, a lovely open-sided room of gold paintwork, red-lacquered wood, lattice lanterns and pictorial wall panels inlaid with mother-of-pearl. Elsewhere in the compound you'll find a fortune-teller, a Chinese medicine stall, and little booths selling devotional paraphernalia.

WAT GA BUANG KIM

Map 5, D4. Express boat to Rajavongse (Rajawong) pier. Bus AC#7, #25 or #53.

Less than 100m northwest up Charoen Krung (New Road)

from Wat Mangkon, a left turn into Rajawong Road, followed by a right turn into Anawong Road and a further right turn into the narrow, two-pronged Soi Krai brings you to the typical neighbourhood temple of **Wat Ga Buang Kim**. Here, as at Thai temples upcountry, local residents socialize in the shade of the tiny, enclosed courtyard and the occasional worshipper drops by to pay homage at the altar. This particular wat is remarkable for its exquisitely ornamented "vegetarian hall", a one-room shrine with a central altarpiece framed by intricately carved wooden tableaux – gold-painted miniatures arranged as if in sequence, with recognizable characters reappearing in new positions and in different moods. The hall's outer wall is adorned with small tableaux, too – the area around the doorway at the top of the stairs peopled with finely crafted ceramic figurines drawn from Chinese opera stories. The other building in the wat compound is a stage used for Chinese opera performances.

WAT CHAKRAWAT

Map 5, C4. Express boat to Rajavongse (Rajawong) pier. Bus #56.

About another 100m to the south, the temple of **Wat Chakrawat** overlooks the Chao Phraya River. The compound is home to several long-suffering crocodiles, not to mention monkeys, dogs and chess-playing local residents. **Crocodiles** have lived in the tiny pond behind the bot for about fifty years, ever since one was brought here after being hauled out of the river, where it had been endangering the limbs of bathers. The original crocodile, stuffed, sits in a glass case overlooking the current generation in the pond.

Across the other side of the wat compound is a grotto housing two unusual **Buddhist relics**. The first is a black silhouette on the wall, decorated with squares of gold leaf and believed to be the Buddha's shadow. Nearby, the statue of a fat monk looks on. The story goes that this monk was so good-looking that he was forever being tempted by the attentions of women; the only way he could deter them was to make himself ugly, which he did by gorging himself into obesity.

PAHURAT

Map 5, B3. Express boat to Saphan Phut pier (Memorial Bridge). Bus AC#7, #53 or #56.

The small square south of the intersection of Chakraphet and **Pahurat** roads, is the focus of the capital's sizeable Indian community. Curiosity-shopping is not as rewarding here as in Chinatown, but if you're interested in buying **fabrics** other than Thai silk this is definitely the place. Pahurat Road is chock-a-block with cloth merchants specializing in everything from curtain and cushion materials, through saree and sarong lengths to wedding outfits and *lakhon* dance costumes complete with accessories. Also here, at the Charoen Krung (New Road)/Triphet Road intersection, is the Old Siam Plaza: its mint-green and cream exterior, resplendent with shutters and balustraded balconies, redolent of a colonial summer palace, and its airy, three-storey interior filled with a strange combination of shops selling either upmarket gifts or hi-tech consumer goods. You'll find a few eateries and an exceptionally good food hall under this roof, too, but Pahurat is renowned for its **Indian restaurants**, and a short stroll along Chakraphet Road will take you past a choice selection of bona fide curry houses and street vendors.

For more information on places to eat in Pahurat, see p.170.

PAHURAT

Thonburi

Bangkok really began across the river from Ratanakosin in the town of **Thonburi**. Devoid of grand ruins and isolated from central Bangkok, it's hard to imagine Thonburi as a former capital of Thailand, but so it was for fifteen years, between the fall of Ayutthaya in 1767 and the establishment of Bangkok in 1782. General Phrya Taksin chose to set up his capital here, strategically near the sea and far from the marauding Burmese, but the story of his brief reign is a chronicle of battles that left little time and few resources to devote to the building of a city worthy of its predecessor. When General Chao Phraya displaced the demented Taksin to become Rama I, his first decision as founder of the Chakri dynasty was to move the capital to the more defensible site across the river. It wasn't until 1932 that Thonburi was linked to its replacement by the **Memorial Bridge**, built to commemorate the one-hundred-and-fiftieth anniversary of the foundation of the Chakri dynasty and of Bangkok, and dedicated to Rama I, whose bronze statue sits at the Bangkok approach. Thonburi retained its separate identity for another forty years until, in 1971, it officially became part of Bangkok.

> **Thonburi has no obvious places to stay, but the guesthouses and restaurants of Banglamphu (see p.136 and p.166) are within easy reach, just across the Chao Phraya River.**

While Thonburi may lack the fine monuments of Thailand's other ancient capitals, it nevertheless contains

Thonburi canal rides

One of the most popular ways of seeing the sights of Thonburi is to embark on a canal tour by **chartering a longtail boat** from Tha Chang, in front of the Grand Palace. These tours follow a set route, taking in Wat Arun and the Royal Barge Museum and then continuing along Thonburi's network of small canals, and charge an average price of B250 per person. There are no official departure times: you just turn up at the pier, haggle with the boatman next in line and jump into his longtail.

A less expensive but equally satisfying alternative is to use the **public longtails** that run bus-like services along back canals from central Bangkok-side piers, departing every ten to thirty minutes and charging B10–30 a round trip. Some of the most accessible routes include: the Khlong Bangkok Noi service from Tha Chang; the Khlong Mon service from Tha Thien, in front of Wat Po; the Khlong Bang Waek service from Tha Saphan Phut, at Memorial Bridge; and the Khlong Om service from Tha Nonthaburi.

If possible, try to avoid going on an organized canal tour to Thonburi's Wat Sai **floating market**, which has become very commercialized, and opt instead for the two-hour trip out of Bangkok to the floating markets of Damnoen Saduak (see p.248). However, if you're short on time, you can join longtail Wat Sai market tours from Tha Chang or from Tha Orienten (at the *Oriental Hotel*). Tours leave at around 7am and cost from B350 per person.

some of the most traditional parts of Bangkok, making it a pleasant and evocative place in which to wander. As well as the imposing riverside structure of **Wat Arun**, Thonburi offers a fleet of royal barges and several moderately interesting temples. In addition, life on this side of the river still revolves around the khlongs, on which vendors of food and household goods paddle their boats through the residential areas, and canalside factories transport their wares to the Chao Phraya River artery. Canalside **architecture** ranges from ramshackle, makeshift homes balanced just above the water – and prone to flooding during the monsoon season – to villa-style residences where the river is kept at bay by lawns, verandahs and concrete. Modern Thonburi, on the other hand, sprawling to each side of Phra Pinklao Road, consists of the prosaic line-up of department stores, cinemas, restaurants and markets found all over urbanized Thailand.

Getting there is simply a matter of crossing the river – use one of the numerous bridges (Memorial and Phra Pinklao are the most central), take a cross-river ferry, or hop on the express ferry, which makes three stops around the riverside Bangkok Noi station, just south of Phra Pinklao Bridge.

WAT ARUN

Map 4, A9. Daily 7am–5pm; B10. Cross-river ferry from Tha Thien.
Almost directly across the river from Wat Po rises the enormous five-pranged **Wat Arun,** the Temple of Dawn, probably Bangkok's most memorable landmark and familiar as the silhouette used in the TAT logo. It's best seen from the river, as you head downstream from the Grand Palace towards the *Oriental Hotel*, but is ornate enough to merit stopping off for a closer look. All boat tours include half an hour here, but – despite the claims of tour operators who'll try to persuade you otherwise – it's easy to visit Wat Arun independently: just take a cross-river ferry from Tha Thien.

A good way to enjoy the night-time, floodlit view of
Wat Arun and Bangkok's other riverside sights is to
join one of the restaurant boats that travel up and
down the Chao Phraya River every evening. See p.170
for recommendations.

A wat has occupied this site since the Ayutthaya period,
though it only became known as the Temple of Dawn in
1768, when General Phrya Taksin reputedly reached his
new capital at the break of day. The temple served as his
royal chapel and housed the recaptured Emerald Buddha
for several years until the image was moved to Wat Phra
Kaeo in 1785. Despite losing its special status after the
relocation, Wat Arun continued to be revered, and was
reconstructed and enlarged to its present height of 104m
by Rama II and Rama III.

The Wat Arun that you see today is a classic prang structure of Ayutthayan style, built as a representation of Mount
Meru, the home of the gods in Khmer mythology.
Climbing the two tiers of the square base that supports the
central prang, you not only get a good view of the river
and beyond, but also a chance to examine the tower's curious decorations. Both this main prang and the four minor
ones that encircle it are covered in bits of broken porcelain,
arranged to create an amazing array of polychromatic flowers. (Local people gained much merit by donating their
crockery for the purpose.) Statues of mythical figures such
as *yaksha* demons and half-bird, half-human *kinnari* support
the different levels and, on the first terrace, the mondops at
each cardinal point contain statues of the Buddha at the
most important stages of his life: at birth (north), in meditation (east), preaching his first sermon (south) and entering
Nirvana (west). The second platform surrounds the base of
the prang proper, whose closed entranceways are guarded

WAT ARUN

by four statues of the Hindu god Indra on his three-headed elephant Erawan. In the niches of the smaller prangs stand statues of Phra Pai, the god of the wind, on horseback.

WAT PRAYOON

Map 2, B6. Express boat to Saphan Phut pier (Memorial Bridge), then walk across the bridge.

Downstream of Wat Arun, beside Memorial Bridge, **Wat Prayoon** is worth visiting for its unusual collection of miniature chedis and shrines, set on an artificial hill constructed on a whim of Rama III's, after he'd noticed the pleasing shapes made by dripping candle wax. Wedged in among the grottoes, caverns and ledges of this uneven mass are numerous shrines to departed devotees, forming a phenomenal gallery of different styles, from traditionally Thai chedis, bots or prangs to such obviously foreign designs as the tiny Wild West house complete with cactuses at the front door. Turtles fill the pond surrounding the mound – you can feed them with the banana and papaya sold nearby. At the edge of the pond stands a memorial to the unfortunate few who lost their lives when one of the saluting cannons exploded at the temple's dedication ceremony in 1836.

About ten minutes' walk upstream from Wat Prayoon, the Catholic church of **Santa Cruz** sits at the heart of what used to be Thonburi's **Portuguese quarter**. The Portuguese came to Thailand both to trade and to proselytize, and by 1856 had established the largest of the European communities in Bangkok: four thousand Portuguese Christians lived in and around Thonburi at this time, about one percent of the total population. The Portuguese ghetto is a thing of the distant past, but this is nonetheless an interesting patch to stroll through, comprising narrow backstreets and tiny shophouses stocked with all manner of goods, from two-baht plastic toys to the essential bottles of chilli sauce.

ROYAL BARGE MUSEUM

Map 2, A3. Daily 8.30am–4.30pm; B10. Express boat to Bangkok Noi pier. Bus AC#3, AC#7, AC#9, AC#11, #124 or #127.

Until about twenty years ago, the king would process down the Chao Phraya River to Wat Arun in a flotilla of royal barges at least once a year, on the occasion of Kathin, the annual donation of robes by the laity to the temple at the end of the rainy season. Fifty-one barges, filling the width of the river and stretching for almost a kilometre, drifted slowly to the measured beat of a drum and the hypnotic strains of ancient boating hymns, chanted by over two thousand oarsmen whose red, gold and blue uniforms complemented the black and gold craft.

The hundred-year-old boats are becoming quite frail, so such a procession is now a rare event – the last was in 1996, to mark the fiftieth anniversary of the king's accession to the throne. The three elegantly narrow vessels at the heart of the ceremony now spend their time moored in the **Royal Barge Museum** on the north bank of Khlong Bangkok Noi. Up to 50m long and intricately lacquered and gilded all over, they taper at the prow into magnificent mythical figures after a design first used by the kings of Ayutthaya. Rama I had the boats copied and, when those fell into disrepair, Rama V commissioned the exact reconstructions still in use today. The most important of the trio is *Sri Suphanahongse*, which bears the king and queen and is instantly recognizable by the 5m-high prow representing a golden swan. In front of it floats *Anantanagaraj*, fronted by a magnificent seven-headed naga and bearing a Buddha image, while the royal children bring up the rear in *Anekchartphuchong*, which has a monkey god from the *Ramayana* at the bow.

The museum is a feature of all canal tours. To **get there** on your own, cross the Phra Pinklao Bridge and take the first left (Soi Wat Dusitaram), which leads to the museum through a jumble of walkways and houses on stilts. Alternatively, take a ferry to Bangkok Noi station; from there follow the tracks until you reach the bridge over Khlong Bangkok Noi, cross it and follow the signs. Either way it's about a ten-minute walk.

Dusit

onnected to Ratanakosin via the boulevards of Rajdamnoen Klang and Rajdamnoen Nok, the spacious, leafy area known as **Dusit** has been a royal district since the reign of Rama V (1860–1910). The first Thai monarch to visit Europe, Rama V returned with radical plans for the modernization of his capital, the fruits of which are most visible in Dusit: notably **Vimanmek Palace** and **Wat Benjamabophit**, the so-called Marble Temple. Today the peaceful Dusit area retains its European feel, and much of the country's decision-making goes on behind the high fences and impressive facades that line its leafy avenues: Government House is here, and the king lives on the eastern edge of the area, in the Chitrlada Palace.

VIMANMEK PALACE

Map 2, E1. Daily 9am–4pm; compulsory free guided tours every 30min, last tour 3pm; B50, or free if you have a Grand Palace ticket, which remains valid for one month. Note that the same **dress rules** apply here as to the Grand Palace (see p.56). Bus AC#10 or #56.

Vimanmek Palace, at the end of the impressive sweep of Rajdamnoen Nok, was built by Rama V as a summer retreat on the little east-coast island of Ko Si Chang, from

The royal white elephants

In Thailand the most revered of all elephants are the so-called **white elephants**. Actually tawny brown albinos, they are considered so sacred that they all, whether wild or captive, belong to the king; Buddhist mythology, which tells how the barren Queen Maya became pregnant with the future Buddha after dreaming that a white elephant had entered her womb. The thirteenth-century King Ramkhamhaeng adopted the beast as a symbol of the great and the divine, and ever since, a Thai king's greatness is measured by the number of white elephants he owns. The present king, Rama IX, has eleven, the largest collection to date.

The most recent addition was first spotted in Lampang in 1992, but experts from the royal household had to spend a year watching its every move before it was given offical "white elephant" status. Key **attributes** include paleness of seven crucial areas – eyes, nails, palate, hair, outer edges of the ears, tail and testicles – and an all-round genteel demeanour, manifested in the way in which it cleans its food before eating or in a tendency to sleep in a kneeling position. Traditionally, an elaborate **ceremony** should take place every time a new elephant is presented to the king: the animal is paraded from its place of capture to Dusit, where it's anointed with holy water before being housed in the royal stables. Recently. though, the ceremonies have been dropped as a cost-cutting measure, and only one of the elephants is now kept inside the palace – the others live in less luxurious rural accommodation.

The expression "white elephant" probably derives from the legend that the kings used to present enemies with one of these creatures, whose upkeep proved so expensive that the recipient went bust trying to keep it.

where it was transported bit by bit in 1901. Constructed entirely of golden teak without a single nail, the L-shaped "Celestial Residence" is encircled by verandahs that look out on to well-kept lawns, flower gardens and lotus ponds. Not surprisingly, Vimanmek soon became the king's favourite palace, and he and his enormous retinue of officials, concubines and children stayed here for lengthy periods between 1902 and 1906. All of Vimanmek's 81 rooms were out of bounds to male visitors, except for the king's own apartments, which were entered by a separate staircase.

A bronze equestrian statue of Rama V stands close to the entrance to the palace compound – walk to the right of the statue, around the Italian Renaissance-style **Throne Hall** (home of the National Assembly until the 1970s), and a little way past the entrance to Dusit Zoo (see below).

On display inside is Rama V's collection of artefacts from all over the world, including *bencharong* ceramics, European furniture and bejewelled Thai betel-nut sets. Considered progressive in his day, Rama V introduced many newfangled ideas to Thailand: the country's first indoor bathroom is here, as is the earliest typewriter with Thai characters, and some of the first portrait paintings – portraiture had until then been seen as a way of stealing part of the sitter's soul.

....

Dusit has no accommodation of its own, but the guest houses of north Banglamphu, near the National Library, are fairly near (see p.137). Restaurants in this area are listed on p.165.

....

DUSIT ZOO

Map 2, E2. Daily 8am–6pm; B20. Bus AC#10 or #56.

Nearby **Dusit Zoo**, once part of the Chitrlada Palace gardens and now a public park, is nothing special, but it does have a few rare animals in its small bare cages. Look out for the Komodo dragon, the world's largest reptile, which lives only on a small part of the Indonesian archipelago and in a few zoos in other parts of the world. The Dusit resident is relatively small as these monsters go: in the wild they can grow to a length of 3m and achieve a weight of 150kg. Also on show are cage-loads of white-handed gibbons, a favourite target of Thai poachers, who make a lot of money by selling them as pets (and to zoos) via Chatuchak Weekend Market and other channels. The zoo used to house several royal white elephants (see box on p.104), but at the time of writing they have all been relocated: one now lives in the grounds of Chitrlada Palace, and the others have been farmed out to less luxurious accommodation in the countryside.

Dusit Zoo can be quite fun for kids; for other child-friendly sights and activities in Bangkok, see p.217.

WAT BENJAMABOPHIT

Map 2, E3. Daily 7am–5pm; B10. Bus AC#3 or AC#9.

Ten minutes' walk southeast from Vimanmek along Sri Ayutthaya Road, **Wat Benjamabophit** is the last major temple to have been built in Bangkok. It's an interesting fusion of classical Thai and nineteenth-century European design, with its Carrara marble walls – hence the touristic tag "The Marble Temple" – complemented by the bot's unusual stained-glass windows, Victorian in style but depicting figures from Thai mythology. Inside, a fine replica of the highly revered Phra Buddha Chinnarat image of Phitsanulok presides over the small room containing Rama V's ashes. The courtyard behind the bot houses a gallery of Buddha images from all over Asia, set up by Rama V as an overview of different representations of the Buddha.

Wat Benjamabophit is one of the best temples in Bangkok to see religious **festivals** and rituals. Whereas monks elsewhere tend to go out on the streets every morning in search of alms, at the Marble Temple the ritual is reversed, and merit-makers come to them. Between about 6 and 7.30am, the monks line up outside the temple gates on Nakhon Pathom Road, their bowls ready to receive donations of curry and rice, lotus buds, incense, even toilet paper and Coca-Cola. The demure row of saffron-robed monks is a sight that's well worth getting up early for. The evening candlelight processions around the bot during the Buddhist festivals of Maha Puja (in February) and Visakha Puja (in May) are among the most entrancing in the country (see p.25).

WAT BENJAMABOPHIT

Downtown Bangkok

Extending east from the rail line and south to Sathorn Road, the **downtown** area is central to the colossal expanse of Bangkok as a whole, but rather peripheral in a sightseer's perception of the city. This is where you'll find the main financial district, around Silom Road; Thailand's most prestigious centre of higher learning, Chulalongkorn University; and the green expanse of **Lumphini Park**. The chief shopping centres cluster around the corner of Rajdamri and Rama I roads, extending east towards Sukhumvit Road and west to Siam Square (not in fact a square, but a grid of small commercial streets on the south side of Rama I Road, between Phrayathai and Henri Dunant roads).

Scattered widely across the downtown area there are just a few attractions for visitors, including the noisy and glittering **Erawan Shrine**, the **Visual Dhamma Gallery**, and three attractive museums housed in traditional teak buildings: the **Suan Pakkad Palace Museum**, **Jim Thompson's House** and the **Kamthieng House**. The infamous **Patpong** district hardly shines as a tourist sight, yet, lamentably, its sex bars provide Thailand's single biggest draw for foreign men.

If you're heading downtown from Banglamphu, allow at least an hour to get to any of the places mentioned here by

bus. To get to the southern part of the area, take an **express boat** downriver and then change onto a bus if necessary. For other parts of the downtown area, it's worth considering the regular **longtails** on Khlong Sen Seb, which runs parallel to Phetchaburi Road.

For details of accommodation downtown see p.149, for restaurants see p.172.

SUAN PAKKAD PALACE MUSEUM

Map 2, H4. Daily 9am–4pm; B80. Bus AC#13, #62 or #72.

In the northern part of downtown, the **Suan Pakkad Palace Museum** stands on what was once a cabbage patch (which gave it its name) but is now one of the finest gardens in Bangkok. The private collection of beautiful Thai objects from all periods is displayed in six traditional wooden houses, which were transported to Bangkok from various parts of the country. You can either take a mediocre guided tour in English (free) or explore the loosely arranged collection yourself (a free handout is usually available and some of the exhibits are labelled).

The Marsi Gallery, attached to Suan Pakkad, has recently opened to host some interesting temporary exhibitions of contemporary art and archeology (daily 9am–6pm; ©246 1775-6 for details).

The highlight is the renovated **Lacquer Pavilion**, across the reedy pond at the back of the grounds. Set on stilts, the pavilion is actually an amalgam of two temple buildings, a *ho trai* (library) and a *ho khien* (writing room), one inside the other, which were found between Ayutthaya and Bang Pa-In. The interior walls are beautifully decorated with gilt on black lacquer: the upper panels depict the life of the Buddha while the lower ones show scenes from the *Ramayana*. Look out especially for the grisly details in the tableau on the back wall, showing the earth goddess drowning the evil forces of Mara. Underneath are depicted some European dandies on horseback, probably merchants, whose presence suggests that the work was executed before the fall of Ayutthaya in 1767.

The carefully observed details of daily life and nature are skilful and lively, especially considering the restraints which the **lacquering technique** places on the artist, who has no opportunity for corrections or touching up: the design has to be punched into a piece of paper, which is then laid on the panel of black lacquer (a kind of plant resin); a small bag of chalk dust is pressed on top so that the dust penetrates the minute holes in the paper, leaving a line of dots on the lacquer to mark the pattern; a gummy substance is then applied to the background areas which are to remain black, before the whole surface is covered in microscopically thin squares of gold leaf; thin sheets of blotting paper, sprinkled with water, are then laid over the panel, which when pulled off bring away the gummy substance and the unwanted pieces of gold leaf that are stuck to it, leaving the rest of the gold decoration in high relief against the black background.

The **Ban Chiang house** has a very good collection of elegant, whorled pottery and bronze jewellery, which the former owner of Suan Pakkad Palace, Princess Chumbot, excavated from tombs at Ban Chiang, the major Bronze Age settlement in the northeast. Scattered around the museum's other five traditional houses, you'll come across some attractive Thai and Khmer religious sculpture among an eclectic jumble of artefacts: fine ceramics as well as some intriguing kiln-wasters, failed pots which have melted together in the kiln to form weird, almost rubbery pieces of sculpture; beautiful betel-nut sets; and some rich teak carvings, including a 200-year-old temple door showing episodes from *Sang Thong*, a folk tale about a childless king and queen who discover a handsome son in a conch shell.

> To the north of Suan Pakkad, the Victory Monument can be seen from way down Phrayathai Road. Erected after the Indo-Chinese War of 1940–41, when Thailand pinched back some territory in Laos and Cambodia while the French were otherwise occupied in World War II, it now commemorates all of Thailand's military glories.

JIM THOMPSON'S HOUSE

Map 6, B3. Mon–Sat from 9am, viewing on frequent 45min guided tours in several languages, last tour 4.30pm; B100, under-25s B40. Longtail boat along Khlong Sen Seb to Phrayathai Rd. Bus AC#2, AC#8, AC#15, #15, #25, AC#29, #29 or #40.

Just northwest of Siam Square, **Jim Thompson's House** is a kind of Ideal Home in elegant Thai style, and a peaceful refuge from downtown chaos. The house was the residence of the legendary American adventurer, entrepreneur, art collector and all-round character whose mysterious disappearance in the jungles of Malaysia in 1967 has made him even more of a legend among Thailand's expat community. Apart from putting together this beautiful home, Thompson's most concrete contribution was to turn traditional silk-weaving from a dying art into the highly successful international industry it is today.

The grand, rambling **house** is in fact a combination of six teak houses, some from as far afield as Ayutthaya and most over two hundred years old. Like all traditional houses, they were built in wall sections hung together without nails on a

The legend of Jim Thompson

Thai silk-weavers, art dealers and conspiracy theorists all owe a debt to **Jim Thompson**, who even now, more than thirty years after his death, remains Thailand's most famous farang. An architect by trade, Thompson left his New York practice in 1940 to join the Office of Strategic Services (later to become the CIA). He took part in clandestine operations in North Africa, Europe and, in 1945, the Far East, where he was detailed to a unit preparing for the invasion of Thailand. When the mission was pre-empted by the Japanese surrender, he served for a year as OSS station chief in Bangkok, forming links that were later to provide grist for endless speculation.

After an unhappy and short-lived stint as part owner of the *Oriental Hotel*, Thompson found his calling in the struggling **silk-weavers** of the area near the present Jim Thompson House. Their traditional product was unknown in the West and had been all but abandoned by Thais in favour of less costly imported textiles. Encouragement from society friends and an enthusiastic write-up in *Vogue* convinced him there was a foreign market for Thai silk, and by 1948 he had founded the Thai Silk Company Ltd. Success was assured when, two years later, the company was commissioned to make the costumes for the Broadway run of *The King and I*. Thompson's celebrated eye for colour combinations and his tireless promotion – in the early days, he could often be seen in the lobby of the *Oriental* with bolts of silk slung over his shoulder, waiting to pounce on any remotely curious tourist – quickly made his name synonymous with Thai silk.

Like a character in a Somerset Maugham novel, Thompson played the role of Western exile to the hilt. Though he spoke no Thai, he made it his personal mission to preserve traditional arts and architecture at a time when most Thais were more keen to emulate the West, assembling his famous Thai house and stuffing it with all manner of Oriental *objets d'art*. At the same time he held firmly to his farang roots and society connections: no foreign gathering in Bangkok was complete without Jim Thompson, and virtually every Western luminary passing through Bangkok – from Truman Capote to Ethel Merman – dined at his table.

If Thompson's life was the stuff of legend, his **disappearance** and presumed death only added to the mystique. On Easter Sunday, 1967, Thompson, while staying with friends in a cottage in Malaysia's Cameron Highlands, went out for a stroll and never came back. A massive search of the area, employing local guides, tracker dogs and even shamans, turned up no clues, provoking a rash of fascinating but entirely unsubstantiated theories. The grandfather of them all, advanced by a Dutch psychic, held that Thompson had been lured into an ambush by the disgraced former prime minister of Thailand, Pridi Panyonyong, and spirited off to Cambodia for indeterminate purposes; later versions, supposing that Thompson had remained a covert CIA operative all his life, proposed that he was abducted by Vietnamese communists and brainwashed. More recently, an amateur sleuth claims to have found evidence that Thompson met a more mundane fate, having been killed by a careless truck driver and hastily buried.

frame of wooden pillars, which made it easy to dismantle them, pile them onto a barge and float them to their new home. Although he had trained as an architect, Thompson had more difficulty in putting them back together again; in the end, he had to go back to Ayutthaya to hunt down a group of carpenters who still practised the old house-building methods. Thompson added a few unconventional touches of his own, incorporating the elaborately carved

THE LEGEND OF JIM THOMPSON

front wall of a Chinese pawn shop between the drawing room and the bedroom, and reversing the other walls in the drawing room so that their carvings faced into the room.

The impeccably tasteful **interior** has been left as it was during Thompson's life, even down to the cutlery on the dining table. Complementing the fine artefacts from throughout Southeast Asia is a stunning array of Thai **arts and crafts**, including one of the best collections of traditional Thai paintings in the world. Thompson picked up plenty of bargains from the Thieves' Quarter (Nakhon Kasem) in Chinatown, before collecting Thai art became fashionable and expensive. Other pieces were liberated from decay and destruction in upcountry temples, while many of the Buddha images were turned over by ploughs, especially around Ayutthaya. Some of the exhibits are very rare, such as a seventeenth-century Ayutthayan teak Buddha, but Thompson also bought pieces of little value and fakes simply for their looks – a shopping strategy that's all the more sensible in the jungle of today's Thai antiques trade.

THE ERAWAN SHRINE

Map 6, H4. Bus AC#4, AC#8, AC#11, AC#13, AC#15, #15, #25 or #40.
For a break from high culture drop in on the **Erawan Shrine** (*Saan Phra Pom* in Thai), at the corner of Ploenchit and Rajdamri roads. Remarkable as much for its setting as anything else, this shrine to Brahma, the ancient Hindu creation god, and Erawan, his elephant, squeezes in on one of the busiest and noisiest corners of modern Bangkok, in the shadow of the *Grand Hyatt Erawan Hotel* – whose existence is the reason for the shrine. When a string of calamities held up the building of the original hotel in the 1950s, spirit doctors were called in, who instructed the owners to build a new home for the offended local spirits: the hotel was then finished without further mishap.

Be prepared for sensory overload: the main structure shines with lurid glass of all colours and the overcrowded precinct around it is almost buried under scented garlands and incense candles. You might also catch a lacklustre group of traditional **dancers** performing here to the strains of a small classical orchestra – worshippers hire them to give thanks for a stroke of good fortune. To increase their future chances of such good fortune, visitors buy a bird or two from the flocks incarcerated in cages here; the bird-seller transfers the requested number of captives to a tiny hand-held cage, from which the customer duly liberates the animals, thereby accruing merit. People set on less abstract rewards will invest in a lottery ticket from one of the physically handicapped sellers: they're thought to be the luckiest you can buy.

THE SNAKE FARM

Map 2, G8. Displays Mon–Fri 10.30am & 2pm, Sat, Sun & holidays 10.30am; B70. Bus AC#2, AC#7.

The **Snake Farm** (also known as the Pasteur Institute or the Queen Saowaba Institute), at the corner of Rama IV and Henri Dunant roads, is a bit of a circus act, but an entertaining, informative and worthy one at that. Run by the Thai Red Cross, it has a double function: to produce snake-bite serums, and to educate the public on the dangers of Thai snakes.

The latter mission involves putting on **displays** that begin with a slick half-hour slide show illustrating, among other things, how to apply a tourniquet and immobilize a bitten limb. Things warm up with a live demonstration of snake handling, which is well presented and safe, and gains a perverse fascination from the knowledge that the strongest venoms of the snakes on show can kill in only three minutes. The climax of the display comes when, having watched a python squeezing great chunks of chicken through its body, the audience is invited to handle a docile Burmese constrictor.

THE SNAKE FARM

Snake's blood and other treats

If you venture into the darker corners of Bangkok, notably the port district of Khlong Toey, you may come across obscure stalls offering restorative glasses of warm **snake's blood**, which appeals mostly to Malaysian, Chinese and Korean visitors. Not just any snake, of course: only poisonous varieties will do, with prices ranging from B100 for a common cobra, through B2000 for a king cobra, up to B30,000 for the rare albino cobra.

Once you've selected your victim from the roadside cages, the proprietor will take the snake behind the stall, hang it up by its head and slit it open with a razor blade. The major artery yields enough blood to fill a wine glass, and when it's been mixed with the bile from the snake's gall bladder, warm whisky and a dash of honey, you down the potion in one. If this doesn't satisfy, delicacies like dried gall bladder and pickled snake genitals might tempt you. But if your health is really in a bad way, all that's left is the shock cure of drinking the **venom**, after it's been mixed with whisky and left standing for quarter of an hour.

There's no evidence to support the claims made for the **medicinal properties** of snakes' innards, but there's no proof to the contrary either. While male impotence remains the main reason for the trade's persistence, the blood is also said to be good for the eyes, for backache, for malodorous urine, and simply to "make happy".

LUMPHINI PARK

Map 2, H8. Bus AC#2, AC#4, AC#7, AC#15, #15 or #62.

If you're sick of cars and concrete, head for **Lumphini Park** (*Suan Lum*), at the east end of Silom Road, where the air is almost fresh and the traffic noise dies down to a low murmur. Named after the town in Nepal where the Buddha was born, the park is arranged around two lakes, where you can join the locals in feeding the turtles and fish with bread or take out a pedalo or a rowing boat (B30 per half-hour), and is landscaped with a wide variety of local trees and numerous pagodas and pavilions, usually occupied by Chinese chess players. In the early morning and at dusk, exercise freaks hit the outdoor gym on the southwest side of the park, or en masse do some jogging along the yellow-marked circuit or some balletic t'ai chi, stopping for the twice-daily broadcast of the king's anthem. The wide open spaces here are a popular area for gay cruising, and you might be offered dope, though the police patrol regularly. For all that, it's not at all an intimidating place.

> **To recharge your batteries in Lumphini Park, make for the garden restaurant, *Pop*, in the northwest corner (see p.174), or the pavement food stalls at the northern edge of the park.**

PATPONG

Map 7, J5. Bus AC#2, AC#4, AC#15 or #15.
Concentrated into a small area between the eastern ends of Silom and Suriwong roads, the neon-lit go-go bars of the **Patpong** district loom like rides in a tawdry sexual Disneyland. In front of each bar, girls cajole passers-by with a lifeless sensuality while insistent touts proffer printed menus detailing the degradations on show. Inside, bikini-clad or topless women gyrate to Western music and play hostess to the (almost exclusively male) spectators; upstairs, live shows feature women who, to use Spalding Gray's

PATPONG

phrase in *Swimming to Cambodia*, "do everything with their vaginas except have babies."

Patpong was no more than a sea of mud when the capital was founded on the marshy riverbank to the west, but by the 1960s it had grown into a flash district of nightclubs and dance halls for rich Thais, owned by a Chinese millionaire godfather who gave his name to the area. In 1969, an American entrepreneur turned an existing teahouse into a luxurious nightclub to satisfy the tastes of soldiers on R&R trips from Vietnam, and so Patpong's transformation into a Western sex reservation began. At first, the area was rough and violent, but over the years it has wised up to the desires of the affluent farang, and now markets itself as a packaged concept of Oriental decadence.

The centre of the skin trade lies along the interconnected sois of **Patpong 1** and **2**, where lines of go-go bars share their patch with respectable restaurants and bookstores, a 24-hour supermarket and *KFC*, the Athlete's Foot shoeshop and an overabundance of pharmacies. By night, it's a thumping theme park, whose blazing neon promises tend towards self-parody, with names like *French Kiss* and *Love Nest*. Budget travellers, purposeful safari-suited businessmen and noisy lager louts throng the streets, and even the most demure tourists – of both sexes – turn out to do some shopping at the night market down the middle of Patpong 1, where hawkers sell fake watches, bags and designer T-shirts. By day, a relaxed hangover descends on the place. Bar-girls hang out at food stalls and cafés in respectable dress, often recognizable only by their faces, pinched and strained from the continuous use of antibiotics and heroin in an attempt to ward off venereal disease and boredom. Farang men slump at the beer bars on Patpong 2, drinking and watching videos, unable to find anything else to do in the whole of Bangkok.

PATPONG

The small dead-end alley to the east of Patpong 2, **Silom 4** (ie Soi 4, Silom Road), hosts Bangkok's hippest nightlife, its bars, clubs and pavements heaving at weekends with the capital's brightest and most overprivileged young things. A few gay venues still cling to Silom 4, but the focus of the scene has recently shifted to **Silom 2**. In between, **Thaniya Road**'s hostess bars and one of the city's swishest shopping centres, Thaniya Plaza, cater mostly to Japanese tourists, while **Soi Tantawan** (Soi 6) to the west of Patpong is beginning to turn into a small ghetto for Korean visitors.

The sex industry

Bangkok owes its reputation as the carnal capital of the world to a thriving **sex industry** fuelled by more than 1000 sex-related businesses. But contrary to the image fostered by the girlie bars of Patpong, the vast majority of Thailand's prostitutes of both sexes (estimated at anywhere between 200,000 and 700,000) work with Thai men, not foreigners.

Prostitution and polygamy have long been intrinsic to the Thai way of life. Until 1910, Thai kings had always kept a retinue of concubines, and the practice was aped by nobles and merchants keen to have lots of sons and heirs. Though the monarch is now monogamous, it is still acceptable practice for men of all classes to keep **mistresses** (known as *mia noi*, or minor wives), and public figures rarely attempt to keep their liaisons secret. For those not wealthy enough to take on *mia noi*, prostitution is a far less costly and equally accepted option. Between 43 and 97 percent of sexually active Thai men are thought to use the services of prostitutes twice a month on average.

The **farang sex industry** began during the Vietnam War, when the American military set up seven bases around

Thailand and the country became a playground for GIs on R&R breaks. When the bases were evacuated in the mid-1970s, tourists moved in to fill the vacuum, and sex tourism has since grown to become an established part of the Thai economy. The two million-plus foreign males who arrive here each year represent a foreign-exchange earnings potential of B50 billion.

The majority of the women who work in the Patpong bars come from the poorest rural areas of north and northeast Thailand. **Economic refugees** in search of a better life, they're easily drawn into an industry where they can make in a single night what it takes a month to earn in the rice fields; a couple of lucrative years in the sex bars is often the most effective way of helping to pay off family debts.

Despite its ubiquity, prostitution has been **illegal** in Thailand since 1960, but sex-industry bosses easily get round the law by registering their establishments as entertainment venues and making payoffs to the police. Sex workers, on the other hand, have no legal rights and will often endure violence rather than face fines and long rehabilitation sentences. In an attempt to redress this iniquitous system, a more stringent **anti-prostitution law** was passed in April 1996, but this has been met with some cynicism, due to the number of influential figures allegedly involved in the sex industry.

In recent years, the spectre of **AIDS** has put the problems of the sex industry into sharp focus: according to WHO, there are currently around 800,000 HIV carriers in Thailand, including an estimated twenty per cent of the country's prostitutes. The wives, girlfriends and new-born children of prostitute-visiting males now constitute the highest risk group. However, as a result of an aggressive campaign by the government, the rate of new infections has dropped significantly, by 54 percent between 1993 and 1995.

Beyond the west end of Silom Road, the old farang trading quarter between Charoen Kung (New Road) and the river is the only area in Bangkok where you could eke out an architectural walk, though it's hardly compelling. Incongruous churches and "colonial" buildings – the best of these the *Oriental Hotel's* Authors' Wing, where nostalgic afternoon teas are served – are hemmed in by Chinatown (see p.88) to the north and the spice shops and *halal* canteens of the Muslim area on Charoen Kung.

BAN KAMTHIENG

Map 8, E6. 131 Soi Asoke (Soi 21), off Sukhumvit Road. Mon–Sat 9am–5pm; B70 (B20 for under 25s). Longtail boat along Khlong Sen Seb to Saphan Asoke pier, then bus #38. Bus AC#1, AC#8, AC#11, AC #13, #38 or #40.

Another reconstructed traditional Thai residence, **Ban Kamthieng** was moved in the 1960s from Chiang Mai to Sukhumvit Road and set up as an ethnological museum by the Siam Society. It differs from both Suan Pakkad and Jim Thompson's House in being the home of a commoner, and although the owner was by no means poor, the objects on display give a fair representation of rural life in northern Thailand.

The house was built on the banks of the River Ping in the mid-nineteenth century and the ground-level display of farming tools and fish traps evokes the upcountry practice of fishing in flooded rice paddies to supplement the supply from the rivers. Upstairs, the main rooms of the house are much as they would have been 150 years ago – the raised floor is polished and smooth, sparsely furnished with only a couple of low tables and seating mats, and a betel-nut set to

BAN KAMTHIENG

hand. Notice how surplus furniture and utensils are stored in the rafters. The rectangular lintel above the door to the inner room is a *hum yon*, carved in floral patterns that represent testicles and designed to ward off evil spirits. Walking along the open verandah between the kitchen and the granary, you'll see areca palm (betel nut) trees to your left: the garden, too, is as authentic as possible.

Next door to Kamthieng House, in the same compound, is the more recently acquired **Sangaroon House**, built here to house the folk-craft collection of Thai architect and lecturer Sangaroon Ratagasikorn. Upon his return to Thailand after studying in America under Frank Lloyd Wright, Sangaroon became fascinated by the efficient designs of rural utensils and began to collect them as teaching aids. Those on display include baskets, fishing pots and *takraw* balls, all of which fulfil his criteria of being functional, simple and beautiful, with no extraneous features.

VISUAL DHAMMA GALLERY

Map 8, E5. Just off Sukhumvit's Soi Asoke (Soi 21), at 44/28. Mon–Fri 1–6pm, Sat 10am–5pm; free. Longtail boat along Khlong Sen Seb to Saphan Asoke pier, then bus #38. Bus AC#1, AC#8, AC#11, AC#13, #38 or #40.

One of Bangkok's most vibrant modern art galleries, the **Visual Dhamma Gallery** houses a permanent collection of paintings by major figures – such as Vasan Sitthiket, Montien Boonma and Pichai Nirand – and temporary shows of less established artists. The gallery was set up in 1981 by Austrian expat Alfred Pawlin to promote pieces with a Buddhist and mythological theme, but over the years has widened its scope to embrace the more abstract work of painters such as Thaiwijit Puangkasemsomboon, and now also functions as an important resource centre on works of the last two decades.

Chatuchak and the outskirts

T he amorphous clutter of Greater Bangkok doesn't harbour many attractions, but there are a handful of places on the **outskirts** of the city which make pleasant half-day outings. Nearly all the places described in this chapter can be reached fairly painlessly by some sort of city transport, either by ferry up the Chao Phraya River, or by city bus.

If you're in Bangkok on a Saturday or Sunday, it's well worth making the effort to visit the enormous **Chatuchak Weekend Market**, the perfect place to browse and to buy. The open-air **Prasart Museum** and **Muang Boran Ancient City** are both recommended for anyone who hasn't got the time to go upcountry and admire Thailand's temples and palaces in situ; both these cultural theme parks boast finely crafted replicas of traditional Thai buildings. Taking a boat ride up the Chao Phraya River makes a nice change to sitting in city-centre traffic, and the upstream town of **Nonthaburi** and the nearby island of **Ko Kred** provide the ideal excuse for doing just that.

CHATUCHAK WEEKEND MARKET

Sat & Sun 7am–6pm. Bus AC#2, AC#3, AC#9, AC#10, or AC#13; about an hour's ride north of Banglamphu or Sukhumvit.

With six thousand open-air stalls to peruse, and wares as diverse as Laotian silk, Siamese kittens and buffalo-horn catapults to choose from, the enormous **Chatuchak Weekend Market** is Bangkok's most enjoyable shopping experience.

Though its primary customers are Bangkok residents in search of inexpensive clothes, home accessories and a strong dose of fun, Chatuchak also has a good number of collector- and tourist-oriented **stalls**. Best buys include antique curios such as amulets and lacquerware, unusual silk and cotton sarongs, cotton weave clothing from the north, jeans, northern crafts, traditional musical instruments, silver jewellery, basketware and ceramics, particularly the five-coloured *bencharong*.

If you're going there to buy something specific, take a copy of *Nancy Chandler's Map of Bangkok*, as it shows the location of all the specialist areas within the market. TAT have also produced a **map** of Chatuchak, which is available free of charge from the TAT counter in the Chatuchak market building on the southwest edge of the market, across the car park.

The Market also has a reputation for dealing in endangered species of **wildlife**, in particular gibbons, palm cockatoos, golden dragon fish, Indian pied hornbills – even tiger and lion cubs. Many of the animals are smuggled across from Laos and Cambodia and then sold at Chatuchak to private animal collectors and foreign zoos, particularly in eastern Europe. It's unlikely that you'll see any of these controversial birds and animals on display, though you're bound to come across fighting cocks around the back (demonstrations are almost continuous), miniature flying squirrels being fed milk through pipettes, and iridescent red and blue Siamese fighting fish, kept in individual jars and shielded from each others' aggressive stares by sheets of cardboard.

There's no shortage of **food** stalls inside the market compound, particularly at the southern end, where you'll find plenty of places serving inexpensive *pat thai* and Isaan snacks. Close by these stalls is a classy little juice bar called *Viva* where you can rest your feet while listening to the manager's jazz tapes. For vegetarian sustenance, head for *Chamlong's* (also known as *Asoke*), an open-air, cafeteria-style restaurant just outside the market on Kamphaeng Phet Road (across Kamphaeng Phet 2 Road), set up by Bangkok's former governor as a service to the citizenry (Sat & Sun 8am–noon). You can **change money** (7am–7pm) in the market building at the south end of the market, across the car park from the stalls area.

THE PRASART MUSEUM

#9, Soi 4A, Soi Krungthep Kreetha, Krungthep Kreetha Road.
Fri–Sun 10am–3pm; B300 including compulsory tour. Bus #93
from Si Phraya Road near River City, or from Phetchaburi or New
Phetchaburi Roads.

Located right out on the eastern edge of the city – and still surrounded by fields – the **Prasart Museum** is an unusual open-air exhibition of traditional Asian buildings, collected and reassembled by wealthy entrepreneur and art lover Khun Prasart. The museum is rarely visited by independent tourists, partly because of its intentionally limited opening hours and inflated admission price, and partly because it takes at least an hour and a half to get here by bus from Banglamphu or Silom, but it makes a pleasant day out and is worth the effort.

Set in a gorgeously lush tropical garden, the museum

THE PRASART MUSEUM

comprises about a dozen replicas of **traditional buildings**, including a golden teak palace inspired by the royal residence now housed at the National Museum, a Chinese temple and water garden, a Khmer shrine, a Sukhothai-era teak library set over a lotus pond, and a European-style mansion, fashionable with Bangkok royalty in the late-nineteenth century. Some of these structures have been assembled from the ruins of buildings found all over Asia, but there's no attempt at purist authenticity – the aim is to give a flavour of architectural styles, not an exact reproduction. Many of the buildings, including the Thai wat and the Chinese temple, were constructed from scratch, using designs dreamed up by Khun Prasart and his team.

All the buildings are beautifully crafted, with great attention paid to carvings and decorations, and many are filled with antique **artefacts**, including Burmese woodcarvings, prehistoric pottery from Ban Chiang and Lopburi-era statuettes. There are also some unusual pieces of royal memorabilia and an exquisite collection of *bencharong* ceramics. Khun Prasart also owns a ceramics workshop which produces reproductions of famous designs; they can be bought either at the museum, or at his showroom, the *Prasart Collection*, on the second floor of the *Peninsular Plaza* shopping centre on Rajdamri Road.

The easiest way to get to the museum is by ordinary **bus** #93, which you can pick up either on Si Phraya Road near River City and the GPO, or anywhere along its route on Phetchaburi and New Phetchaburi roads. The #93 terminates on Krungthep Kreetha Road, but you should get off a couple of stops before the terminus, at the first stop on Krungthep Kreetha Road, as soon as you see the sign for the Prasart Museum (about 1hr 15 mins bus ride from Si Phraya). Follow the sign down Soi Krungthep Kreetha, go past the golf course and, after about a 15-minute walk, turn off down Soi 4A.

MUANG BORAN ANCIENT CITY

Map 1, I6. 33km southeast of the city centre. Daily 8am–5pm; B50, kids B25. Bus AC#8, AC#11 or #25 to Samut Prakan, then a songthaew.

The brochure for **Muang Boran Ancient City** sells the place as a sort of cultural fast-food outlet – "a realistic journey into Thailand's past in only a few hours, saving you the many weeks of travel and considerable expense of touring Thailand yourself". The open-air museum is a considerably more authentic experience than its own publicity makes out, showcasing past and present Thai artistry and offering an enjoyable introduction to the country's architecture.

Some of Muang Boran's ninety-odd buildings are **originals**, including the rare scripture library rescued from Samut Songkhram. Others are painstaking **reconstructions** from contemporary documents (the Ayutthaya-period Sanphet Prasat palace is a particularly fine example) or **scaled-down copies** of famous monuments such as the Grand Palace. A sizeable team of restorers and craftspeople maintains the buildings and helps keep some of the traditional techniques alive; if you come here during the week you can watch them at work.

NONTHABURI

Map 1, H5.

A trip to **Nonthaburi**, the first town beyond the northern boundary of Bangkok, is just about the easiest jaunt you can make from the centre of the city and affords a perfect opportunity to experience a small slice of rural Thailand without even having to board a bus. Nonthaburi is the last stop upriver on the Chao Phraya Express **boats**, only 45 minutes from Phra Athit pier (every 15min), and is also served by the less reliable Laemthong Express.

MUANG BORAN ANCIENT CITY, NONTHABURI

The ride is half the fun in itself, weaving round huge, crawling rice barges and tiny canoes, and the slow pace of the boat gives you plenty of time to take in the sights on the way. Once out of the centre, you'll pass the royal boathouse in front of the National Library on the east bank, where you can glimpse the minor ceremonial boats which escort the grand royal barges. The nearer you get to Nonthaburi, the less you see of the riverbanks, which are increasingly obscured by houses on stilts and houseboats – past the Singha brewery with its manicured lawns and topiary garden, you'll see a community of people who live on the huge teak vessels used to carry rice, sand and charcoal.

Disembarking at Nonthaburi, you immediately get the feeling of being out in the sticks, despite the noisy bus terminal that confronts you: the pier, on the east bank of the river, is overrun by a market that's famous for the quality of its fruit; the Provincial Office across the road is covered in rickety old wooden latticework; and the short promenade, its lampposts hung with models of the town's famous durian fruit (see box on p.129), lends a seaside atmosphere. To break up your trip with a slow, scenic drink or lunch, you'll find a floating seafood **restaurant**, *Rim Fung*, to your right at the end of the prom which, though a bit overpriced, is quiet and breezy.

If you're thirsty for more cruising on the water, take a longtail boat from Nonthaburi pier up Khlong Om (round trip 45min; B10): the canal, lined with some grand suburban mansions, traditional wooden houses, temples and durian plantations, leads almost out into open country.

Durians

The naturalist Alfred Russel Wallace, eulogizing the taste of the **durian**, compared it to "rich butter-like custard highly flavoured with almonds, but intermingled with wafts of flavour that call to mind cream cheese, onion sauce, brown sherry and other incongruities". He neglected to discuss the smell of the fruit's skin, which is so bad – somewhere between detergent and dogshit – that durians are barred from Thai hotels and aeroplanes.

The different **varieties** bear strange monikers which do nothing to make them more appetizing: "frog", "golden pillow", "gibbon" and so on. However, the durian has fervent admirers, perhaps because it's such an acquired taste, and because it's considered a strong aphrodisiac. Aficionados discuss the varieties with as much subtlety as if they were vintage champagnes, and they treat the durian as a social fruit, to be shared around despite a price tag of up to B2500 each.

Durian season is roughly April to June and the most famous durian orchards are around Nonthaburi, where the fruits are said to have an incomparably rich and nutty flavour due to the fine clay soil. If you don't smell them first, you can recognize durians by their sci-fi **appearance**: the shape and size of a rugby ball, but slightly deflated, they're covered in a thick, pale-green shell which is heavily armoured with short, sharp spikes (*duri* means "thorn" in Malay). By cutting along one of the faint seams with a good knife, you'll reveal a white pith in which are set a handful of yellow blobs with the texture of a bad soufflé: this is what you eat. The taste is best when the smell is at its highest, about three days after the fruit has dropped. Be careful when out walking: due to its great weight and sharp spikes, a falling durian can lead to serious injury, or even an ignominious death.

DURIANS

Wat Chalerm Phra Kiat

Set in relaxing grounds on the west bank of the river, elegant **Wat Chalerm Phra Kiat** provides an unexpected touch of urban refinement amid a grove of breadfruit trees. From the Nonthaburi pier, you can either squeeze into one of the regular longtails going upriver (a 5min ride) or take the ferry straight across the Chao Phraya then walk up the river bank for ten minutes.

The beautifully proportioned temple, which has been lavishly restored, was built by Rama III in memory of his mother, whose family lived in the area. Entering the walls of the temple compound, you feel as if you're coming upon a stately folly in a secret garden, and a strong Chinese influence shows itself in the unusual ribbed roofs and elegantly curved gables, decorated with pastel ceramics. The restorers have done their best work inside: look out especially for the simple, delicate landscapes on the shutters.

KO KRED

Map 1, H4. Acces via *Laemthong Express* boats, or via rush-hour green-flag *Chao Phraya Express* boats, to Pakkred (at least an hour), then by longtail taxi boat or shuttle boat to Ko Kred.

About 7km north of Nonthaburi, the tiny island of **Ko Kred** lies in a particularly sharp bend in the Chao Phraya, cut off from the east bank by a waterway created to make the cargo route from Ayutthaya to the Gulf of Thailand just that little bit faster. This artificial island is something of a time capsule: a little oasis of village life completely at odds with the metropolitan chaos just ninety minutes downriver. Roughly ten square kilometres in all, Ko Kred has no roads, just a concrete path that circles its circumference, with a few arterial walkways branching off towards the interior. Villagers, the majority of whom are ethnic Mons, use the fifteen-strong fleet of motorbike taxis to cross their island, but as a sightseer you're much better off on foot: a round-island walk takes less than an hour and a half and it's practically impossible to get lost.

There are no sights as such on Ko Kred, but its lushness and comparative emptiness make it a perfect place in which to wander. You'll no doubt come across one of the island's **potteries** and kilns, which churn out the regionally famous earthenware flower-pots and small water-storage jars and employ a large percentage of the village workforce. The island's clay is also very rich in nutrients and therefore excellent for fruit-growing, and banana trees, coconut palms, pomelo, papaya and durian trees all grow in abundance on Ko Kred, fed by an intricate network of irrigation channels that crisscrosses the interior. In among the orchards, the Mons have built their wooden houses, mostly in traditional style and raised high above the marshy ground on stilts. A couple of attractive riverside wats, a school and a few diminutive general stores complete the picture.

The **access** point for Ko Kred is **Pakkred**, the terminus for all *Laemthong Express* boats, as well as for a few rush-hour green-flag *Chao Phraya Express* boats (see p.47), the latter docking 50m south of the former. The direct *Laemthong* boats from Bangkok take at least an hour. Alternatively, you can take a *Chao Phraya Express* boat to Nonthaburi (see p.127) and travel on to Pakkred from here on a *Laemthong* boat (30mins). From Pakkred, which is on the east bank of the Chao Phraya, the easiest way of getting across to the island is to hire a longtail boat, although shuttle boats operate at the river's narrowest point at Wat Sanam Nua, about a kilometre's walk or a short cycle-rickshaw ride south of the Pakkred boat piers.

Ko Kred is not on the tourist trail and farang visitors are still a rarity here, but the riverside *Song Fung* restaurant, beside the Chao Phraya Express pier in Pakkred, offers a detailed English-language menu, with over 170 Chinese, Thai and seafood dishes from which to choose.

KO KRED

LISTINGS

Accommodation

Bearing in mind Bangkok's appalling traffic jams, you should think carefully about what you want to do in the city before deciding which part of town to stay in. The other consideration is price, as certain parts of the city are significantly more expensive than others.

For double rooms under B450, your widest choice lies with the **guesthouses** of Banglamphu and the smaller, dingier travellers' ghetto that has grown up around Soi Ngam Duphli, off the south side of Rama IV Road. Bangkok guesthouses are tailored to the independent traveller's needs and range from cramped, no-frills crash pads to airier places with private bathrooms. Unless you pay a cash deposit in advance, bookings are rarely accepted by guesthouses, but it's often useful to phone ahead and establish whether a place is full already – during peak season (roughly Nov–Feb) you may have difficulty getting a room after noon.

Moderate and **expensive** rooms are mainly concentrated downtown around Siam Square and in the area between Rama IV Road and Charoen Krung (New Road), along Sukhumvit Road, and to a lesser extent in Chinatown. Air-conditioned rooms with hot-water bathrooms can be had for as little as B500 in these areas, but for that you're looking at a rather basic cubicle. You'll probably have to pay more like B1000 for smart furnishings and a

Accommodation prices

Throughout this guide, guesthouses and hotels have been categorized according to the price codes given below. These categories represent the minimum you can expect to pay in the high season (roughly Nov–Feb & July–Aug) for a double room. If travelling on your own, expect to pay anything between sixty and one hundred percent of the rates quoted for a double room.

The top-whack hotels will add seven percent tax and a ten-percent service charge to your bill – the price codes below are based on net rates after taxes have been added.

① under B150	④ B300–450	⑦ B1000–1500
② B150–200	⑤ B450–650	⑧ B1500–3000
③ B200–300	⑥ B650–1000	⑨ over B3000

swimming pool, or B3000 and over for a room in a five-star, international chain hotel.

Many of the expensive hotels listed in this guide offer special **deals for families**, usually allowing one or two under-12s to share their parents' room for free, so long as no extra bedding is required. It's also often possible to cram two adults and two children into the double rooms in inexpensive and mid-priced hotels (as opposed to guesthouses), as beds in these places are usually big enough for two.

BANGLAMPHU

Nearly all backpackers head straight for **Banglamphu**, Bangkok's long established traveller's ghetto, which is within easy reach of the Grand Palace and other major sights in Ratanakosin. At its heart stands the legendary **Khao San Road**, crammed with guesthouses, dodgy travel agents and ethnic clothes stalls. Travellers who pre-

Getting to and from Banglamphu

All the guesthouses listed lie only a few minutes' walk from either the Phra Athit **express boat** stop (Map 3, A7) or the Thewes express boat stop (Map 3, A7). Public **longtail boats** also ply the three khlongs in the area.

Useful **bus** routes in and out of Banglamphu include AC#3 and AC#9 for Chatuchak Weekend Market, AC#11 from both the Eastern and Southern bus terminals, AC#15 and ordinary #15 to Siam Square, #53 to Hualamphong train station and, in the opposite direction, to the Grand Palace, and #56 to Chinatown. **Airport Bus** #A2 also has several stops in Banglamphu.

fer to avoid the Khao San hustle head for nearby **Soi Chana Songkhram**, which encircles the wat of the same name, to **Phra Athit**, running parallel to the Chao Phraya River; or the residential alleyways of **Trok Mayom** and **Damnoen Klang Neua**. A 25-minute walk north from Khao San Road brings you to the even quieter **Sri Ayutthaya Road**, behind the National Library, the newest and best-value accommodation centre in Banglamphu, where rooms are larger, guesthouses smaller, and the atmosphere more typically Thai.

INEXPENSIVE AND MODERATE

Apple Guesthouse
Map 3, B7. 10/1 Phra Athit ©281 6838.
One of the few remaining guesthouses in the capital where you actually live in a Thai family home. The atmosphere is personal and friendly, though rooms are small and a bit grotty. B50 dorm beds are also available. ①

Chai's House

Map 3, B8. 49/4–8 Soi Rongmai ©281 4901, fax 281 8686.
Quietish place, away from most other guesthouses, with large, clean, simple rooms. None have bathrooms, but some have air-con. The rate is per person, which makes singles better value than doubles. ③–④

Chart Guesthouse

Map 3, C8. 58–60 Khao San Rd ©282 0171.
Clean, comfortable enough hotel in the heart of backpacker land. Rooms in all categories are a little cramped, but they all have windows. Most have bathroom and some have air-con. ②–④

J House

Map 3, C8. 1 Trok Mayom ©281 2949.
Simple rooms – some with private bathroom – in a traditional wooden house, located (unusually for Banglamphu) among old-fashioned Thai homes in a narrow alley. ①–③

Khao San Palace Hotel

Map 3, D8. 139 Khao San Rd ©282 0578.
One of several recently renovated, clean and well-appointed smallish hotels in Banglamphu. All rooms have attached bathrooms, and those at the top of the range have air-con and TV. Avoid the rooms overlooking Khao San Road, as they can be noisy at night. ④–⑤

There's no need to resort to a dip in the stinky Chao Phraya River – drop in to Khao San Road's public swimming pool instead, round the back of *Buddy Beer Bar*, which charges B100 a session.

ACCOMMODATION: BANGLAMPHU

Lek House

Map 3, D8. 125 Khao San Rd ℂ282 4927.

Classic old-style Khao San Road guesthouse; rooms are small and pretty basic, with shared facilities, but the place is less shabby than many others in the same price bracket. ②

Marco Polo Hostel

Map 3, E7. 108/7–10 Khao San Rd ℂ281 1715.

This mini hotel in the heart of the backpackers' ghetto offers the least expensive rooms of their kind in the area. Rooms all have air-con and showers, which makes them good value, but some have no window. ④

Merry V

Map 3, B6. 35 Soi Chana Songkhram ℂ282 9267.

Large, efficiently run budget favourite, located away from the Khao San Road scrum, but within easy reach of it. Rooms are basic and slightly cramped, with shared facilities, but the place is kept scrupulously clean. ①

My House

Map 3, B6. 37 Soi Chana Songkhram ℂ282 9263.

Popular place in one of the quieter corners of Banglamphu, offering a range of fairly basic but exceptionally clean rooms, including some with attached bathrooms, and some with air-con. ③–⑤

Nat II

Map 3, G9. 91–95 Post Office Rd ℂ282 0211.

Small place in a fairly quiet location, though you may be woken by the 5am calls from the neighbourhood mosque. Rooms are large and clean but otherwise unremarkable. ①–②

New Siam Guesthouse

Map 3, B6. 21 Soi Chana Songkhram ℂ282 4554, fax 281 7461.
Comfortably kitted out, modern and well-maintained hotel-style rooms; all with fans and windows, and plenty of clothes hooks. The mid-priced rooms have private bathrooms, and the most expensive have hot-water showers, air-con and towels. A definite notch above the typical Banglamphu guesthouse. ③–⑤

New World House

Map 3, D5. Samsen 2 ℂ281 5605.
Good-value, large, unadorned rooms, equipped with desks, showers and air-con. They're a bit soulless, but worth considering for extended stays of three months and over; long-stay rates start at B5500 per month. ④–⑤

Peachy Guesthouse

Map 3, B7. 10 Phra Athit Rd ℂ281 6471.
Somewhat sporadic management – the office is frequently unstaffed – but clean if spartan air-con and fan-cooled rooms, some with private baths, and a pleasant garden with bar. Popular with long-stay guests. Try to negotiate a room away from the second-floor communal area, as the TV can attract a noisy crowd of late-night viewers. ①–⑤

Pra Arthit Mansion

Map 3, B6. 22 Phra Athit Rd ℂ280 0744, fax 280 0742.
Recommended mid-range place that offers very good rooms with air-con, TV, hot water and mini-bar. Somewhat lacking in atmosphere, but staff are friendly and the location is both quiet and convenient. ⑥

> **Banglamphu is well stocked with Internet cafés –
> about two dozen at the last count, many of them on
> Khao San Road.**

7 Holder Guesthouse

Map 3, F9. 216/2–3 Soi Damnoen Klang Neua ©281 3682.
Clean and modern place round the back of Khao San Road.
Rooms are simply furnished and none have private bathrooms,
though a few have air con. ②–④

Sawasdee Bangkok Inn

Map 3, D8. On a tiny soi connecting Khao San Rd with the parallel
Trok Mayom ©280 1251, fax 281 7818.
Easily spotted because of its mauve-painted facade, this popular
and efficiently run mini-hotel has a good atmosphere and a range
of comfortable rooms; the cheapest are a bit cramped and have no
bathroom, while the priciest include air-con and TV, which makes
them good value. You can get Thai massage therapy and lessons
on the premises, and there's an attractive garden eating area. ③–④

Shanti Lodge

Map 3, E1. Soi 16, Sri Ayutthaya Rd ©281 2497.
Quiet, attractively furnished and comfortable rooms make this
deservedly the most popular place in the National Library area,
25 minutes' walk north of Khao San Road. All rooms share
bathrooms. There's a good veggie restaurant downstairs and the
management is welcoming. ③

Siam Oriental

Map 3, D8. 190 Khao San Rd ©629 0311.
Hotel-style guesthouse right in the middle of Khao San Road,
offering smallish but good value rooms, all with attached bathrooms; towels provided. Some air-con. ③–⑤

Sweety

Map 3, F9. 49 Rajdamnoen Klang, but access is from Post Office
Rd ©280 2191, fax 280 2192.
Popular place that's one of the most inexpensive in Banglamphu;
it's nicely located away from the fray but convenient for both

Khao San Rd and Rajdamnoen buses. Rooms are very small but they all have windows, and the beds have thick mattresses; some have private bath. ①–③

Tavee Guesthouse

Map 3, E1. Soi 14, 83 Sri Ayutthaya Rd ©282 5983.
Good-sized rooms in this quiet, friendly place that's the cheapest in the National Library quarter. None of the rooms have attached bathrooms, but some have air-con. Dorm beds for B80. ②–④

Villa

Map 3, C4. 230 Samsen 1 ©281 7009.
Banglamphu's most therapeutic guesthouse is a lovely old Thai house and garden with just ten large rooms, each idiosyncratically furnished in simple, semi-traditional style. Bathrooms are shared, and the price depends on the size of the room. ③–④

EXPENSIVE

Royal Hotel

Map 3, C9. 2 Rajdamnoen Klang Rd ©222 9111, fax 224 2083.
Used mostly for conferences, this hotel is conveniently located just five minutes' stroll from Sanam Luang and a further ten or so from the Grand Palace, though getting to Khao San Road entails a life-endangering leap across two very busy main roads. Although the facilities are perfectly adequate with air-con in all rooms, the place lacks atmosphere and is not exactly plush for the price. ⑦

Thai Hotel

Map 3, H4. 78 Pracha Thipatai Rd ©282 2831, fax 280 1299.
Comfortable enough place that seems popular with Asian tourists and businesspeople, but a little overpriced, considering

its slightly inconvenient location away from the best of Banglamphu's shops and restaurants. All rooms have air-con and there's a decent sized pool. ⑦

Vieng Thai Hotel

Map 3, D6. Ram Bhuttri Rd ℗280 5392, fax 281 8153.
This is the best of the options in the upper price bracket: it's convenient for the shops and restaurants of Khao San Road and Banglamphu, and is geared towards tourists not businesspeople. All rooms here have air-con, TV, hot water and mini-bar, and though the older (cheaper) rooms are rather faded, the smart new deluxe versions are well worth the extra money. There's a big pool, and a cultural show is staged in the hotel every Saturday. ⑦

CHINATOWN AND HUALAMPHONG STATION AREA

Not far from the Ratanakosin sights, **Chinatown (Sampeng)** is one of the most vibrant and typically Asian parts of Bangkok. Staying here, or in one of the sois around the nearby **Hualamphong Station**, can be noisy, but there's always plenty to look at. Some travellers base themselves here to get away from the travellers' scene in Banglamphu.

Getting to and from Chinatown and Hualamphong

Useful **bus** routes for Chinatown include AC#7, #25 and 53, which all go to Ratanakosin (for Wat Po and the Grand Palace); for full details see p.54. There's also a handy long-tail **boat** service from Hualamphong Station to Banglamphu (Map 5, H6).

Bangkok Center

Map 5, H6. 328 Rama IV Rd ℂ238 4848, fax 236 1862.
Handily placed upmarket option just across the road from the
train station. Rooms are smartly furnished, and they all have
air-con and TV; there's a pool and restaurant on the premises,
and service is efficient. ⑧

The Chinatown Hotel

Map 5, F5. 526 Yaowarat Rd ℂ225 0203, fax 226 1295.
Classy Chinese hotel in the heart of the gold-trading district.
Comfortably furnished rooms, all with air-con and TV. Kids
under 12 can share parents' rooms for free. ⑦–⑧

FF Guesthouse

Map 5, I7. 338/10 Trok La-O, off Rama IV Rd ℂ233 4168.
The closest budget accommodation to the station – cross Rama
IV Road, walk left for 200m, and then right down Trok La-O
to the end of the alley. A bit of a last resort, with spartan but
just about passable rooms and very basic shared facilities. ②

Krung Kasem Sri Krung Hotel

Map 5, H5. 1860 Krung Kasem Rd ℂ225 0132, fax 225 4705.
Excellent-value mid-range Chinese hotel just 50m across the
khlong from the station. Rooms are spacious and reasonably
furnished, and they all have air-con and TV. ⑤

New Empire Hotel

Map 5, G6. 572 Yaowarat Rd ℂ234 6990, fax 234 6997.
Medium-sized hotel right in the thick of the Chinatown bus-
tle, offering average mid-priced rooms with showers and air-
con. ⑤

TT Guesthouse (TT2)

Map 2, E7. 516 Soi Sawang, off Maha Nakorn Rd ℂ236 2946, fax
236 3054.

The best budget place in the station area; cross Rama IV Road, walk left for 250m, right down Maha Nakorn Road, left down Soi Sawang and straight on under the flyover, following the signs for *TT*. Clean, friendly and well run, though significantly more expensive than *FF*, with good noticeboards and traveller-oriented facilities, including left luggage at B7 a day and a small library. All rooms share bathrooms, and there are B100 dorm beds. ③

White Orchid Hotel

Map 5, F5. 409–421 Yaowarat Rd ©226 0026, fax 225 6403.
One of the plushest hotels in Chinatown, right at the hub of the gold-trading quarter. All rooms have air-con and TV, and there's a *dim sum* restaurant on the premises. If you book your room through the Pacto PC&C travel agency in Room 100 at Hualamphong Station, you should get a discount of up to twenty percent. ⑥–⑧

DOWNTOWN: AROUND SIAM SQUARE AND PLOENCHIT ROAD

The area around **Siam Square** – not really a square, but a grid of shops and restaurants between Phrayathai and Henri Dunant roads – and nearby **Ploenchit Road** are as central as you can get in Bangkok, handy for all kinds of shopping and nightlife, and for Hualamphong Station. There's no budget accommodation of note here, but a few scaled-up guesthouses have sprung up alongside the expensive hotels. Concentrated in their own "ghetto" on **Soi Kasemsan 1**, which runs north off Rama I Road just west of Phrayathai Road and is the next soi along from Jim Thompson's House (see p.111), these offer an informal guesthouse atmosphere, with hotel comforts – air-con and en-suite hot-water bathrooms – at moderate prices.

Getting to and from Siam Square and Ploenchit Road

Airport bus #A1 crosses the western end of Ploenchit Road in front of the Erawan Shrine on its way down Rajdamri Road, while the closest #A2 gets to this area is the corner of Phrayathai and Petchaburi roads. Dozens of other buses of all kinds run through the area, most passing the focal junction by the Erawan Shrine. Probably the most useful for travellers are those which stop near Soi Kasemsan 1, including AC#2 (south to Silom Road or north to Chatuchak Weekend Market), AC#8 (west to Ratanakosin and east along Sukhumvit Road), AC and ordinary #15 (Ratanakosin one way, Silom Road the other), and AC and ordinary #29 (Airport–Hualamphong Station). Soi Kasemsan 1 is five minutes' walk from the Khlong Sen Seb **longtail boat** stop at Phrayathai Road, and adventurous guests at the *Hilton* are very handily placed for the stop at Wireless (Witthayu) Road.

MODERATE

A-One Inn

Map 6, C4. 25/13 Soi Kasemsan 1, Rama I Rd ©215 3029, fax 216 4771.

The original upscale guesthouse, and still justifiably popular, with helpful staff. Bedrooms come in a variety of sizes, including family rooms, and the broad range of facilities includes a reliable left-luggage room, a tour service, satellite TV and a sociable café. ⑤

The Bed & Breakfast

Map 6, C3. 36/42 Soi Kasemsan 1, Rama I Rd ©215 3004, fax 215 2493.

Bright, clean, family-run and friendly, though the rooms – carpeted and with en-suite telephones – are a bit cramped. As the name suggests, breakfast, of a continental nature, is included. ⑤

Wendy House
Map 6, C4. 36/2 Soi Kasemsan 1, Rama I Rd ℂ216 2436–7, fax 216 8053.
As cramped as the name suggests, with no frills in the service, but clean and comfortable enough. TV in every room, and a small restaurant on the ground floor. ⑤

White Lodge
Map 6, C4. 36/8 Soi Kasemsan 1, Rama I Rd ℂ216 8867, fax 216 8228.
Well-maintained, shining white cubicles and a welcoming, if slightly eccentric, family-style atmosphere, with very good continental breakfasts at *Sorn's* next door. ⑤

EXPENSIVE

Chom's Boutique Inn
Map 6, L4. 888/37–9 Ploenchit Rd ℂ254 0056–63, fax 254 0054.
Small, tasteful hotel, popular with businesspeople, owned and well run by the family who founded the ground-breaking Imperial hotel group. Continental breakfast, included in the price, is served in the hotel's good restaurant, *Chom's Thai Kitchen.* ⑦

Hilton International
Map 6, K2. Nai Lert Park, 2 Wireless Rd ℂ253 0123, fax 253 6509.
Luxury hotel with beautiful, expansive gardens, in which are set a landscaped swimming pool, jogging track, tennis courts and health club, overlooked by many of the spacious, balconied bedrooms. Good French and Chinese restaurants, and a 24hr deli-café that's popular, post-clubbing, with bright young things. ⑨

Jim's Lodge

Map 6, L7. 125/7 Soi Ruam Rudee, Ploenchit Rd ©255 3100–3, fax 253 8492.

In a relatively peaceful residential area, handy for the British and American embassies, luxurious international standards on a small scale and at bargain prices; no swimming pool, but a roof garden with outdoor jacuzzi. ⑦

Le Meridien President

Map 6, I4. 971 Ploenchit Rd ©656 0444, fax 656 0555.

Now part of the Forte group, this thirty-year-old landmark has recently rejuvenated itself with the building of a huge new Tower Wing, aimed primarily at business travellers. Handily placed for the Erawan Shrine and shopping, the hotel has no less than seven restaurants, as well as the usual spa and health club; room rates compare very favourably with those of other five-star hotels in Bangkok. ⑨

Regent

Map 6, H6. 155 Rajdamri Rd ©251 6127, fax 253 9195.

The stately home of Bangkok's top hotels, offering a choice between large, well-endowed rooms and resort-style "cabanas" with private patios in the landscaped gardens. Afternoon tea is served under extravagant Thai murals in the grand lobby, and facilities include a health club and spa, and the highly acclaimed *Spice Market* Thai restaurant. ⑨

Siam Inter-Continental

Map 6, F3. 967 Rama I Rd ©253 0355-7, fax 253 2275.

Elegant, offbeat, low-rise modern Thai buildings in a quiet haven opposite Siam Square. The huge gardens encompass a golf-driving range, jogging trails and tennis. ⑨

Siam Orchid Inn

Map 6, I3. 109 Soi Rajdamri, Rajdamri Rd ©251 4417, fax 255 3144.

Very handily placed behind the Narayana Phand souvenir centre. A friendly, cosy place with an ornately decorated lobby, a tasty restaurant with live music in the evenings, and air-con, hot water, cable TV, mini-bars and phones in the comfortable bedrooms. ⑦

DOWNTOWN: SOUTH OF RAMA IV ROAD

South of Rama IV Road, the left bank of the river contains a full cross-section of places to stay. At the eastern edge there's **Soi Ngam Duphli**, a ghetto of budget guesthouses which is often choked with traffic escaping the jams on Rama IV Road. Though the neighbourhood is generally on the slide, the best guesthouses, tucked away on quiet **Soi Saphan Khu**, can just about compare with Banglamphu's finest. A disadvantage for lone travellers is that, of the bottom-end places listed below, only *Freddy's 2* and *Madam* offer decent single rates.

Getting to and from the southern downtown area

The big advantage of staying at the western edge of this area is that you'll be handily placed for Chao Phraya **express boats**, with useful stops at Harbour Department (*River View Guesthouse*), Wat Muang Kae (*Newrotel*), the *Oriental Hotel* and Sathorn (*Shangri-La*). Indeed, if you're staying anywhere in this area and travelling by public transport to Ratanakosin, you're best off catching a bus to the nearest express-boat stop and finishing your journey on the water. The most useful **bus** for Soi Ngam Duphli is likely to be AC#7, which among other things would allow you to check out alternative accommodation in Banglamphu if necessary, while countless buses run along Silom Road, including airport bus #A1.

Some medium-range places are scattered between Rama IV Road and the river, ranging from the notorious (the *Malaysia*) to the sedate (the *Bangkok Christian Guesthouse*). The area also lays claim to the capital's biggest selection of top hotels, which are among the most opulent in the world. It's also good for eating and shopping, with a generous sprinkling of embassies for visa-hunters.

INEXPENSIVE

Freddy's 2 Guesthouse
Map 7a. 27/40 Soi Sri Bamphen ©286 7826, fax 213 2097.
Popular, clean, well-organized guesthouse with a variety of rooms and plenty of comfortable common areas, including a café and beer garden at the rear. Rather noisy. ②

Lee 3 Guesthouse
Map 7a. 13 Soi Saphan Khu ©286 3042, fax 679 7045.
The best of the four Lee family guesthouses spread around this and the adjoining sois. Decent and quiet, with reasonably-sized rooms, though stuffy. ②

Lee 4 Guesthouse
Map 7a. 9 Soi Saphan Khu ©286 7874.
Simple, secure, airy rooms with en-suite cold-water bathrooms, priced according to size, in a dour modern tower at the entrance to the alley. ②–③

Madam Guesthouse
Map 7a. 11 Soi Saphan Khu ©286 9289, fax 213 2087.
Cleanish, often cramped rooms, with or without their own bathrooms, in a warren-like wooden house next door to *Lee 3*. Friendly, but sometimes a bit raucous at night. ①–③

Madras Lodge

Map 7, F7. 31/10–11 Trok Vaithi, opposite the *Narai Hotel*, Silom Rd ℗235 6761, fax 236 4771.

A ten-minute walk down a quiet lane off the south side of Silom Road, this rather ramshackle place above an Indian vegetarian café (see p.178) is run by a friendly, venerable emigré from South India. Rooms vary widely – some sport holes in the wall and dangling wires – but the towels and bedding are clean; choose either a fan and shared bathroom, or air con with en-suite hot water. ③–⑤

Sala Thai Daily Mansion

Map 7a. 15 Soi Saphan Khu ℗287 1436.

The pick of the Soi Ngam Duphli area. A clean and efficiently run place, with large, tastefully designed rooms, at the end of a quiet, shaded alley; a roof terrace makes it all the more pleasant. ③

TTO Guesthouse

Map 7a. 2/48 Soi Sri Bamphen ℗286 6783, fax 287 1571.
Rough, poorly designed but clean and spacious rooms, each with fridge, fan or air con, phone and hot-water bathroom, in a friendly establishment down a quiet alley off the south side of Soi Sri Bamphen. ③–④

MODERATE

Bangkok Christian Guesthouse

Map 7, K7. 123 Soi 2, Saladaeng Rd ℗233 6303, fax 237 1742.
Missionary house off the eastern end of Silom Road whose plain air-con rooms with hot-water bathrooms surround a quiet lawn. At the bottom of this price code, with breakfast included; good deals for singles. ⑦

Charlie House

Map 7a. 1034/36–37 Soi Saphan Khu ©679 8330-1, fax 679 7308.
Decent mid-range alternative to the crashpads of Soi Ngam
Duphli: bright, air-chilled lobby and small, slightly battered
bedrooms with minimal floral decor, hot-water bathrooms, air
con, TV and phone, in a modern tower close to Rama IV
Road. ⑤

Four Brothers Best House

Map 7a. 1034/31 Soi Saphan Khu ©679 8822-4, fax 679 8822.
Chaotic contrast to nearby *Charlie's*, with a run-down recep-
tion strewn with Chinese shrines, but the rooms are OK if you
prioritize facilities: air con, hot water and TV. ④

Malaysia Hotel

Map 7a. 54 Soi Ngam Duphli ©679 7127-36, fax 287 1457.
Big rooms with air con and hot-water bathrooms, some with
fridge, TV and video. Swimming pool (B50 per day for non-
guests) and reasonably priced Internet access (email:
malaysia@ksc15.th.com). Once a travellers' legend, now a sleaze
pit, with probably the surliest staff in Thailand. ⑤–⑥

Newrotel

Map 7, C5. 1216/1 New Rd ©630 6995, fax 237 1102.
Smart, clean, prettily decorated and very good value, between
the GPO and the *Oriental Hotel*, with air con, hot-water bathrooms, fridges and cable TV; the price includes American or
Chinese breakfast. ⑥

Niagara

Map 7, G7. 26 Soi Suksa Witthaya ©233 5783, fax 233 6563.
No facilities other than a coffee shop at this hotel off the south
side of Silom Road, but the clean bedrooms, with air con, hot-
water bathrooms, and telephones are a snip. ⑤

River View Guesthouse

Map 2, D7. 768 Soi Panurangsri, Songvad Rd ©235 8501, fax 237 5428.

Large but unattractive rooms, with fan and cold water at the lower end of the range, air con, hot water, TVs and fridges at the top. Great views over the bend in the river, especially from the top-floor restaurant, and handy for Chinatown, Hualamphong Station and the GPO. To find it through a maze of crumbling Chinese buildings, head north for 400m from River City shopping centre along Soi Wanit 2, before following signs to the guesthouse to the left. ⑤–⑥

EXPENSIVE

Dusit Thani Hotel

Map 7, L6. 946 Rama IV Rd ©236 0450-9, fax 236 6400.

Centrally placed top-class establishment on the corner of Silom Road, geared for both business and leisure, with very high standards of service. Many of the elegant rooms enjoy views of Lumphini Park and the sleek downtown high-rises. The hotel is famous for its restaurants, including the top-floor *Tiara*, which has probably the most spectacular vistas in Bangkok. ⑨

La Residence

Map 7, G5. 173/8–9 Suriwong Rd ©233 3301, fax 237 9322.

Small, intimate hotel above *All Gaengs* restaurant; the cutesy rooms stretch to mini-bars and cable and satellite TV. At the lower end of this price code, with decent rates for singles. ⑧

Montien Hotel

Map 7, J4. 54 Suriwong Rd ©233 7060-9, fax 236 5219.

Grand, airy and solicitous luxury hotel on the corner of Rama IV Road, with a strongly Thai character. It's very handily placed for business and nightlife, and famous for the astrologers who dispense predictions to Bangkok's high society in the lobby. ⑨

ACCOMMODATION DOWNTOWN: SOUTH OF RAMA IV ROAD

Oriental Hotel

Map 7, B5. 48 Oriental Ave, off New Rd ℗236 0400, fax 236 1937. One of the world's best. Effortlessly stylish riverside hotel, with immaculate service (1200 staff to around 400 rooms, and a neat little trick with matchsticks so they can make up your room while you're out). It's long outgrown the original premises, an atmospheric, colonial-style wooden building, now dubbed the Authors' Wing – indeed, there can't be many famous scribes who haven't stayed here, with suites named after a motley crew descending from Joseph Conrad through Graham Greene to Barbara Cartland. ⑨

Pinnacle

Map 7a. 17 Soi Ngam Duphli ℗287 0111-31, fax 287 3420. Bland but reliable international-standard place, close to Rama IV Road, with jacuzzi, fitness centre and scenic top-floor cocktail lounge; rates, which are at the lower end of this price code, include breakfast. ⑧

Shangri-La

Map 7, B7. 89 Soi Wat Suan Plu, New Rd ℗236 7777, fax 236 8579. Grandiose establishment voted, for what it's worth, top hotel in the world by *Condé Nast Traveler* readers in 1996. It boasts the longest river frontage of any hotel in Bangkok, and makes the most of it, with gardens, restaurants – including the award-winning *Salathip* for Thai cuisine – and two pools by the Chao Phraya; the two accommodation wings are linked by free tuk-tuk if you can't be bothered to walk. A list of facilities as long as your arm leaves nothing to chance; good deals are offered to families with children. ⑨

Sukhothai

Map 7, L9. 13/3 Sathorn Thai Rd ℗287 0222, fax 287 0228. The most elegant of Bangkok's top hotels, its decor inspired by the walled city of Sukhothai. Low-rise accommodation coolly furnished in silks, teak and granite, amid gardens set well back from the main road. Excellent Italian and Thai restaurants. ⑨

Swiss Lodge

Map 7, J7. 3 Convent Rd ©233 5345, fax 236 9425.

Swish, friendly, good-value, solar-powered boutique hotel, just off Silom Road and ideally placed for business and nightlife. The imaginatively named theme restaurant *Café Swiss* serves fondue, raclette and all your other Swiss favourites, while the tiny terrace swimming pool confirms the national stereotypes of neatness and clever design. ⑨

YMCA Collins International House

Map 7, L8. 27 Sathorn Thai Rd ©287 1900, fax 287 1996.

First-class facilities, including swimming pool and gym, with no frills. Its adjacent sister concern, the *YWCA Hostel* (©286 1936), was closed for renovation at the time of writing, but has in the past offered equally good value for money at lower rates (air-con rooms with hot-water bathrooms, and a swimming pool). ⑧

SUKHUMVIT ROAD

Although this is not the place to come if you're on a tight budget, **Sukhumvit Road** is a good area for mid-range hotels and small, well-appointed "inns", many of which are clustered together in a little enclave known as Soi 11/1. The four- and five-star hotels on Sukhumvit tend to be oriented more towards business travellers than tourists, but what they lack in glamour they more than make up for in facilities. Advance reservations are accepted at all places listed below, and are recommended during high season.

Staying here gives you a huge choice of restaurants, bars and shops, on Sukhumvit and the adjacent Ploenchit roads, but you're a long way from the main Ratanakosin sights, and the sheer volume of traffic on Sukhumvit means that travelling by bus across town can take an age.

Getting to and from Sukhumvit Road

Useful **buses** for getting from Sukhumvit to Ratanakosin include AC#8 and #25; #25 and #40 go to Hualamphong Station and Chinatown, and AC#13 goes to Chatuchak Weekend Market. Full details of bus routes are given on p.44. **Airport bus** #A3 has stops all the way along Sukhumvit Road .

A much faster way of getting across town is to hop on one of the **longtail boats** that ply the canals: Khlong Sen Seb, which begins at Phanfa near Democracy Monument in the west of the city, runs parallel with part of Sukhumvit Road and has stops at the northern ends of Soi Nana Neua (Soi 3) and Soi Asoke (Soi 21), from where you can either walk down to Sukhumvit Road itself, hop on a bus, or take a motorbike taxi.

MODERATE

The Atlanta

Map 8, A6. Far southern end of Soi 2 ©252 1650, fax 656 8123. Classic old-style hotel with lots of character, welcoming staff, and some of the cheapest rooms on Sukhumvit. The atmosphere is straight out of colonial times – palm trees in the little courtyard writing tables in the lobby – and the hotel restaurant has a huge Thai menu with lots of vegetarian dishes. The rooms are simple and a bit scruffy, but all have bathrooms and some have air-con and hot water. ④–⑤

Bangkok Inn

Map 8, B9. Soi 11/1 ©254 4834, fax 254 3545. A cosy, friendly little hotel just a stone's throw from the main drag. All rooms have air-con, shower, fridge and TV. ⑥

Grand Inn

Map 8, B4. Soi 3 *©*254 9021, fax 254 9020.

Very central small hotel, with reasonably priced, spacious rooms, all of which have air-con, TV and fridge. Good value. ⑥–⑦

Miami Hotel

Map 8, C9. Soi 13 *©*253 5611, fax 253 1266.

Popular, long-established budget hotel built around a swimming pool. Rooms are large and clean, if slightly shabby; most have attached bathroom, and some have air-con and TV. ③–⑤

Narry's Inn

Map 8, B9. Soi 11/1 *©*254 9184, fax 254 3568.

Very similar in style and facilities to the neighbouring *Bangkok Inn*, but slightly cheaper. Rooms are large and air-conditioned, and all have TVs and fridges. ⑤–⑥

Premier Travelodge

Map 8, C5. Soi 8 *©*251 3031, fax 253 3195.

Well-equipped small hotel offering good value rooms with shower, bath, air-con, fridge and TV. ⑤–⑥

SV Guesthouse

Map 8, D5. Soi 19 *©*253 1747.

Some of the least expensive beds in the area. Rooms are scruffy but just about adequate, and most of them share bathrooms. Some air-con. ③–④

Uncle Rey's Guesthouse

Map 8, B5. Soi 4 *©*252 5565, fax 253 8307.

Reasonably priced place that's quiet considering its central location and proximity to the Soi Nana strip of bars. Rooms are shabby but clean enough, and all have air-con and shower. ④–⑤.

ACCOMMODATION: SUKHUMVIT ROAD

Amari Boulevard Hotel
Map 8, C4. Soi 7 ©255 2930, fax 255 2950.
Medium-sized, unpretentious and friendly top-notch accommodation. All rooms enjoy fine views of the Bangkok skyline, and the deluxe ones have private garden patios as well. There's a well-placed rooftop swimming pool, a fitness centre and several restaurants. ⑨

Ambassador Hotel
Map 8, B10. Between sois 11 and 13 ©254 0444, fax 253 4123.
Sprawling hotel complex on Sukhumvit, with an unenticingly dark lobby area, but an excellent range of facilities that includes more than a dozen restaurants. ⑧–⑨

Imperial Queen's Park
Map 8, G9. Soi 22 ©261 9000, fax 261 9530.
Enormous, swish high-rise hotel, whose large, comfortable rooms are nicely decorated with Thai-style furnishings. Facilities include two swimming pools, snooker tables, a fitness centre, and six restaurants. Access can be a problem because it's so far down Sukhumvit Road, which also makes it feel rather isolated. ⑨

JW Marriott Hotel
Map 8, B4. Between sois 2 and 4 ©656 7700, fax 656 7711.
Brand new, central deluxe hotel geared towards business travellers, offering comfortable rooms with sophisticated phone systems and data ports. Facilities include three restaurants, a swimming pool, spa and fitness centre. ⑨

Landmark Hotel
Map 8, C5. Between sois 6 and 8 ©254 0404, fax 253 4259.
One of the most luxurious hotels on Sukhumvit, oriented

towards the business traveller, with all 415 rooms linked up to a central database providing information on the stock exchange, airline schedules and so on. Easy access to the restaurants and shops in the adjacent Landmark Plaza, plus a fitness club and pool on the premises. ⑨

Rex Hotel

Soi 34 ℗259 0106.

Adequate rooms, all with air-con, TV, hot water, and use of pool. Its location close to the Eastern Bus Terminal makes it convenient for east-coast connections, but too isolated from the best of Sukhumvit for a longer stay. ⑦–⑧

Sheraton Grande Sukhumvit

Map 8, D6. Between sois 12 and 14 ℗653 0333, fax 653 0400.

Deluxe accommodation with all the trimmings you'd expect from an upmarket chain hotel. Facilities include a swimming pool and fitness club, a spa with a range of treatment plans, and the classy *Golden Lotus* Chinese restaurant. Kids of 17 and under go free if sharing adults' room. ⑨

Eating

Bangkok boasts an astonishing fifty thousand **places to eat** – that's almost one for every hundred citizens – ranging from grubby streetside noodle shops to the most elegant of restaurants. Despite this glut, an awful lot of tourists venture no further than the front doorstep of their guesthouse, preferring the dining-room's ersatz Thai or Western dishes to the more adventurous fare to be found in even the most touristy accommodation areas.

Thai restaurants of every type are found all over the city. The air-con **standard Thai** places, patronized by office workers and middle-class families, almost always work out to be excellent value, with massive menus of curries, soups, rice and noodle dishes, and generally some Chinese dishes as well; the Banglamphu and Democracy areas have an especially high concentration of these. The best **gourmet Thai** restaurants, operating from the downtown districts around Sukhumvit and Silom roads, definitely merit an occasional splurge. At the other end of the scale there are simple **street stalls**, fronted by a few tables and stools, and specializing in one type of food, or even a single dish. These are so numerous in Bangkok that we can only flag a few of the most promising areas – but wherever you're staying, you'll hardly have to walk a block in any direction before encountering something cheap and very edible.

Of the non-Thai cuisines, Chinatown naturally rates as the most authentic district for pure **Chinese** food; likewise neighbouring Pahurat, the capital's Indian enclave, is best for unadulterated **Indian** dishes – though here, as in Chinatown, many establishments are nameless and transient, so it's hard to make recommendations.

Fast food comes in two forms: the mainly Thai version, which stews canteen-style in large tin trays on the upper floors of department stores all over the city, and the old Western favourites like *McDonald's* and *KFC* that mainly congregate around Siam Square and Ploenchit Road – an area that also has its share of decent Thai and foreign restaurants.

Few Thais are **vegetarian**, but in the capital it's fairly easy to find specially concocted Thai and Western veggie dishes, usually at tourist-oriented eateries. Even at the plainest street stall, it's rarely impossible to persuade the cook to rustle up a vegetable-only fried rice or noodle dish. If you're vegan you'll need to stress that you don't want egg when you order, as eggs get used a lot; cheese and other dairy produce, however, don't feature at all in Thai cuisine.

Hygiene is a consideration when eating anywhere in Bangkok, but being too cautious means you'll end up spending a lot of money and missing out on some real treats – you can be pretty sure that any noodle stall or curry shop that's permanently packed with customers is a safe bet. Thais don't drink water straight from the tap, and nor should you: plastic bottles of drinking water (*nam plao*) are sold everywhere for B5–10, as well as the full multinational panoply of soft drinks.

As soft-drink bottles are returnable, don't be surprised if a shopkeeper or stallholder pours the contents into a small plastic bag, perhaps with some crushed ice, deftly fastens the bag with an elastic band and inserts a straw, rather than charging you extra for taking away the bottle.

EATING

A food and drink glossary

Noodles (kwáy tiãw or ba mìi)

Ba mìi	Egg noodles
Kwáy tiãw (sên yaì/sên lék)	White rice noodles (wide/thin)
Ba mìi kràwp	Crisp fried egg noodles
Kwáy tiãw/ba mìi haêng	Rice noodles/egg noodles fried with egg, small pieces of meat and a few vegetables
Kwáy tiãw/ba mìi nám (mǔu)	Rice noodle/egg noodle soup, made with chicken broth (and pork balls)
Kwáy tiãw/ba mìi nâ rât (mǔu)	Rice noodles/egg noodles fried in gravy-like sauce with vegetables (and pork slices)
Pàt thai	Thin noodles fried with egg, beansprouts and tofu, topped with ground peanuts
Pàt siyú	Wide or thin noodles fried with soy sauce, egg and meat

Rice (khâo) and rice dishes

Khâo	Rice
Jók	Rice breakfast porridge
Khâo man kài	Slices of chicken served over marinated rice
Khâo nâ kài/pèt	Chicken/duck served with sauce over rice
Khâo niãw	Sticky rice
Khâo pàt kài/mǔu/kûng/phàk	Fried rice with chicken/pork/shrimp/vegetables
Khâo rât kaeng	Curry over rice
Khâo tôm	Rice soup

Stir-fries, curries (kaeng), soups, salads and seafood

Kaeng kài/néua/pèt/ plaa dùk/sôm	Chicken/beef/duck/catfish/ fish and vegetable curry
Kài pàt nàw mái	Chicken with bamboo shoots
Kài pàt mét mámûang	Chicken with cashew nuts
Kài pàt khǐng	Chicken with ginger
Kûng chúp paêngthâwt	Prawns fried in batter
Pàt phàk bûng	Morning glory fried in garlic and bean sauce
Pàt phàk lǎi yàng	Stir-fried vegetables
Plaa (mǔu) prîaw wǎan	Sweet and sour fish (pork)
Plaa nêung páe sá	Whole fish steamed with vegetables and ginger
Plaa rât phrík	Whole fish cooked with chillies
Sôm tam	Spicy papaya salad
Thâwt man plaa	Fish cakes
Tôm khàa kài	Chicken coconut soup
Tôm yam kûng	Hot and sour prawn soup

Fruit (phǒnlamái)

Fàràng	Guava (year-round)
Khanǔn	Jackfruit (year-round)
Klûay	Banana (year-round)
Lamyai	Longan (July–Oct)
Línjìi	Lychee (April–May)
Mámûang	Mango (March–June)
Ngáw	Rambutan (May–Sept)
Málákaw	Papaya (year-round)
Mákhǎam	Tamarind (Dec–Jan)
Mánao	Lemon/lime (year-round)
Mangkùt	Mangosteen (April–Sept)
Mapráo	Coconut (year-round)
Sàppàròt	Pineapple (year-round)
Sôm	Orange (year-round)

Sôm oh	Pomelo (Oct–Dec)
Taeng moh	Watermelon (year-round)
Thúrian	Durian (April–June)

Sweets (khanŏm)

Khanŏm beuang	Small crispy pancake folded over with coconut cream and strands of sweet egg
Khâo lăam	Sticky rice, coconut cream and black beans cooked and served in bamboo tubes
Khâo niăw daeng	Sticky red rice mixed with coconut cream
Khâo niăw thúrian/ mámûang	Sticky rice mixed with coconut cream, and durian/mango
Klûay khàek	Fried banana
Lûk taan chêum	Sweet palm kernels served in syrup
Săngkhayaa	Coconut custard
Tàkôh	Jelly (jello) topped with coconut cream

Drinks (khreuang deùm)

Bia	Beer
Chaa ráwn	Hot tea
Chaa yen	Iced tea
Kaafae ráwn	Hot coffee
Mâekhŏng	Thai brand-name rice whisky (Mekhong)
Nám klûay	Banana shake
Nám mánao/sôm	Fresh, bottled or fizzy lemon/orange juice
Nám plaò	Drinking water (boiled or filtered)
Nom jeùd	Milk
Sohdaa	Soda water

Ordering

I am vegetarian	*Phŏm* (male)/*diichăn* (female) *kin jeh*
Can I see the menu?	*Khăw duù menu?*
I would like . . .	*Khăw . . .*
With/without	*Sai/mâi sai*
Can I have the bill please?	*Khăw check bin?*

In the more expensive restaurants you may have to pay a **service charge** and ten percent government **tax**. In the listings below, telephone numbers are given for the more popular or out-of-the-way places, where bookings may be advisable.

How to eat Thai food

Thai food is eaten with a **fork** (left hand) and a **spoon** (right hand); there is no need for a knife as food is served in bite-sized chunks, which are forked onto the spoon and fed into the mouth. **Chopsticks** are provided for noodle dishes, and the sticky rice (*khao niaw*) available in northeastern Thai restaurants is always eaten with the **fingers** of the right hand, rolled into small balls and dipped into chilli sauces. Never eat with the fingers of your left hand, which is used for washing after going to the toilet.

Instead of being divided into courses, a Thai meal – even the soup – is served all at once, and shared communally, so that complementary taste combinations can be enjoyed. The more people, the more taste and texture sensations; if there are only two of you, it's normal to order at least three dishes, plus your own individual plates of steamed rice, while three diners would order at least four dishes and so on. Only put a serving of one dish on your rice plate at each time, and then only one or two spoonfuls.

Bland food is anathema to Thais, and restaurant tables usually come decked out with a **condiment** set featuring chopped chillies in watery fish sauce, sugar, and dried and ground red chillies – and often extra ground peanuts and a bottle of chilli ketchup as well. If you do bite into a chilli, the way to combat the searing heat is to take a mouthful of plain rice – swigging water just exacerbates the sensation.

BANGLAMPHU AND DEMOCRACY AREA

Chochana
Map 3, C7. Off Chakrabongse Rd, between the Shell petrol station and the police station.
Daily 11am–11pm.
Inexpensive Israeli restaurant, serving hearty platefuls of workaday falafels, hummus, salads and dips. It's attached to a guesthouse patronized mainly by Israeli travellers, so the food is reasonably authentic, and a good option for vegetarians.

Dachanee
Map 3, H4. 18/2 Pracha Thipatai Rd, near *Thai Hotel*.
Popular with local office workers, this air-con restaurant serves up moderately priced standard Thai fare such as fiery *tom yam* as well as tasty extras like tofu- and beansprout-stuffed *khanom buang* (crispy pancakes).

Dragon Eyes
Map 3, D3. Samsen/Wisut Kasat junction.
Mon–Sat 6pm–midnight.
This small, mid-priced restaurant is popular with young Thai couples and has a lively atmosphere. It serves stylish renditions of standard Thai dishes – try the *khao pat* with added fruit and nuts, or the chilli-fried chicken with cashews – as well as more unusual fare. There's a huge selection of bar drinks as well, and, as you'd expect from a place managed by a *Bangkok Post* music critic, a fine range of music.

For advice on getting to this area on public transport see p.42, and for a more detailed breakdown of useful bus routes see p.44.

Fresh Corner

Map 3, C8. West end of Trok Mayom/Damnoen Klang Neua.

Daily approximately 10am–10pm.

Makeshift alleyway restaurant, comprising two tiny cubicles and a few alleyside tables for customers. One cubicle serves a small but scrumptious menu of inexpensive Thai food, including a recommended potato curry with tofu; the other does ten different blends of freshly brewed coffee, plus espressos and cappucinos.

Hemlock

Map 3, B7. 53 Phra Athit Rd, opposite the express boat pier.

Mon–Sat 5pm–2am.

Small, stylish air-con restaurant that's deservedly very popular with students and young Thai couples. Offers a long, mid-priced menu of unusual Thai dishes, including banana flower salad, coconut and mushroom curry, grand lotus rice and various *larb* and fish dishes. Good veggie selection too. Highly recommended.

Isaan restaurants

Map 2, D3. Behind the Rajdamnoen Boxing Stadium on Rajdamnoen Nok Rd.

There's at least five restaurants in a row here, all of them serving inexpensive northeastern fare to hungry boxing fans: take your pick for hearty plates of *kai yang* and *khao niaw*.

Kainit

Map 2, C4. Thanon Titong, next to Wat Suthat.

Daily 11am–11pm.

Rather formal Italian restaurant that's mainly patronized by expats, but also works fine as a lunchtime treat after visiting Wat Suthat next door. The pizza and pastas are tasty but expensive.

Kaloang

Map 3, D1. Beside the river at the far western end of Sri Ayutthaya Rd.

Daily 11am–11pm.

Flamboyant service and excellent seafood attracts a predominantly Thai clientele to this pricey open-air restaurant located beside the Chao Phraya River. Try the fried rolled shrimps served with a sweet dip, the roast squid cooked in a piquant sauce, or the steamed butter fish.

Lotus Café

Map 3, D8. Khao San Rd.

Archetypal travellers' haven, with only a few tables, an emphasis on wholesome ingredients, and yoga posters on the walls. The small menu includes delicious home-made brown bread, a range of tasty sandwich fillings, muesli and yoghurt.

May Kaidee

Map 3, G8. Off Tanao Rd, down the soi with the *Royal Fashion* sign.
Daily until about 9pm.

Simple, very inexpensive permanent soi-side foodstall serving the best vegetarian food in Banglamphu. Try the tasty green curry with coconut, the curry-fried tofu with vegetables or the sticky black-rice pudding.

Na Pralan

Map 4, C5. Almost opposite the Gate of Glorious Victory, Na Phra Lan Rd.
Mon–Sat 10am–10pm.

Technically in Ratanakosin but very close to Banglamphu, this small café is ideally placed for refreshment before or after a tour of the Grand Palace. Popular with students, it occupies a quaint old shophouse with battered, arty decor and air con. The mid-priced menu is well thought out and has some unusual twists, offering tasty daily specials – mostly one-dish meals with rice – and a range of Thai desserts, coffees, teas and beers.

Royal India

Map 3, D8. Opposite *Hello Café* on Khao San Rd.

Daily 11am–11pm.

Excellent, reasonably priced Indian food at this very popular branch of the Pahurat original. Dishes taste authentic and are served in copious quantities. Service is not exactly speedy, but you can fill in the gaps by watching the movies that play every night in the dining area.

Sorn Daeng

Map 3, G10. Southeast corner of Democracy Monument.
Daily 10am–10pm.
The main customers at this large air-con restaurant are local office workers, so the menu offers a good range of standard, fairly inexpensive Thai fare. The southern curries are recommended, particularly the rich sweet beef *kaeng matsaman*.

So Ying Thai

Map 2, C4. Intersection of Tanao and Bamrung Muang roads.
Busy and moderately priced if rather characterless family restaurant, serving up family-sized portions of Thai standards such as chicken and bamboo shoots, plus less common ones, like fried frog in curry sauce.

Tang Teh

Map 3, D3. Corner of Samsen and Wisut Kasat roads.
Daily noon to 2.30pm & 6–11pm.
Unusual, quality Thai restaurant, with contemporary art on the walls and high-class food on the menu. The fried catfish with cashews and chilli sauce is recommended, as are the superb fishcakes and the steamed sea bass with Chinese plum sauce. There's also a fairly interesting veggie menu, and tasty home-made ice cream, all at moderate prices.

Wang Nah

Map 3, A8. Phra Athit Rd, under Phra Pinklao Bridge.
Daily 11am–11pm.

Sizeable, mid-priced seafood menu served at this breezy location beside the Chao Phraya River.

Yod Dam

Map 3, G6. Opposite Wat Bowoniwes at 365/1 Phra Sumen. Cosy, wood-beamed restaurant done out like a curio shop and serving authentically fiery Thai dishes such as roast duck salad, steamed freshwater fish and pork steamed in bamboo; some Chinese specialities too. Moderately priced.

Yok Yor

Map 3, C3. Tha Wisut Kasat pier, Wisut Kasat Rd.
Daily 11am–11pm.

Riverside restaurant in two sections, which sends a boatload of diners down to Rama IX Bridge and back every evening: departs 8pm, returns 10pm. The food is definitely nothing special – there's more choice before the boat sets off and leaves the main kitchen behind – but it's the most inexpensive of a host of similar operations, and the floodlit views of Wat Arun, Wat Phra Kaeo and others are worth the B50 cover charge.

CHINATOWN AND PAHURAT

Chong Tee

Map 5, H7. 84 Soi Sukon 1, Traimit Rd, between Hualamphong station and Wat Traimit.

This typical, long-standing, no-frills Chinese restaurant is known for its delicious and inexpensive pork satay and sweet toast.

For advice on getting to this area on public transport see p.42, and for a more detailed breakdown of useful bus routes see p.44.

Hua Seng Hong
Map 5, F5. 371 Yaowarat Rd.

Not too hygienic, but the food is good and reasonably priced. Sit outside on the jostling pavement for delicious egg noodle soup with pork, duck or *wonton*, or good-value shark's fin soup. Inside the air-con restaurant, the main thrust is fish and seafood (try the asparagus with scallop), but also on offer are pricey Chinese specialities like goose feet, smoked whole baby pig and bird's nest.

> **Every evening, the stall just outside *Hua Seng Hong* on Yaowarat Road sells cheap and delicious *bua loy nga dam nam khing*, soft rice dumplings stuffed with bittersweet black sesame in ginger soup.**

Maturot
Map 5, F4. Soi Texas, Yaowarat Rd.
Evenings only, until late.

In a soi famous for its seafood stalls, the fresh, meaty prawns, accompanied by *pak bung fai daeng* (fried morning glory) and *tom yam kung*, stand out. Prices range from inexpensive to moderate.

Royal India
Map 5, B3. Just off Chakraphet Rd.
Daily 11am–11pm.

Serves the same excellent and highly authentic curries as its Banglamphu branch, but attracts an almost exclusively Indian clientele. Prices are very reasonable and portions large.

White Orchid Hotel
Map 5, F5. 409–421 Yaowarat Rd.
Dim sum 11am–2pm & 5–10pm.

Recommended for its fairly pricey *dim sum*, with bamboo baskets of prawn dumplings, spicy spare ribs, stuffed beancurd and the like, served in three different portion sizes. All-you-can-eat lunchtime buffets are also worth considering at B130 per person.

You Sue Vegetarian

Map 5, I6. 75m east of Hualamphong Station at 241 Rama IV Rd. Cheap and cheerful Chinese vegetarian café, directly across the road from the sign for the *Bangkok Centre Hotel*. Standard curries and Chinese and one-pot dishes are made with high-protein meat substitutes. Not worth making a special outing for, but handy for the station.

....

Nearly all Bangkok's Chinese restaurants stop serving meat for the duration of the nine-day Vegetarian Festival in October, flying special yellow flags to show that they're upholding the community's tradition.

....

DOWNTOWN: AROUND SIAM SQUARE AND PLOENCHIT ROAD

Bali

Map 6, L5. 15/3 Soi Ruam Rudee ©250 0711.
Mon–Sat 11am–10pm, Sun 5–10pm.
Top-notch, authentic Indonesian food and homely, efficient service in a cosy old house with garden tables just off Ploenchit Road. Prices per dish are mostly moderate, or blow out on a seven-course *rijstaffel* for B180.

Ban Khun Phor

Map 6, F5. 458/7–9 Soi 8, Siam Square ©250 1252.
Daily 11am–11pm.
Traditional music and rustic atmosphere in dark-wood rooms scattered with antiques, with good, moderately priced Thai specialities; food spiced to order.

For advice on getting to this area on public transport see p.42, and for a more detailed breakdown of useful bus routes see p.44.

Kirin Restaurant

Map 6, D5. 226/1 Soi 2, Siam Square ©251 2326-9.

Daily 11am–2pm & 6–10pm.

Swankiest, best and most expensive of many Chinese restaurants in the area; for a blow-out, order the delicious *ped pak king*, duck cooked with vegetables and ginger.

Mah Boon Krong Food Centre

Map 6, C5. Sixth floor of MBK shopping centre, corner of Rama I and Phrayathai roads, opposite Siam Square.

Daily 10am–10pm.

Increase your knowledge of Thai food: ingredients, names and pictures of inexpensive dishes (including some vegetarian ones) from all over the country are displayed at the various stalls. A beer terrace, open in the evenings, affords good views of the cityscape.

Noble House

Map 6, K2. *Hilton International Hotel*, Nai Lert Park, 2 Wireless Rd ©253 0123.

Daily 11.30am–2pm & 6.30–10pm.

Top-notch Cantonese restaurant which has been beautifully modelled on an old Chinese trading house. Prices, not surprisingly, are very high, especially for the more esoteric delicacies, but the excellent *dim sum*, prepared by a Hong Kong chef, is very reasonable if ordered by the dish (B40).

Phong Lan

Map 6, J8. 239 Soi Sarasin, down a side soi, just west of Soi Lang Suan ©651 9368.

Daily 10am–11pm.

Vietnamese favourite, which doesn't make the most of its location in a grand former embassy: the muzak and the somewhat institutional decor are disappointing. However, the service is very attentive and the moderately priced food excellent: try the *miang sod sai kung*, rice papers filled with vegetables, mint, rice and prawns, and the *yum-sao*, chicken salad flavoured with Vietnamese mint leaf, and leave room for dessert.

Pop

Map 6, H9. Northwest corner of Lumphini Park.

Daily 6am–8pm.

Informal garden restaurant that's popular for breakfasts and passable *dim sum* lunches, though a bit close to busy Soi Sarasin for true peace. Standard inexpensive Chinese and Thai dishes (especially northeastern food such as *nam tok* and *som tam*) are also on offer, as well as a decent range of ice creams and drinks.

Sarah Jane's

Map 6, K8. Ground Floor, Sindhorn Tower 1, 130–132 Witthayu Rd ©650 9992–3.

Daily 11am–10pm.

Long-standing, moderately priced restaurant, popular with Bangkok residents from Isaan (the northeast of Thailand), serving excellent, simple northeastern food. It's run by an American – and offers a smaller range of Italian dishes – but the *kai yang* (barbecued chicken) and *som tam* (papaya salad) are supremely authentic nonetheless; try also the *neua nam tok* (barbecued beef salad) and the *yam pla dook foo* (finely chopped catfish, deep fried until crispy, with a mango topping). The new premises are slick but unfussy, and can be slightly tricky to find at night towards the rear of a modern office block.

Sorn's

Map 6, C4. 36/8 Soi Kasemsan 1, Rama I Rd ©215 5163.

Daily 6.30am–10pm.

In this quiet lane of superior guesthouses, a laid-back, open-air hangout strewn with plants and vines, with an atmosphere like a beachside guesthouse restaurant. A photographer and long-time resident of the US, Sorn serves up delicious, moderately priced versions of standard Thai dishes – the *tom kha kai* is especially good – as well as Western meals, varied breakfasts, good coffee and Amarit beer on draught.

Whole Earth

Map 6, J7. 93/3 Soi Langsuan ©252 5574.
Daily 11.30am–2pm & 5.30–11pm.

The best veggie restaurant in Bangkok, serving interesting, moderately priced Thai and Indian-style food, plus some dishes for carnivores and delicious fresh fruit smoothies; twee but relaxing atmosphere and good service. In the upstairs room (not always open), you can eat sprawled on cushions at low tables.

Zen

Map 6, H4. 6th floor, World Trade Center, corner of Ploenchit and Rajdamri roads ©255 6462.
Daily 10.30am–10pm.

Expensive but good-value Japanese restaurant with wacky wooden design, modern but nodding to traditional Japanese themes, and seductive booths. Among a huge range of dishes, the complete meal sets (with pictures to help you choose) are delicious and filling, and the soups are particularly good; reasonably priced beer.

DOWNTOWN: SOUTH OF RAMA IV ROAD

Akane Japanese Noodle

Map 7, F6. 236 Silom Rd, between sois 16 and 18.
Daily 11am–9pm.

Deliciously authentic *soba*, *udon*, *ramen* and *sushi* dishes, some surprisingly moderately priced, in unpretentious café-style surroundings next to the *Narai Hotel*, and handy after shopping or before hitting Silom's nightlife.

All Gaengs

Map 7, G5. 173/8–9 Suriwong Rd ℂ233 3301.
Mon–Fri 11am–2pm & 6.30–10pm, Sat & Sun 6.30–10pm.
Large moderately priced menu of tasty curries (*gaeng* or *kaeng*) and spicy Thai salads (*yam*) served in cool, modern, air-con surroundings underneath *La Residence* hotel – a good place to fire yourself up for the nightclubs over on Silom Road.

Ban Chiang

Map 7, D7. 14 Soi Srivieng, Surasak Rd ℂ236 7045.
Daily 11am–2pm & 5–10.30pm.
Fine central and northeastern Thai cuisine – try the *kaeng liang*, a delicious broth chock full of vegetables and shrimps – at moderate to expensive prices. The restaurant can be difficult to find, off the western end of Silom Road down towards Sathorn Road, but rewards persistence with an elegant, surprisingly quiet setting in an old wooden house with garden tables.

Bussaracum

Map 7, F8. 139 Sethiwan Building, Pan Rd ℂ266 6312-8.
Daily 11am–2pm & 5–9.30pm.
Superb "royal" Thai cuisine, offering recipes created for the court which until recently were kept secret from the common folk. Only top-quality ingredients are used, and great care is taken over the look of individual dishes, which are often decorated with carved fruit and vegetables. Expensive, but well worth it.

For advice on getting to this area on public transport see p.42, and for a more detailed breakdown of useful bus routes see p.44.

Chai Karr

Map 7, D6. 312/3 Silom Rd ℗233 2549.

Daily 10am–9pm.

Small restaurant, fifteen minutes' walk west of the main Silom action, opposite the *Holiday Inn*. Traditional wooden decor is the setting for a wide variety of moderately priced Thai and Chinese dishes, followed by liqueur coffees and coconut ice cream.

Charuvan

Map 7, J6. 70–2 Silom Rd, near the entrance to Soi 4.

Daily 9am–9pm.

Clean basic restaurant, lackadaisical verging on rude, with a walled-in air-con room. Specializing in inexpensive and tasty duck on rice – the beer's a bargain too – it's popular with both Soi 4 clubbers and Patpong barflies.

Deen

Map 7, E6. 786 Silom Rd.

Mon–Sat 11am–9.30pm.

Small, neat, well-lit café with air con (no smoking), almost opposite Silom Village. It draws most of its clientele from the Islamic south of Thailand, serving fairly cheap Thai and Chinese standard dishes with a southern twist, as well as spicy Indian-style curries and southern Thai specialities such as *grupuk* (crispy fish) and *roti* (Muslim pancakes).

Harmonique

Map 7, C4. 22 Soi 34, Charoen Krung (New Rd) ℗237 8175.

Mon–Sat 11am–10pm.

Relaxing, welcoming restaurant, on the lane between Wat Muang Kae express-boat pier and the GPO, that's well worth a trip: tables are scattered throughout several converted houses decorated with antiques, and a quiet, leafy courtyard, and the moderately priced Thai food is varied and excellent – among the seafood specialities, try the crab curry.

Himali Cha-Cha

Map 7, C6. 1229/11 Charoen Krung (New Rd) ©235 1569.

Daily 11am–3.30pm & 6–11.30pm.

Fine, moderately priced north Indian restaurant a short way down an alley to the south of GPO, founded by a character who was chef to numerous Indian ambassadors, and now run by his son; homely atmosphere, attentive service and a good vegetarian selection.

Laicram

Map 7, K6. 2nd floor, Thaniya Plaza, Thaniya Rd.

Daily 10.30am–3pm & 5–10pm.

Proficient, moderately expensive restaurant tucked away in a shopping centre off the eastern end of Silom Road. On offer are plenty of unusual specialities from around Thailand on a huge menu, plus loads of veggie dishes and traditional desserts (*khanom*).

Le Bouchon

Map 7, J5. 37/17 Patpong 2, near Suriwong Rd ©234 9109.

Daily 11am–2pm & 6pm–midnight.

Cosy, welcoming bar-bistro that's much frequented by the city's French expats, offering pricey French home cooking on a regularly changing menu; the lamb with rosemary sauce is strongly recommended, as is booking.

Madras Lodge and Café

Map 7, F7. 31/10–11 Trok Vaithi, opposite the *Narai Hotel*, Silom Rd.

Daily lunch and dinner.

A ten-minute walk off the side of Silom Road, this simple café with neat pink decor and a few tables on the quiet alley is run by a long-term emigré from Madras. On offer is a long, cheap menu of delicious food from the subcontinent, both veggie and carnivorous, including a wide choice of south Indian *dosas*.

Ranger Ranger

Map 7a. Mahamek Driving Range, south end of Soi Ngam Duphli, by Ministry of Aviation compound.

Daily 10am–10.30pm.

Unusual location by a golf driving range, but the setting for this moderately priced restaurant is pastoral cute, on stilted, tree-shaded platforms above a quiet, lotus-filled pond. Specialities include serpent-head fish, catfish and *yam hua pree*, gooey and delicious banana flower salad with dried shrimp and peanuts; some veggie dishes are available and the service is friendly and attentive.

Ratree Seafood

Map 7, K6. Soi 1, Silom Rd.

Daily, evenings only.

Famous street stall with twenty or so tables, surrounded by many similar competitors, at the eastern end of Silom Road opposite Thaniya Plaza. On offer are all manner of fresh seafood – barbecued fish and *poo chak ka chan* (oily, orange, medium-sized sea crabs) are the specialities – and noodle soup.

Ratstube

Map 7a. Goethe Institut, 18/1 Soi Ngam Duphli (round corner on Soi Attakarn Prasit) ℗286 4528.

Daily 10am–10pm.

Delicious but pricey German favourites – lots of flesh, including home-made veal sausages, and *sauerkraut* – in elegant, classy surroundings in the German cultural centre. Save some room, if you can, for blueberry pie or caramel *koepfchen*. There's also a good, inexpensive Thai cafeteria (daytime only) in the grounds outside.

Savoury

Map 7, F7. 60 Pan Rd ℗236 4830.

Mon–Sat 11am–2pm & 6–10pm.

Expensive but excellent European food, recommended for a splurge. The setting, above the ground-floor Artist's Gallery, is romantic, and service friendly and courteous.

Sui Heng

Map 7, A9. Mouth of Soi 65, Charoen Krung (New Rd).

Daily, evenings only, until late.

In a good area for stall-grazing, south of Sathorn Bridge, a legendary Chinese street vendor who has been selling one dish for over seventy years: *khao man kai*, tender boiled chicken breast served with delicious broth and garlic rice.

Trattoria Da Roberto

Map 7, J6. Patpong Plaza (1st floor), Patpong 2.

Daily 11.30am–midnight.

Informal haven at the epicentre of sleaze-land, which somehow retains an easy-going family atmosphere. The pricey seafood, pizzas and pastas wouldn't win any prizes, but they're palatable enough for the area.

SUKHUMVIT ROAD

Ambassador Hotel Asian Food Centre

Map 8, B10. Inside the *Ambassador Hotel* complex, between sois 11 and 13.

Daily 11am–10pm.

Inexpensive street-level canteen with about thirty stalls selling Japanese, Vietnamese, Chinese, Korean and regional Thai dishes; also vegetarian fare, both Thai and European. Food is bought with coupons, which are sold (and refunded) from a booth at the entrance.

For advice on getting to this area on public transport see p.42, and for a more detailed breakdown of useful bus routes see p.44.

Bangkapi Terrace

Map 8, B10. On the edge of the *Ambassador Hotel* complex, between sois 11 and 13.

Open 24-hours.

Streetside 24hr coffee-shop, billed as Bangkok's most popular after-hours meeting place. Workaday rice, noodle and Western standards.

Cabbages and Condoms

Map 8, D7. Soi 12.

Daily 11am–10pm.

Run by the Planned Parenthood Association of Thailand, this popular place offers good, mid-priced authentic Thai food in the Condom Room, relaxed scoffing of barbecued seafood in the beer garden, and free condoms for all diners. Recommended dishes include the honey roast chicken, the beef curry, and the chicken and coconut soup.

De Meglio

Map 8, C4. Soi 11.

Daily 11.30am–2.30pm & 5.30–11pm.

Upmarket Italian restaurant presided over by a chef who was trained by Anton Mosiman. Many of the antipasti are unusual Thai-Italian hybrids, and both the linguini with clams and the crab cannelloni with fennel salad are recommended. Authentic wood-fired pizzas are a house speciality.

Haus München

Map 8, D5. Soi 15.

Daily 10am–1am.

Large but moderately priced helpings of authentic German and Austrian classics, from pigs' knuckles to *bratwurst*, served in a restaurant that's modelled on a Bavarian lodge. There's usually some recent German newspapers to peruse here too.

Lemongrass

Map 8, H9. Soi 24.

Daily 11.30am–2.30pm & 5.30–11pm.

Scrumptious Thai nouvelle cuisine served in the elegant surroundings of a converted traditional house; a vegetarian menu is
available on request. Prices range from moderate to expensive.

Mrs Balbir's

Map 8, B9. Soi 11/1.

Daily 11am–11pm.

Deservedly popular veg and non-veg Indian restaurant run by
TV cook Mrs Balbir. Specialities include the spicy dry chicken
and lamb curries (*masala kerai*) and the daily all-you-can-eat
veggie buffet, which is recommended at B150 per person.
Indian cookery courses are held here every week – see p.222
for details.

Nipa

Map 8, C5. Third floor of Landmark Plaza, between sois 6 and 8.

Daily 11.30am–2.30pm & 5.30–11pm; last orders at 10.15pm.

Tasteful traditional Thai-style place with a classy, fairly pricey
menu that features an adventurous range of dishes, including
spicy fish curry, several *masaman* and green curries, excellent
somtam and mouthwatering braised spare ribs. Also offers a
sizeable vegetarian selection. Regular cookery classes are held
here – see p.222 for details.

Pasta 'n' noodles

Map 8, C5. Corner of Soi 9.

Daily 10am–10pm.

Novel Eurasian fast food joint where you choose your noodle
or pasta base (from penne to Singapore noodles) and then select
your sauce (such as tuna, tomato and herb, or peanut, coconut
and basil). Hardly haute cuisine, but a satisfying place for lunch.

Seafood Market
Map 8, H10. 89 Soi 24.

Daily 11.30am–11.30pm.

More of a pink-neon supermarket than a restaurant: you pick
your fish off the racks ("if it swims, we have it") and then
choose how you want it cooked. Go for the novelty and choice
rather than the atmosphere or fine cuisine. Mid-priced.

Suda Restaurant
Map 8, E6. Soi 14.

Daily 11am–midnight.

Unpretentious and inexpensive locals' hangout serving standard
rice and noodle dishes, plus some fish: the fried tuna with
cashews and chilli is recommended.

Thai Ruam Ros
Map 8, A3. Soi 1.

Daily 10am–10pm.

The sizeable, mid-priced menu of typical but unexceptional
Thai, Chinese and Mexican dishes makes this a good place for
lunch, but not such an exciting prospect for dinner.

Yong Lee
Map 8, D6. Corner of Soi 15.

Mon–Sat 11.30am–9.30pm.

One of the few unpretentious, up-country style rice-and-
noodle shops on Sukhumvit. Run by a Chinese family, its rates
are inexpensive, considering the competition.

Nightlife

For many of Bangkok's visitors, nightfall in the city is the signal to hit the **sex bars**, the neon sumps that disfigure three distinct parts of town: along Sukhumvit Road's Soi Cowboy (between sois 21 and 23) and Nana Plaza (Soi 4), and, most notoriously, in the two small sois off the east end of Silom Road known as Patpong 1 and 2. But within spitting distance of the beer bellies flopped onto Patpong's bars lies **Silom 4**, Bangkok's most happening after-dark haunt, pulling in the cream of Thai youth and tempting an increasing number of travellers to stuff their party gear into their rucksacks: Soi 4, the next alley off Silom Road to the east of Patpong 2, started out as a purely gay area but now offers a range of styles in gay, mixed and straight pubs, dance bars and clubs.

For a more casual drink, join the less adventurous Thai youth and yuppie couples who pack out the **music bars** concentrated around Soi Langsuan and Sarasin Road on the north side of Lumphini Park, and scattered randomly over the rest of the city. The atmosphere in these places is as pleasant as you'll find in a Bangkok bar, but don't expect anything better than Western covers and bland jazz from the resident musicians. Look out for inflated drink prices in the popular bars – a small bottle of Mekhong whisky can cost up to five times what a guesthouse would charge.

Local whisky is a lot better value than beer, and Thais think nothing of consuming a bottle a night, heavily diluted with soda water or coke and ice. The most widely available brand is Mekhong; distilled from rice, it's quite palatable once you've stopped expecting it to taste like Scotch.

Away from the cutting edge of imported sounds, Bangkok has its fair share of **discos** which churn out Thai and Western chart hits. Besides those listed on the following page, there are nightclubs in most of the deluxe hotels, notably the *Ambassador* and *Dusit Thani*; all charge an admission price which often includes a couple of free drinks.

BARS

For convenient drinking, we've split the recommended bars into three central areas. In **Banglamphu**, bars tend either to be backpacker-oriented, in which case they usually have pool tables or back-to-back video showings, or style-conscious student hangouts, where the decor sets the tone and the clientele rarely includes more than a handful of foreigners. Many of the **downtown** music bars attract both foreign and Thai drinkers, though the Patpong joints are aimed squarely at farangs, and if you end up in one of these you must be prepared to shell out up to B600 for a small beer. Many Patpong bars trumpet the fact that they have no cover charge, but almost every customer gets ripped off in some way, and stories of menacing bouncers are legion. **Sukhumvit Road** watering holes tend to be either British-style pubs or girlie bars.

During the cool season (Nov–Feb), an evening out at one of the seasonal **beer gardens** is a pleasant way of soaking up the urban atmosphere (and the traffic fumes). You'll find them in hotel forecourts or sprawled in front of shopping centres – the huge beer garden that sets up in front of the World Trade Centre on Rajdamri Road is extremely popular, and recommended; beer is served in pitchers here and bar snacks are available too.

BANGLAMPHU AND HUALAMPHONG

About Café
Map 5, H5. Five minutes' walk from Hualamphong Station at 402 Maitri Chit Rd.

Daily 7pm–midnight.

Arty café-bar that's popular with trendy young Thais. There's a gallery space upstairs and exhibits usually spill over into the ground floor eating and drinking area, where tables and sofas are scattered about in an informal and welcoming fashion.

For advice on getting to Banglamphu on public transport see p.137; for Hualamphong see p.143. For a more detailed breakdown of useful bus routes see p.44.

Banana Bar and Easy Bar
Map 3, D9. Trok Mayom/Damnoen Klang Neua.

Daily from about 6pm.

Half a dozen tiny cubbyhole bars open up on this alley every night, each with just a handful of alleyside chairs and tables, loud music on the tape player, and a trendy bartender.

Boh
Map 4, B8. Tha Thien, Maharat Rd.

Daily 7pm–midnight.

Not quite in Banglamphu, but within easy striking distance in Ratanakosin. When the Chao Phraya express boats stop running around 7pm, this bar takes over the pier with its great sunset views across the river. Beer and Thai whisky with accompanying spicy snacks and loud Thai pop music – very popular with Silpakorn and Thammasat university students.

Buddy Beer

Map 3, E8. Khao San Rd.

Daily from about 11am–2am.

Huge, airy, backpackers' pub with pool tables and streetside seating that makes this the perfect place for watching the action on Khao San Road – and for bumping into travellers you never thought you'd see again. And if you need to drown your sorrows in a different way, you can nip round the back for a dip in *Buddy Beer's* public swimming pool.

Damnoen

Map 3, E10. Tanao Rd.

Daily 6pm–2am.

One of several student-oriented bars along this road, this is a small cosy hideaway whose wooden tables, quirky decor and mellow music give it the feel of a place for intense discussions. There are plenty of beers and whiskies on the menu, plus some food too.

Gulliver's Traveller's Tavern

Map 3, C8. Corner of Khao San Rd and Chakrabongse Rd.

Daily 11am–6am.

Huge, popular, American-style bar/restaurant with several TV monitors, each showing a different sports channel. Table football, pool table, and reasonably priced beer.

Gypsy Pub

Map 3, C5. West end of Phra Sumen Rd.

Mon–Sat 6pm–2am.

Friendly, medium-sized bar attracts a youthful and predominantly Thai clientele with its nightly live music (of varying quality).

BARS: BANGLAMPHU AND HUALAMPHONG

Jai Yen

Map 3, A7. Next to Tha Phra Athit pier.

Daily 11am–10pm.

Its riverside location next to Banglamphu's main express boat pier makes *Jai Yen* a pleasant and breezy place for a drink – especially after the boats stop running at around 6pm. Inexpensive beer, and some food also available.

No Name Bar

Map 3, D7. Khao San Rd.

Daily from about 6pm.

Small, low-key drinking-spot at the heart of the backpackers' ghetto. The dim lighting, decent tape collection and competitively priced beer make this a popular place.

Spicy

Map 3, F10. Tanao Rd.

Nightly 6pm–2am.

Fashionably modern, neon-lit youthful hangout, mainly patronized by students from the nearby university. Best for beer, whisky and snacks, but serves main dishes too.

DOWNTOWN BANGKOK

The Barbican

Map 7, K5. Soi Thaniya, east end of Silom Rd.

Daily 11am–1am.

Stylishly modern fortress-like decor to match the name: dark woods, metal and undressed stone. With Guinness on tap and the financial pages posted above the urinals, you could almost be in a smart City of London pub – until you look out of the windows onto the soi's incongruous Japanese hostess bars.

For advice on getting to this area see pp.146 and 149. For a more detailed breakdown of useful bus routes see p.44.

BARS: DOWNTOWN BANGKOK

Blue's Bar

Map 6, I9. 231/16 Soi Sarasin.

Mon–Fri 6pm–1am, Sat & Sun 6pm–midnight.

Long-standing, friendly, blue-painted haunt, trendiest in a row
of similar bars between Rajdamri Road and Soi Lang Suan,
where young creative types drink to British indie sounds.

Brown Sugar

Map 6, I9. 231/19–20 Soi Sarasin ©250 0103.

Mon–Sat 11am–2am, Sun 5pm–1am.

Lively joint, acknowledged as the capital's top jazz venue, that
manages to be both chic and homely. Happy hour of sorts at
the well-stocked but pricey bar daily 3–9.30pm. House jazz
band Mon–Sat from 9.30pm, Sunday jam from 9.30pm.

Dallas Pub

Map 6, F5. Soi 6, Siam Square ©255 3276.

Daily 7pm–2am.

In complete contrast to the sophisticated *CM2* nightclub
opposite, a typical dark, noisy hangout in the "songs for life"
tradition – Thai folk music blended with Western progressive
and folk rock. Lots of fun: singalongs to decent live bands,
dancing round the tables, and friendly, casual staff.

Delaneys

Map 7, J6. 1/5 Convent Rd, off the east end of Silom Rd ©266 7160.

Daily 11am–1am.

Blarney Bangkok-style: a warm, relaxing Irish pub, tastefully
done out in wood, iron and familiar knick-knacks and packed
with expats on Friday nights. Guinness and Kilkenny bitter on
tap (happy hour 4–7pm), very expensive Irish food such as
Belfast chaps (fried potatoes) and good veggie options, as well
as a fast-moving rota of house bands.

BARS: DOWNTOWN BANGKOK

Hard Rock Café
Map 6, E5. Soi 11, Siam Square ℂ251 0792-4.

Daily 11am–2am.

Genuine outlet of the famous international chain – yes, you can buy the T-shirt. Big sounds including live bands nightly from around 10.30pm, brash enthusiasm, bank-breaking prices.

Hyper
Map 7, J6. Soi 4, Silom Rd.

Daily 9pm–2am.

Long-standing Soi 4 people-watching haunt, with laid-back dance music and a fun crowd.

Old West
Map 6, I9. 231/17 Soi Sarasin ℂ252 9510.

Daily 6pm–1am.

Slightly expensive but buzzing saloon, complete with swing doors, with nightly live music from local bands from about 10.30pm onwards (requests usually taken); popular with Thai and expat thirtysomethings.

Saxophone
Map 2, H3. 3/8 Victory Monument (southeast corner), Phrayathai Rd ℂ246 5472.

Daily 7.30pm–2am.

Lively bar hosts nightly blues, folk, jazz and rock bands (from around 9pm onwards), and attracts a good mix of Thais and farangs. Relaxed drinking atmosphere, reasonable prices and good Thai food.

Tapas Bar
Map 7, J6. Soi 4, Silom Rd.

Daily 6pm–2am.

Small, mellow, Spanish-oriented bar, whose outside tables, near the entrance to the soi, are probably the best spot for checking out the comings and goings on Silom 4; no tapas, but good beers and decent espresso.

....

Maison du Vin **on the second floor of the Thaniya Plaza, Silom Road, sell a better-than-passable Chateau de Loei red and white wine, made by an eccentric Frenchman from grapes grown on the slopes of Phu Reua in northeast Thailand.**

....

SUKHUMVIT ROAD

The Bull's Head
Map 8, H8. Soi 33/1 (behind *Villa*).
Mon–Fri 11.30am–2.30pm & 5.30pm–1am; Sat & Sun 11am–1am.
Easy-going British-style pub that's extremely popular with expat drinkers. If you're longing for a taste of home, you can indulge in baked potatoes and apple crumble with custard. Regular music and quiz events, plus a friendly crowd of regulars.

....

For advice on getting to this area see p.155, and for a more detailed breakdown of useful bus routes see p.44.

....

Cheap Charlies
Map 8, A8. Soi 11.
Daily from 3pm.
Hugely popular sidewalk bar with standing room only – but at a bargain B30 for a bottle of beer it's worth the discomfort.

Imageries by the Glass
Map 8, H10. Soi 24, Sukhumvit Rd.
Daily 6.30–11pm.
Air-conditioned bar that's usually packed out with Thai yuppies, but is nothing special. There's nightly music from the in-house jazz-fusion band, and the drinks are moderately priced.

BARS: SUKHUMVIT ROAD

Manet Club, Renoir Club, Van Gogh Club

Map 8, H6. Soi 33, Sukhumvit Rd.

Daily 4pm–midnight.

Three-in-a-row small, very similar, not-at-all-Parisian bars, of interest mainly for their air-conditioning and happy hours, which run daily from 4–9pm.

Old Dutch

Map 8, E6. Soi 23, Sukhumvit Rd, at the mouth of the Soi Cowboy strip.

Daily 11am–1am.

Cool, dark, peaceful oasis at the edge of Sukhumvit's frenetic sleaze. The reasonably priced menu and a large stock of current US and European newspapers make this a good daytime or early evening watering hole.

Paulaner Bräuhaus

Map 8, H10. President Park, end of Soi 24 ©661 1210.

Daily 5pm–1am.

German restaurant that's chiefly of interest for its in-house micro-brewery, located within view of the dining area. At weekends, you should reserve ahead if you want to eat as well as drink.

CLUBS AND DISCOS

CM²

Map 6, F5. *Novotel*, Soi 6, Siam Square.

Daily 7pm–2am; admission price depends on what's on.

More theme park than nightclub, with various, barely distinct entertainment zones, including *Club La Femme*, sporting suggestively padded walls, for women only. Drinks are pricey.

Details of Bangkok's gay nightlife are given on p.197.

Deeper
Map 7, J6. Soi 4, Silom Rd.

Free, except Fri & Sat B150 including one drink.

Long-running hardcore dance club, done out in metal and black to give an underground feel.

Peppermint
Map 7, J6. Patpong 1.

Daily 9pm–4am; free.

No-nonsense chart-sound dance club, popular with travellers and Thais. Drinks are moderately priced.

Rome Club
Map 7, J6. 90–96 Soi 4, Silom Rd.

Daily 7pm–3am; B100 including one drink (B200 including two drinks Fri & Sat).

Once the city's leading gay nightclub, recently one of its most fashionable mixed venues, but as we went to press, we heard that it was in financial trouble and open only at weekends. If it survives the financial crisis (consult *Bangkok Metro*), it's well worth checking out for its slick drag show, good sounds and sound system, and large dancefloor.

Spasso
Map 6, H5. *Grand Hyatt Erawan Hotel*, 494 Rajdamri Rd ©254 1234.

Mon–Sat 10pm–1am; free.

One of the best upmarket venues in town, surprisingly lively, with regular live music and special events. The beautiful decor stretches to a mosaic dancefloor and hand-painted alcoves. Great pizzas from a wood-fired oven and good, though very pricey cocktails.

Taurus
Map 2, L8. Soi 26, Sukhumvit Rd.

Daily 6.30pm–2am; B500 including two drinks.

CLUBS AND DISCOS

Swanky, well-designed place on various levels which accommodate a balconied disco with plenty of room to dance, a couple of eateries, and a pub with live bands. You'll need to dress up to get in. Opposite is its US-style microbrewery, *Taurus Brew House*.

Gay Bangkok

Bangkok's **gay scene** is mainly focused on mainstream venues like karaoke bars, restaurants, massage parlours, gyms, saunas and escort agencies. Most of the action happens on Silom 4 (near Patpong), on the more exclusive Silom 2 (towards Rama IV Road), and at the rougher, mostly Thai bars of Sutthisarn Road near the Chatuchak Weekend Market. The scene is heavily male, and there are hardly any lesbian-only venues, though quite a few gay bars are mixed. As with the straight scene, the majority of gay bars feature go-go dancers and live sex shows. Those listed here do not.

Buddhist tolerance and a national abhorrence for confrontation and victimization combine to make Thai society relatively unfussed about homosexuality, if not exactly positive about same-sex relationships. There is no mention of homosexuality at all in Thai **law**, which means that the age of consent for gay sex is sixteen, the same as for heterosexuals. Although excessively physical displays of affection are frowned upon for both heterosexuals and homosexuals, Western gay couples should get no hassle about being seen together in public – it's much more acceptable, and common, in fact, for friends of the same sex (gay or not) to walk hand-in-hand, than for heterosexual couples to do so.

Further information

Anjaree PO Box 322, Rajdamnoen PO, Bangkok 10200, ✆ & fax 477 1776; email *anjaree@hotmail.com* Lesbian group that fights for homosexual rights and can povide some info on lesbian life in the city.

Dreaded Ned's Website *www.dreadedned.com* Lots of interesting background on gay life in Thailand, plus listings of almost every gay venue in the country.

Metro *bkkmetro.com* Bangkok's monthly English-language listings magazine publishes up-to-date reviews of gay bars and clubs in the city. Available from bookshops and 7–11 stores.

Pink Ink *www.khsnet.com/pinkink* Thailand's first English-language gay and lesbian newsletter is available from certain gay venues and, in truncated form, online. It carries listings, gossip columns and plenty of other interesting stuff.

Utopia *www.utopia-asia.com* Bangkok's gay and lesbian centre (see p.198) maintains a useful Web site with lots of good links.

If you're in Bangkok for the first time, you might be interested in the **gay friends** service offered by the Utopia gay and lesbian centre (see p.198). These gay, English-speaking Bangkok residents are called Thai Friends and are keen to show tourists the sights of Bangkok. It's a strictly non-sexual arrangement and can be organized through the Utopia centre or via their Web site. Utopia can also arrange tourist accommodation in a gay hotel on Sukhumvit Road; contact the centre for details.

GAY BARS AND CLUBS

At the Time
Map 2, I1. 81, Soi 7, Paholyothin Rd (Soi Aree), opposite the Yosawadee Building.
Daily 6pm-2am.
Newish lesbian/mixed restaurant and bar.

Disco Disco
Map 7, K6. Soi 2, Silom Rd.
Daily 9pm–2am.
Small, well-designed bar/disco, with reasonably priced drinks and good dance music for a fun crowd of young Thais.

DJ Station
Map 7, K6. Soi 2, Silom Rd.
Daily 10pm–2am; B100 including one drink (B200 including two drinks Fri & Sat).
Highly fashionable but unpretentious disco, which gets packed at weekends, attracting a mix of Thais and foreigners. A cabaret show is staged every day at midnight.

JJ Park
Map 7, K6. 8/3 Soi 2, Silom Rd.
Classy, Thai-oriented bar/restaurant, for relaxed socializing rather than raving, with live Thai music and karaoke.

Khrua Silom
Map 7, K6. 60/10–11 Silom Rd (in soi beside 7–11).
This fun, unpretentious club-style café has a karaoke machine and always seems to be packed out with with gay Thai students.

Kitchenette
First floor, Duchess Plaza, 289, Soi 55, Sukhumvit Rd (Soi Tonglaw).

Daily 4pm–1am.
Friendly, mixed café/bar that's a bit of a hike from the main action on Sukhumvit. Attracts an older, lesbian crowd. Live music on Friday and Saturday nights.

Sphinx
Map 7, J6. 98–104 Soi 4, Silom Rd.
Mon–Thur & Sun 7pm–12.30am, Fri & Sat until 1am.
Chic decor, terrace seating and good food attract a fashionable crowd to this ground-floor bar and restaurant.

Telephone Bar
Map 7, J6. 114/11–13 Soi 4, Silom Rd.
Daily 8pm–2am.
This smart, long-standing eating and drinking venue has good Thai cuisine and a terrace on the alley. It's best known, however, for its telephones: each table inside has a phone with a clearly displayed number so you can call up other customers.

GAY MEETING PLACES

Babylon
Map 2, I9. 50 Soi Attakarn Prasit, Sathorn Thai Rd, next to the Austrian Embassy ©213 2108.
Weekdays 5–11pm (B170), weekends 3pm–midnight (B200).
The least sleazy, most luxurious sauna complex in the city, with a bar, restaurant, roof garden and well-endowed gym.

Utopia
Map 8, F5. 116/1 Soi 23 (Soi Sawadee), Sukhumvit Rd ©259 9619;
www.utopia-asia.com
Daily noon–midnight.
Bangkok's first gay and lesbian community centre is a good

place to find out what's happening on the gay scene and to meet other men and women. It has a café, noticeboards, gallery and shop.

Entertainment

Traditional **Thai dancing** is the most accessible of the capital's performing arts, and can be seen at the National Theatre and a number of tourist-oriented restaurants. **Thai boxing** can be equally theatrical and is well worth watching: the live experience at either of Bangkok's two main national stadiums far outshines the TV coverage.

CINEMAS

Central Bangkok has over forty **cinemas**, many of which show recent American and European releases with their original dialogue and Thai subtitles. Most cinemas screen shows four times a day: programmes are detailed every day in the *Nation* and *Bangkok Post*, and listings and reviews appear in the monthly listings magazine, *Bangkok Metro*; cinema locations are printed on *Nancy Chandler's Map of Bangkok*. Seats cost from B50 to B100, depending on the plushness of the cinema; at all cinemas, you'll be expected to stand for the king's anthem, which is played before every performance.

CULTURE SHOWS

Many tourist restaurants feature nightly culture shows – usually a hotchpotch of Thai dancing and classical music, with a martial arts demonstration thrown in. In some cases there's a set fee for dinner and show, in others the performance is free but the à la carte prices are slightly inflated.

Baan Thai

Soi 32, Sukhumvit Rd.

Nightly at 9pm.

Housed in a traditional teak home, this is a pleasant setting for the nightly performances of traditional Thai dance. Audiences are served a set meal during the show.

Silom Village

Map 7, E6. Silom Rd.

Nightly at 8pm.

The outdoor restaurant inside this complex of tourist shops stages a free cultural show every evening to go with its à la carte menu.

Vieng Thai Hotel

Map 3, D6. Ram Bhuttri Rd, Banglamphu, ©280 5392.

Every Sat; call to check times and reserve a place.

Banglamphu's smartest hotel puts on a cultural show every week, for which it charges B300, including a full Thai dinner.

SHRINE DANCING

Thai dancing is performed for its original **ritual purpose**, usually several times a day, at the Lak Muang Shrine behind the Grand Palace and the Erawan Shrine on the corner of Ploenchit Road (Map 6, H4). Both shrines have resident troupes of dancers who are hired by worshippers to perform *lakhon chatri*, a sort of *khon* dance-drama, to thank benevolent spirits for answered prayers. The dancers are always dressed up in full gear and accompanied by musicians, but the length, number of dancers and complexity of

Traditional dance-drama

Drama pretty much equals **dance** in Thai theatre, and many of the traditional dance-dramas are based on the Hindu epic the *Ramayana* (in Thai, *Ramakien*), a classic adventure tale of good versus evil which is taught in all the schools (see p.62 for an outline of the story).

The most spectacular form of traditional Thai theatre is khon, a stylized drama performed in masks and elaborate costumes by a troupe of highly trained classical dancers. There's little room for individual interpretation in these dances, as all the movements follow a strict choreography that's been passed down through generations: each graceful, angular gesture depicts a precise event, action or emotion which will be familiar to educated *khon* audiences. The dancers don't speak, and the story is chanted and sung by a chorus who stand at the side of the stage, accompanied by a classical *phipat* orchestra.

A typical *khon* performance features several of the best-known **Ramayana** episodes, in which the main characters are recognized by their masks, headdresses and heavily brocaded costumes. Gods and humans don't wear masks, but it's generally easy enough to distinguish the hero Rama and heroine Sita from the action; they always wear tall gilded headdresses and often appear in a threesome with Rama's brother Lakshaman. Monkey masks are always open-mouthed, almost laughing, and come in several colours: the monkey army chief Hanuman always wears white, and his two right-hand men – Nilanol, the god of fire and Nilapat, the god of death – wear red and black respectively. In contrast, the demons have grim mouths, clamped shut or snarling out of usually green faces: Totsagan, king of the demons, wears a green face in battle and a gold one during peace, but always sports a two-tier headdress carved with two rows of faces.

the dance depends on the amount of money paid by the supplicant: a price list is posted near the dance area. The musicians at the Erawan Shrine are particularly highly rated, though the almost comic apathy of the dancers there doesn't do them justice.

Padung Cheep in Banglamphu specializes in selling papier mâché reproductions of the masks used in classical Thai dance-dramas. See p.215.

THAI BOXING

The violence of the average **Thai boxing** match may be off-putting to some, but spending a couple of hours at one of Bangkok's two main stadiums can be immensely entertaining, not least for the enthusiasm of the spectators and the ritualistic aspects of the fights.

Bouts, advertised in the English-language newspapers, are held in the capital every night of the week at the **Rajdamnoen Stadium**, next to the TAT office on Rajdamnoen Nok Avenue (Mon & Wed 7pm; Thurs 5pm & 9pm; Sun 2pm & 6pm), and at **Lumphini Stadium** on Rama IV Road (Tues & Fri 6pm; Sat 5pm). Tickets go on sale one hour before and, unless the boxers are big stars, start at B200, rising to B800 for a ringside seat. You might have to queue for a few minutes, but there's no need to get there early unless there's a really important fight on. Sessions usually feature ten bouts, each consisting of five three-minute rounds (with two-minute rests in between each round), so if you're not a big fan it may be worth turning up an hour late, as the better fights tend to happen later in the billing. It's more fun if you buy one of the less expensive standing tickets, enabling you to witness the wild gesticulations of the betting aficionados at close range.

Rituals of the ring

Thai boxing (*muay Thai*) enjoys a following similar to football in Europe: every province has a stadium and whenever a fight is shown on TV you can be sure that large noisy crowds will gather round the sets in streetside restaurants and noodle shops.

There's a strong spiritual and **ritualistic** dimension to *muay Thai*, adding grace to an otherwise brutal sport. Each boxer enters the ring to the wailing music of a three-piece *phipat* orchestra, often flamboyantly attired in a lurid silk robe over the statutory red or blue boxer shorts. The fighter then bows, first in the direction of his birthplace and then to the north, south, east and west, honouring both his teachers and the spirit of the ring. Next he performs a slow dance, claiming the audience's attention and demonstrating his prowess as a performer.

Any part of the body except the head may be used as an **offensive weapon** in *muay Thai*, and all parts except the groin are fair targets. Kicks to the head are the blows which cause most knockouts. As the action hots up, so the orchestra speeds up its tempo and the betting in the audience becomes more frenetic. It can be a gruesome business, but it was far bloodier before modern boxing gloves were made compulsory in the 1930s – combatants used to wrap their fists with hemp impregnated with a face-lacerating dosage of ground glass.

THEATRE

National Theatre
Map 4, E2. ✆224 1342.
Phone lines open Mon–Fri 8.30am–4.30pm.

The usual programme at Bangkok's main venue for traditional dance and theatre comprises khon (classical) and likay (folk) theatre, and the occasional nang thalung (shadow-puppet play). Tickets for these start at around B100. As these can be quite long and esoteric performances, tourists often prefer the special medley shows, performed by students from the attached College of the Performing Arts, where the evening is broken up into bite-sized portions of dance, drama and music, often brought in from different parts of the country. Medley shows usually take place on the last Friday and Saturday of every month (more regularly Nov–May); tickets start at B40. Programme details can be checked by calling the theatre or TAT.

Consult the monthly listings magazine *Bangkok Metro* for details of current theatre and cinema programmes.

Chalermkrung Royal Theatre

Map 5, B1. 66 Charoen Krung (New Rd), on the intersection with Triphet Rd in Pahurat next to *Old Siam Plaza* ©222 1854.
This recently renovated historical theatre shows contemporary Thai drama and comedy most of the week, but occasionally stages traditional, tourist-friendly dance-dramas. Call the theatre for details of the current programme.

Thailand Cultural Centre

In the far northern part of the city on Ratchadapisek Rd ©231 4257.
The city's major venue for showcasing contemporary Thai drama and comedy is inconveniently located on the fringes of Bangkok. As well as innovative drama, it also puts on regular kids' theatre shows.

THEATRE

Shopping

Bangkok has a good reputation for **shopping**, particularly for silk, gems, fashions and English-language books. Antiques and handicrafts are good buys too, and some shops stock curiosities from the most remote regions of the country.

Downtown Bangkok is full of smart, multi-storied **shopping plazas** with names like Siam Centre, the Emporium and the Amarin Plaza, which is where you'll find the majority of the city's fashion stores, as well as those selling designer goods, and bookshops. The plazas tend to be pleasantly air-conditioned and thronging with trendy young Thais, but they don't hold much interest for tourists unless you happen to be looking for a new outfit.

You're more likely to find useful items in one of the city's numerous **department stores**, most of which are also scattered about the downtown areas. The Central department stores (on Silom and Ploenchit roads) are probably the city's best, but Robinson's, on Sukhumvit Soi 19, Rajdamri Road and at the Silom/Rama IV junction) are also good.

Most of the department stores and tourist-oriented shops listed here keep late hours, opening at 10 or 11am every day including Sunday, and closing at about 9pm.

For travellers, spectating, not shopping, is apt to be the main draw of Bangkok's neighbourhood **markets** – notably the bazaars of Chinatown (see p.143) and the spectacular early morning Pak Khlong Talat flower market just west of Memorial Bridge. The massive Chatuchak Weekend Market is an exception, being both a tourist attraction and a marvellous shopping experience – see p.124 for details. If you're planning on some serious market exploration, get hold of the idiosyncratic *Nancy Chandler's Map of Bangkok*, which includes special sections on the main shopping areas. Except for Chatuchak, most markets operate daily from dawn till early afternoon; early morning is often the best time to go to beat the heat and crowds.

ANTIQUES

Bangkok is the entrepôt for the finest Thai, Burmese and Cambodian **antiques**, but the market has long been sewn up, so don't expect to happen upon any undiscovered treasure. Even experts admit that they sometimes find it hard to tell real antiques from fakes, so the best policy is just to buy on the grounds of attractiveness. The *River City* shopping complex devotes its third and fourth floors to a bewildering array of pricey treasures and holds an auction on the first Saturday of every month (viewing during the preceding week). The other main area for antiques is the stretch of Charoen Krung (New Road) that runs between the GPO and the bottom of Silom Road. Here you'll find a good selection of reputable individual businesses specializing in wood carvings, bronze statues and stone sculptures culled from all parts of Thailand and neighbouring countries as well. Most antiques require an export permit.

BOOKS

English-language **bookstores** in Bangkok are always well stocked with everything to do with Thailand, and most carry fiction classics and popular paperbacks as well. The capital's few **secondhand** bookstores are surprisingly poor value, but you might turn up something worthwhile – or earn a few baht by selling your own cast-offs – in the shops and stalls along Khao San Road.

Asia Books

Maps 6, 7 and 8. Branches on Sukhumvit Rd between sois 15 and 19, in Landmark Plaza between sois 4 and 6, and in Emporium between Sois 22 and 24; in Peninsula Plaza on Rajdamri Rd; in Siam Centre on Rama I Rd; and in Thaniya Plaza near Patpong off Silom Rd.

English-language bookstore that's especially recommended for its books on Asia – everything from guidebooks to cookery books, novels to art (the Sukhumvit 15–17 branch has the best Asian selection). Also keeps bestselling novels, and coffee-table books.

Books Kinokuniya

Map 8, G8. Third floor of the *Emporium* shopping centre, between sois 22 and 24 on Sukhumvit Rd.

Huge English-language bookstore, with a broad range of books ranging from bestsellers to travel literature and from classics to sci-fi; not so hot on books about Asia though.

Central department stores

Map 6, J4 and 7, E6. On Silom and Ploenchit roads, and at several other less convenient locations.

Reasonably good books department, which stocks paperback fiction, maps and reference books in English.

DK (Duang Kamol) Books

Maps 6 and 8. Branches on the third floor of the *MBK* shopping centre, corner of Rama I and Phrayathai roads; at 244–6 Soi 2, Siam Square; and at 180/1 Sukhumvit Rd between sois 8 & 10.

One of Thailand's biggest bookseller chains, *DK* is especially good for maps and books on Thailand.

DK International Book Forum

Miles from the city centre in the Seacon Square shopping complex, 904 Moo 6, Srinakarin Rd.

Billed as Southeast Asia's largest bookshop, this megastore stocks half a million titles in English and hosts exhibitions, meet-the-author sessions and other literary events.

Shaman Books

Map 3, E8 and D8. Two branches on Khao San Rd, Banglamphu. The best stocked and most efficient second-hand bookshop in the city, where all books are displayed alphabetically as well as being logged on to the computer – which means you can locate your choice in seconds. Lots of books on Asia (travel, fiction, politics and history) as well as a decent range of novels and general interest books. Don't expect bargains though.

Ton's Booksellers

Map 3, F7. 327/5 Ram Bhuttri Rd, Banglamphu. Small but thoughtfully selected range of English-language books, and currently the only outlet for new books in Banglamphu. Particularly strong on Thai novels in translation, Buddhist philosophy, Thai cookery and Thai language.

CLOTHES AND THAI SILK

Noted for its thickness and sheen, **Thai silk** became internationally recognized only about forty years ago after the efforts of American Jim Thompson (see p.113). Much of it comes from the northeast, but you'll find the lion's share of outlets and tailoring facilities in the capital. Prices start at about B350 per yard for two-ply silk (suitable for thin shirts and skirts), B500 for four-ply (for suits).

Bangkok can be a great place to have **tailored clothes** made: materials don't cost much, and work is often completed in just 24 hours. On the other hand, you may find yourself palmed off with artificial silk and a suit that falls apart in a week. Inexpensive silk and tailoring shops crowd Silom, Sukhumvit and Khao San roads, but many people opt for hotel tailors, preferring to pay more for the security of an established business. Be wary of places offering ridiculous deals – when you see a dozen garments advertised for a total price of less than $200, you know something's fishy – and look carefully at the quality of samples before making any decision. If you're staying in Banglamphu, keep an eye on guesthouse noticeboards for cautionary tales from other travellers.

Khao San Road is lined with stalls selling low-priced **ready-mades**: the tie-dyed shirts, baggy cotton trousers, fake Levi's and ethnic-style outfits are all aimed at backpackers and New Age hippies; the stalls around *New World* department store have the best range of inexpensive Thai fashions in this area. For the best and latest fashions however, you should check out the shops in the *Siam Centre* and the *Siam Discovery Centre* across from Siam Square. **Shoes** and **leather goods** are good buys in Bangkok, being generally hand-made from high-quality leather and quite a bargain: check out the "booteries" along Sukhumvit Road.

Ambassador Fashions

Map 8, A9. Sukhumvit Soi 11.

Long-established and reputable tailor, well versed in making both men's and women's wear. Clothes can be made within 24 hours if necessary.

Emporium

Map 8, G8. Between sois 22 and 24 on Sukhumvit Rd.

Enormous and rather glamorous shopping plaza, with a good range of fashion outlets, from exclusive designer wear to trendy high-street gear. Brand names include DKNY and Max Mara.

Jim Thompson's Thai Silk Company

Map 7, K5. 9 Suriwong Rd.

A good place to start looking for traditional Thai fabric, or at least to get an idea of what's out there. Stocks silk and cotton by the yard and ready-made items from dresses to cushion covers, which are well designed and of good quality, but pricey. Also has a home furnishings section and a good tailoring service.

Khanitha

Map 7, J5 and B5. Branches at 111/3–5 Suriwong Rd and the *Oriental* hotel.

Specialize in women's suits, eveningwear, and dressing gowns, tailored from the finest Thai silk.

Mah Boon Krong (MBK)

Map 6, C5. At the Rama I/Phrayathai intersection.

Labyrinthine shopping centre which houses hundreds of small, mostly fairly inexpensive outlets, including plenty of high-street fashion shops.

Peninsula Plaza

Map 6, H5. Rajdamri Rd.

Considered to be the most upmarket shopping plaza in the city, so come here for (genuine) Louis Vuitton and the like.

Siam Centre

Map 6, E4. Across the road from Siam Square.

Particularly good for big name designer fashions as well as lesser-known labels; Kookai and Soda Pop are typical outlets.

SHOPPING: CLOTHES AND THAI SILK

211

Counterfeit culture

Faking it is big business in Bangkok, a city whose copyright regulations carry about as much weight as its anti-prostitution laws. Forged **designer clothes** and accessories are the biggest sellers; street vendors along Silom, Sukhumvit and Khao San roads will flog you a whole range of inexpensive lookalikes, including Louis Vuitton bags, Armani jeans, Levi 501s, Rayban sunglasses, and Lacoste shirts – even YSL underpants.

Along Patpong, after dark, plausible would-be **Rolex** and **Cartier** watches from Hong Kong and Taiwan go for about B500 – and are fairly reliable considering the price. If your budget won't stretch to a phony Rolex Oyster, there's plenty of opportunities for smaller expenditure at the stalls concentrated on Khao San Road, where pirated **music cassettes** are sold at a fraction of the normal price. Quality is usually fairly high but the choice is often less than brilliant, with a concentration on mainstream pop and rock albums. Finally, several stallholders along Khao San Road even make up passable international **student** and **press cards** – though travel agencies and other organizations in Bangkok aren't so easily fooled.

Siam Discovery Centre

Map 6, E4. Across the road from Siam Square.

Flash designer gear, including plenty of name brands like Dolce and Gabanna, Morgan, Max Mara and YSL.

GEMS AND JEWELLERY

Bangkok boasts the country's best **gem and jewellery** shops, and some of the finest lapidaries in the world, making this *the* place to buy cut and uncut stones such as rubies, blue sapphires and diamonds. The most exclusive gem outlets are scattered along Silom Road – try Mr Ho's at number 987 – but many tourists prefer to buy from hotel shops, like Kim's inside the *Oriental*, where reliability is assured. Other recommended outlets include Johnny's Gems at 199 Fuang Nakhon Road, near Wat Rajabophit in Ratanakosin, Merlin et Delauney at 1 Soi Pradit, off Suriwong Road, and Uthai Gems, at 28/7 Soi Ruam Rudee, off Ploenchit Road. For cheap and cheerful silver earrings, bracelets and necklaces, you can't beat the traveller-oriented jewellery shops along Khao San Road in Banglamphu.

While it's unusual for established jewellers to fob off tourists with glass and paste, a common **sales** technique is to charge a lot more than what the gem is worth based on its carat weight. Get the stone tested on the spot, and ask for a written guarantee and receipt. Be extremely wary of touts and the shops they recommend. Unless you're an experienced gem trader, don't even consider buying gems in bulk to sell at a supposedly vast profit elsewhere: many a gullible traveller has invested thousands of baht on a handful of worthless multi-coloured stones. If you want independent professional advice or precious stones certification, contact the *Asian Institute of Gemological Sciences*, located inside the Jewelry Trade Center Building, 919/298 Silom Road (©267 4315-9).

HANDICRAFTS AND TEXTILES

Many of the shopping plazas have at least one classy handicraft outlet, and competition keeps most prices in the city at upcountry levels. Handicraft sellers in Banglamphu tend to tout a limited range compared to the shops downtown, but several places on Khao San Road sell reasonably priced triangular pillows (*mawn khwaan*) in traditional fabrics, which make fantastic souvenirs but are heavy to post home. This is also a good place to pick up Thai shoulder bags woven to all specifications and designs, with travellers' needs in mind. The cheapest place to buy traditional textiles – including sarongs, triangular pillows and farmers' shirts – is **Chatuchak Weekend Market** (see p.124), and you might be able to nose out some interesting handicrafts here too.

Come Thai

Map 6, H4. Second floor of the Amarin Plaza (the Sogo building) on Ploenchit Rd; currently has no English sign, but easily spotted by its carved wooden doorframe.

Impressive range of unusual handwoven silk and cotton fabrics, much of it made up into traditional-style clothes such as Chinese mandarin shirts and short fitted jackets.

Kealang

Map 6, H4. 2nd floor of the Amarin Plaza (the Sogo building) on Ploenchit Rd.

Stocks a huge variety of traditional style five-coloured *bencharong* pots and vases, as well as other multicoloured Thai-Chinese ceramics.

Khomapastr

Map 7, C3. 1st floor of River City shopping complex, which has its own express-boat pier near Charoen Krung (New Rd).

Unusual choice of attractive patterned fabrics, in lengths or made up into quirky cushion covers.

Krishna's

Map 8, A10. Between sois 9 and 11, Sukhumvit Rd.

The four-storey building is crammed full of artefacts from all over Asia and, though mass-produced metallic statuettes and Balinese masks seem to dominate, there are enough interesting curios (such as Nepalese jewellery and Japanese netsuke) to reward a thorough browse.

The Legend

Map 6, H4. Second floor of Amarin Plaza (the Sogo building) on Ploenchit Rd, and third floor of Thaniya Plaza on Silom Rd.

Stocks a small selection of well-made Thai handicrafts, from wood and wickerware to fabrics and ceramics, at reasonable prices.

Narayana Phand

Map 6, H4. 127 Rajdamri Rd.

This government souvenir centre was set up to ensure the preservation of traditional crafts and to maintain standards of quality, and makes a good one-stop-shop for last-minute presents. Huge assortment of very reasonably priced goods from all over the country, including *khon* masks and shadow puppets, musical instruments and kites, niello ware and celadon, and hill-tribe crafts.

Padung Cheep

Map 3, B8. Chakrabongse Rd, Banglamphu.

Specialist outlet for traditional theatrical masks made of papier mâché, including those worn by characters in *khon* dramas, plus comic masks and some miniature souvenir versions. Also stocks some costume dolls.

Prayer Textile Gallery

Map 6, D4. 197 Phrayathai Rd, on the corner of Rama I Rd.

Traditional fabrics from the north and the northeast, as well as from Laos and Cambodia. The selection is good, but prices for these textiles are getting surprisingly high, particularly those now classified as antiques.

Rasi Sayam

Map 8, F4. A 10-min hike down Sukhumvit Soi 23, opposite *Le Dalat Vietnamese* restaurant.

Mon–Sat 9am–5.30pm.

Very classy handicraft shop, specializing in eclectic and fairly

SHOPPING: HANDICRAFTS AND TEXTILES |

215

pricey decorative and folk arts such as tiny betel-nut sets woven from *lipao* fern, sticky rice lunch baskets, coconut wood bowls, and *mut mee* textiles.

Silom Village

Map 7, E6. 286/1 Silom Rd, just west of Soi Decho.
A complex of wooden houses that attempts to create a relaxing, upcountry atmosphere as a backdrop for its pricey fabrics and occasionally unusual souvenirs, such as grainy *sa* paper made from mulberry bark.

Taekee Taekon

Map 3, B5. Across from the whitewashed fort on Phra Athit in Banglamphu – no English sign, but easy to spot.
Small shop with a spectacular array of traditional silk and cotton textiles, sarongs and scarves. Also stocks some interesting coconut wood buttons, plus a few items of silver jewellery.

Thai Celadon

Map 8, E7. Sukhumvit Soi 16 (aka Ratchadapisek Rd).
Classic celadon stoneware made without commercial dyes or clays and glazed with the archetypal blues and greens that were invented by the Chinese to emulate the colour of precious jade. Mainly dinner sets, vases and lamps, plus some figurines.

SHOPPING: HANDICRAFTS AND TEXTILES

Kids' Bangkok

T hais are very tolerant of children so you can take them almost anywhere without restriction, and they always help break the ice with strangers. Aside from the usual **precautions**, watch out for crazy traffic, rabid dogs, cats and monkeys (see p.21), and fiery hot chillis (see p.165).

Some hotels offer **discounts** for children's accommodation (see p.136 for details), and most of the theme parks and amusement centres listed below knock off at least a few baht, though Bangkok buses and boats do not. The main drawback with Bangkok's kid-centred activities is that most of them are located a long way from the city centre.

THEME PARKS AND AMUSEMENT CENTRES

Adventureland

Seacon Square, 904 Sri Nakarin Rd. Bus #133 from Sukhumvit Soi 77. Mon–Fri 11am–9pm, Sat & Sun 10am–10pm; free entry, but you pay for rides and activities (B40–80) with coupons.

Fun activities and amusement rides for kids, including exciting go-kart circuits and a rollerblade rink – all equipment, including helmets and knee pads are available for hire. There's also a "stimulator" cinema, a rollercoaster, and a "swinging ship".

Dream World

Nakhon Nayok Rd, ten minutes' drive north of Don Muang Airport. Bus #39 or #59 to Rangsit, then songthaew or tuk-tuk.

Mon–Fri 10am–5pm, Sat & Sun 10am–7pm; B90, kids B70.

Enjoyable outdoor theme park that has different zones – such as Fantasy Land, Dream Garden and Adventure Land – each of them with special rides. Most kids like the water rides best.

Magic Land

72 Phaholyothin Rd, about 2km north of Chatuchak Weekend Market, near Central Plaza. Bus AC#2, AC#3, AC#9 or AC#13.

Mon–Fri 10am–5.30pm, Sat & Sun 10am–7pm; B60, kids B50.

Disneyland-style theme and amusement park, which feature a good number of fairground rides plus some water parks.

MBK Magic Land

Map 6, D5. 8th Floor, Mah Boon Krong Shopping Centre, at the Rama I/Phrayathai intersection. Bus AC#2, AC#8, AC#15, #15, #25, #29 or #40.

Mon–Fri 10.30am–6.30pm, Sat & Sun 10.30am–8pm; free.

Centrally located amusements centre in one of downtown Bangkok's oldest shopping centres. Contains fairly tame indoor fairground rides, costing from B15 a go.

....

Kids also usually enjoy Muang Boran Ancient City (see p.127), riding the pedalo boats in Lumphini Park (see p.117), and taking longtail boat trips on the Thonburi canals (see p.97). The annual spring kite festival is also fun (see p.25).

....

Siam Water Park

101 Sukhapiban 2 Rd, on the far eastern edge of town. Bus #27 from Victory Monument.

Mon–Fri 10am–6pm, Sat & Sun 9am–7pm; B200, kids B100.

Popular water park that boasts some of the longest waterslides in the country, along with all manner of whirlpools, swimming pools, and pools that get churned up by artificial surf. There's also a mini-zoo and a botanical garden.

ZOOS AND SAFARI PARKS

Dusit Zoo
Map 2, E2. Rajdamnoen Nok Avenue, Dusit. Bus AC#10 or #56.
Daily 8am–6pm; B20.

This public park – once part of the Chitrlada Palace gardens – now houses a fairly ordinary municipal zoo. Perhaps the most spectacular inhabitant of its dreary cages is an enormous lizard known as the Komodo dragon. The world's largest reptile, it's only found in the wild in a remote corner of Indonesia, where it can grow to a length of 3m; the Dusit dragon is relatively small by comparison. Also on show are cage-loads of white-handed gibbons.

Safari World
99 Ramindra Rd, Minburi. Bus #26 from Victory Monument to Minburi, then a direct minibus to *Safari World*.
Daily 9am–4.30pm; B400, kids B300.

Said to be Southeast Asia's largest wildlife park, Safari World centres on a drive-through safari park, which is home to an assortment of lions, rhinos, giraffes, zebras and monkeys. (If you don't have your own car, you can drive through the park in a Safari World coach.) There's also a sea-life area with dolphins and sea lions, and a bird park with a walk-in aviary.

Directory

AIRLINES Aeroflot, Regent House, 183 Rajdamri Rd ✆251 0617-18;
Air France, Charn Issara Tower, 942/51 Rama IV Rd ✆233 9477;
Air India, c/o SS Travel Service, 10/12 Convent Rd ✆235 0557;
Air Lanka, Charn Issara Tower, 942/34–35 Rama IV Rd ✆236
4981; Biman Bangladesh Airlines, Chongkolnee Building, 56
Suriwong Rd ✆235 7643-4; British Airways, 14 Fl, Abdullrahim
Place, opposte Lumphini Park, 990 Rama IV Rd ✆636 1747;
Canadian Airlines, Maneeya Centre, 518/5 Ploenchit Rd ✆251
4521; Cathay Pacific, Ploenchit Tower, 898 Ploenchit Rd ✆263
0606; China Airlines, Peninsula Plaza, 153 Rajdamri Rd ✆253
4242–3; Egyptair, CP Tower, 313 Silom Rd ✆231 0505-8; Finnair,
12 Fl, Sathorn City Tower, 175 Sathorn Thai Rd ✆635 1234;
Garuda, Lumphini Tower, 1168/77 Rama IV Rd ✆285 6470-3;
Gulf Air, Maneeya Building, 518/5 Ploenchit Rd ✆254 7931-4;
Japan Airlines, 254/1 Rajadapisek Rd ✆274 692 5151; KLM, 19
Fl, Thai Wah Tower 2, 21/133 Sathorn Thai Rd ✆679 1100 extn
11; Korean Air, Kongboonma Building, 699 Silom Rd ✆635 0465;
Lao Aviation, Silom Plaza, Silom Rd ✆236 9822-3; Lauda Air, Wall
Street Tower, 33/37 Suriwong Rd ✆267 0873-9; Lufthansa, Q-
House, Soi 21 Sukhumvit Rd ✆264 2400; Malaysia Airlines,
Ploenchit Tower, 898 Ploenchit Rd ✆263 0565-71; Myanmar
Airlines, 23 Fl, Jewelry Trade Center Bldg, Unit H1, 919/298 Silom
Rd ✆630 0338; Northwest, 4 Fl, Peninsula Plaza, 153 Rajdamri
Rd ✆254 0789; Olympic Airways, 4 Fl, Charn Issara Tower,

942/133 Rama IV Rd ✆237 6141; Pakistan International (PIA), 52 Suriwong Rd ✆234 2961-5; Philippine Airlines, Chongkolnee Building, 56 Suriwong Rd ✆233 2350-2; Qantas, 14 Fl, Abdullrahim Place, opposte Lumphini Park, 990 Rama IV Rd ✆636 1747; Royal Air Cambodge, 17 Fl, Two Pacific Place Bldg, Room 1706, 142 Sukhumvit Rd ✆653 2261-6; Royal Nepal, 9 Fl, Phyathai Plaza Bldg, 128 Phyathai Rd ✆216 5691-5; Singapore Airlines, Silom Centre, 2 Silom Rd ✆236 0440; Swissair, 21 Fl, Abdullrahim Place, opposite Lumphini Park, 990 Rama IV Rd ✆636 2160; Thai International, 6 Lan Luang Rd ✆280 0060; United Airlines, Regent House, 183 Rajdamri Rd ✆253 0558; Vietnam Airlines, 7 Fl, Ploenchit Center Bldg, Sukhumvit Soi 2 ✆656 9056–8.

AIRPORT ENQUIRIES International departures ✆535 1254 or 535 1386; international arrivals ✆535 1310 or 535 1301; domestic departures ✆535 1192; domestic arrivals ✆535 1253.

AMERICAN EXPRESS c/o Sea Tours, 128/88–92, 8 Fl, Phyathai Plaza, 128 Phyathai Rd, Bangkok 10400 ✆216 5759, fax 216 5757. Amex poste restante is held for 60 days and can be collected Mon–Fri 8.30am–5.30pm, Sat 8.30am–noon. For lost cards or cheques call ✆273 0044 (cards, office hours) ✆273 5296 (travellers' cheques, office hours), or ✆273 0022 (after hours).

CAR RENTAL Theoretically, foreigners need an international driver's licence, but some companies accept national licences. Prices for a small car range from B1000 to B1500 per day; petrol costs about B12–15 a litre. Avis, Head Office, 2/12 Witthayu (Wireless) Rd ✆255 5300, and at the *Dusit Thani Hotel*, Rama IV Rd ✆236 0450, the *Grand Hyatt Erawan Hotel*, 494 Rajdamri Rd ✆254 1234, and the *Sukhothai Bangkok Hotel*, 13/3 Sathorn Thai Rd ✆287 0222. Also at the *Amari Airport Hotel*, Don Muang International Terminal ✆566 1020. Hertz, Head Office, 420 Soi 71, Sukhumvit Rd ✆382 0293, and at Don Muang Domestic Terminal ✆535 3004.

CONTRACEPTIVES Condoms (known as *meechai*) are sold in all pharmacies, but other contraceptives should be brought from home.

COOKERY CLASSES The *Nipa Thai* restaurant ℂ254 0404 ext. 4823, runs one- to five-day cookery courses on demand, and regular fruit-carving lessons (Mon–Sat 2–4pm) at the restaurant on the 3rd Floor of the Landmark Plaza, between sois 6 and 8 on Sukhumvit Rd. *Mrs Balbir's* restaurant on Soi 11 Sukhumvit Rd ℂ651 0498, holds regular classes in Thai cookery (Fri 10.30–11.30) and Indian cookery (Tues 10.30–noon).

CRIME Theft and pickpocketing are the main problems. Most travellers prefer to carry their valuables at all times, but it's also sometimes possible to leave them in a hotel or guesthouse locker – the safest lockers are those which require your own padlock, as there are occasional reports of valuables being stolen by hotel staff. Padlock your luggage when leaving it in hotel or guesthouse rooms, as well as when consigning it to storage or taking it on public transport. Never buy anything from touts, and in the case of travel agents call the relevant airline first to make sure you're holding a verified ticket before paying up. Violent crime against tourists is not common, but it does occur. Obvious precautions include locking accessible windows and doors at night, preferably with your own padlock, and not travelling alone at night in a taxi or tuk-tuk. Drug smuggling carries a maximum penalty of death and will almost certainly get you from five to twenty years in a Thai prison.

DEPARTURE TAXES International: B500, domestic: B30.

DISABLED TRAVEL Thailand makes few provisions for its disabled citizens and this obviously affects the disabled traveller. For example, wheelchair users will have a hard time negotiating the uneven pavements, which are high to allow for flooding and invariably lacking in dropped kerbs, and will find it difficult to board buses and trains. Even crossing the road can be a trial, where it's usually a question of climbing steps up to a bridge rather than taking a ramped underpass. On the other hand, most disabled travellers find Thais only too happy to offer assistance where they can, and the country's top hotels are wising up to the need to provide decent facilities.

ELECTRICITY Supplied at 220 volts AC.

EMAIL AND INTERNET ACCESS Most cybercafés charge between B3 and B5 per minute online. There's usually an extra charge for printing out emails, and a small charge for receiving emails at the cybercafé's email address. Bangkok's best cybercafés include: *Hello Internet Café* at 63 Khao San Rd, Banglamphu (*hellopub@loxinfo.co.th* daily 10am–2am); *Cybercafé* on the 2nd Floor of the Ploenchit Center, Soi 2 Sukhumvit Rd (*cybercafé@chomanan.co.th* daily 10am–9.30pm); *Cyberia*, on the corner of Soi 24 Sukhumvit Rd (*kulthep@cyberia.co.th* Sun–Wed 10.30am–11pm, Thurs–Sat 10.30am–midnight); and *Byte in a Cup*, on the 4th floor of *Siam Discovery Centre*, Rama 1 Rd (*www.byte-in-a-cup.com* daily 10am–7pm).

EMBASSIES AND CONSULATES Australia, 37 Sathorn Thai Rd ✆287 2680; Burma (Myanmar) 132 Sathorn Nua Rd ✆233 2237; Canada, Boonmitr Building, 138 Silom Rd ✆237 4125; China 57/2 Rajdapisek Rd ✆245 7033; India 46 Soi 23, Sukhumvit Rd ✆258 0333-6; Indonesia 600–602 Phetchaburi Rd ✆252 3135-40; Ireland, United Flour Mill Building, 205 Rajawong Rd ✆223 0876; Laos 520 Ramkhamhaeng Soi 39 ✆539 6667-8; Malaysia 15 Fl, Regent Hse, 183 Ratchadamri Rd ✆254 1700-5; Nepal 189 Soi 71, Sukhumvit Rd ✆391 7240; Netherlands, 106 Witthayu (Wireless) Rd ✆254 7701-5; New Zealand, 93 Witthayu (Wireless) Rd ✆254 2530; Singapore 129 Sathorn Thai Rd ✆286 2111; UK, 1031 Wireless Rd ✆253 0191-9; US, 20 Witthayu (Wireless) Rd ✆205 4000; Vietnam 83/1 Witthayu (Wireless) Rd ✆251 5835-8).

EMERGENCIES For all emergencies, call the tourist police on ✆ 1699.

IMMIGRATION OFFICE About 1km down Soi Suan Plu, off Sathorn Thai Rd (Mon–Fri 8am–noon © 1–4pm; ©287 3101-10). Visa extension takes about an hour.

LANGUAGE COURSES *AUA*, 179 Rajdamri Rd ©252 8170) runs regular Thai language courses.

LAUNDRIES If you don't want to entrust your clothes to a guest-house laundry service, there are a couple of self-service laundries on Khao San Rd.

LEFT LUGGAGE At Don Muang airport (B40 per day) and Hualamphong train station (B20 per day; most hotels and guest houses will store bags by the week at much more reasonable rates (B7–10 per day).

MASSAGE Traditional Thai massage sessions and courses are held at Wat Po (see p.65), and at *Sawasdee Bangkok Inn* in Banglamphu (p.141).

NEWSPAPERS The two daily English-language papers, the *Bangkok Post* and the *Nation*, are sold at most newsstands in the capital.

PHARMACIES English-speaking staff at Boots the Chemist, on the corner of Soi 33, Sukhumvit Rd (©252 8056) and at other pharmacies across the city.

POLICE The Tourist Assistance Center (TAC) deals with tourist-related crimes and complaints and has an office in the TAT headquarters on Rajdamnoen Nok Avenue, Bangkok (daily 8.30am–4.30pm; ©281 5051). In emergencies, always contact the English-speaking tourist police, toll-free on ©1699.

POSTAL SERVICES The GPO is at 1160 Charoen Krung (New Rd), a few hundred metres left of the exit for Wat Muang Kae express-boat stop. Poste restante can be collected Mon–Fri 8am–8pm, Sat, Sun & hols 8am–1pm; letters are kept for three months. If staying in Banglamphu, use the poste restante at the post office on Soi Sibsam Hang, opposite Wat Bowoniwes (Mon–Fri 8.30am–5pm, Sat 9am–noon). Letters should be addressed c/o Poste Restante, Banglamphubon PO, Bangkok 10203 and are kept for two months. You can also send and receive faxes there on ℂ281 1579. Poste restante can also be sent to the Sukhumvit Road post office between sois 2 and 4, c/o Nana PO, Sukhumvit Rd, Bangkok 10112.

TELEPHONES Payphones come in three colours: red for local calls (use medium-sized one-baht coins only; you get three minutes per B1; blue or stainless steel for long-distance calls within Thailand (these gobble up B5 coins and are generally unreliable); and green cardphones for either, for which you buy a phonecard in any denomination from B25 to B240 from hotels, post offices and shops. The least expensive place to make international calls is the public telephone office in the compound of the GPO on Charoen Krung Rd (aka New Rd), which is open 24hr and also offers a fax service and a free collect call service (see above for location details). The post offices at Hualamphong Station, on Sukhumvit Rd and on Soi Sibsam Hang in Banglamphu also have international telephone offices attached, but these close at 8pm. Many private telephone offices claim that they offer the same rates as the public phone offices, but this is rarely the case. Calling out of Thailand, dial ℂ001 and then the relevant country code. For international directory enquiries call ℂ100. For directory assistance in English dial ℂ13.

TIME Bangkok is seven hours ahead of GMT, twelve hours ahead of Eastern Standard Time and three hours behind Sydney.

TRAVEL AGENCIES Diethelm Travel, Kian Gwan Building II, 140/1 Witthayu (Wireless) Rd ℂ255 9150. Domestic and international flights and tours; particularly good on travel to Burma, Cambodia, Laos and Vietnam. Educational Travel Centre, c/o *Royal Hotel*, 2 Rajdamnoen Rd ℂ224 0043. Exotissimo, 755 Silom Rd ℂ223 1510; and 21/17 Soi Nana Tai, Sukhumvit Rd ℂ253 5240. NS

Tours, c/o *Vieng Thai Hotel*, Ram Bhuttri Rd, Banglamphu ✆629 0509. Pacto PC&C, Room 100 in the Hualamphong Station concourse ✆226 5711. STA Travel, 14 Fl, Wall Street Tower, 33 Suriwong Rd ✆236 0262.

VISAS FOR BURMA, CAMBODIA, LAOS AND VIETNAM Entry formalities change frequently, so check with relevant embassies (see above for addresses). **Burma** (Myanmar): four-week visas from the embassy (B300; one day). **Cambodia**: no embassy in Bangkok, but entry requirements are currently quite lax and some (but not all) passport holders can get 30-day visas on arrival, for which one passport photo is required; for more information contact tour operators and travel agents listed above. **Laos**: fifteen-day visas on arrival at Vientiane Airport and at the Friendship Bridge in Nong Khai for US$50. One-month visas available through many travel agents in Bangkok (B2500; can take up to a week), or direct from the Laos embassy (B300–2000 depending on nationality; two days). **Vietnam**: thirty-day visas from the Vietnamese embassy (B800; four days), or from a travel agent.

EXCURSIONS FROM BANGKOK

Bang Pa-In

Little more than a roadside market, the village of **Bang Pa-In** (Map 1, H2), 60km north of Bangkok, has been put on the tourist map by its extravagant and rather surreal **Royal Palace**, even though most of the buildings can be seen only from the outside. King Prasat Thong of Ayutthaya first built a palace on this site, 20km down the Chao Phraya River from his capital, in the middle of the seventeenth century. It remained a popular royal country residence until it was abandoned a century later when the Thai capital was moved to Bangkok. In the middle of the nineteenth century, however, the advent of steamboats shortened the journey time upriver, and the palace enjoyed a revival: Rama IV built a modest residence here, which his son King Chulalongkorn (Rama V), in his passion for Westernization, knocked down to make room for the eccentric melange of European, Thai and Chinese architectural styles visible today.

Bang Pa-In can easily be visited on a day-trip from Bangkok. At a pinch, you could also take in a visit to Ayutthaya (see p.233), though that wouldn't really leave you enough time to get the most out of the extensive remains of the former capital.

THE PALACE COMPLEX

Daily 8.30am–3.30pm; B50.

Set in manicured grounds on an island in the Chao Phraya River, and ranged around an ornamental lake, the **palace complex** is flat and compact – a free brochure from the ticket office gives a diagram of the layout. On the north side of the lake stand a two-storey, colonial-style residence for the royal relatives and the Italianate **Warophat Phiman** (Excellent and Shining Heavenly Abode), which housed Chulalongkorn's throne hall and still contains private apartments where the present royal family sometimes stays. A covered bridge links this outer part of the palace to the **Pratu Thewarat Khanlai** (The King of the Gods Goes Forth Gate), the main entrance to the inner palace, which was reserved for the king and his immediate family. The high fence which encloses half of the bridge allowed the women of the harem to cross without being seen by male courtiers. You can't miss the photogenic **Aisawan Thiphya-art** (Divine Seat of Personal Freedom) in the middle of the lake: named after King Prasat Thong's original palace, it's the only example of pure Thai architecture at Bang Pa-In. The elegant tiers of the pavilion's roof shelter a bronze statue of Chulalongkorn.

In the inner palace, the **Uthayan Phumisathian** (Garden of the Secured Land) was Chulalongkorn's favourite house, a Swiss-style wooden chalet painted in bright two-tone green. After passing the **Ho Withun Thasana** (Sage's Lookout Tower), built so that the king could survey the surrounding countryside, you'll come to the main attraction of Bang Pa-In, the **Phra Thinang Wehart Chamrun** (Palace of Heavenly Light). The mansion and its contents were shipped from China and presented as a gift to Chulalongkorn in 1889 by Chinese merchants living in Bangkok. You're allowed to take off your shoes and feast your eyes on the interior, which drips with fine porcelain and embroidery, ebony furniture inlaid with mother-of-pearl and fantastically intricate woodcarving. This residence – a masterpiece of Chinese design – was the favourite of Rama VI, whose carved and lacquered writing table can be seen on the ground floor.

The simple marble **obelisk** behind the Uthayan Phumisathian was erected by Chulalongkorn to hold the ashes of Queen Sunandakumariratana, his favourite wife. In 1881, Sunanda, who was then 21 and expecting a child, was taking a trip on the river here when her boat capsized. She could have been rescued quite easily, but the laws concerning the sanctity of the royal family left those around her no option: "If a boat founders, the boatmen must swim away; if they remain near the boat [or] if they lay hold of him [the royal person] to rescue him, they are to be executed." Following the tragedy, King Chulalongkorn became a zealous reformer of Thai customs and strove to make the monarchy more accessible.

Turn right out of the main entrance to the palace grounds and cross the river on the small cable car, and you'll come to the greatest oddity of all: **Wat Nivet Dhamapravat**. A grey Buddhist viharn in the style of a Gothic church, it was built by Chulalongkorn in 1878, complete with wooden pews and stained-glass windows.

PRACTICALITIES

The best way of getting to Bang Pa-In from Bangkok is by early-morning **train** from Hualamphong station (7.05am & 8.30am). The journey takes just over an hour, and all trains continue to Ayutthaya (20 daily; 30min). From Bang Pa-In station (notice the separate station hall built by Chulalongkorn for the royal family) it's a two-kilometre hike to the palace, or you can take a samlor (tricycle rickshaw) for about B30. Slow **buses** leave Bangkok's Northern Terminal every twenty minutes and stop at Bang Pa-In market, a samlor ride from the palace, after about two hours, before continuing to Ayutthaya (30min).

Luxury cruises from Bangkok to Ayutthaya (see p.235) make a stop at Bang Pa-In.

Every Sunday, the Chao Phraya Express boat company (©222 5330) runs a **river tour** to Bang Pa-In, taking in Wat Phailom (Nov–June), a breeding ground for open-billed storks escaping the cold in Siberia, or Wat Chalerm Phra Kiet (July–Oct; see p.130), plus a shopping stop at Bang Sai folk arts and handicrafts centre. The boat leaves Bangkok's Maharat pier (off Maharat Road by Wat Mahathat in Ratanakosin) at 8am, stopping also at Phra Athit pier in Banglamphu, and returns at 5.30pm. Tickets, available from the piers, are B280, not including lunch and admission to the palace.

Ayutthaya

In its heyday as the booming capital of the Thai kingdom from the fourteenth to the eighteenth centuries, **Ayutthaya** (Map 1, H2) was so well endowed with temples that sunlight reflecting off their gilt decoration was said to dazzle from 5km away. Wide, grassy spaces today occupy much of the atmospheric site 80km north of Bangkok, which now resembles a graveyard for temples: grand, brooding red-brick ruins rise out of the fields, satisfyingly evoking the city's bygone grandeur. A few intact buildings help form an image of what the capital must have looked like, while three fine museums flesh out the picture.

The core of the ancient capital was a four-kilometre-wide **island** at the confluence of the Lopburi, Pasak and Chao Phraya rivers, which was once encircled by a twelve-kilometre wall, crumbling parts of which can be seen at the Phom Phet fortress in the southeast corner. A grid of broad roads now crosses the island, with recent buildings jostling uneasily with the ancient remains; the hub of the modern town rests on the northeast bank of the island around the junction of U Thong and Chao Phrom roads, although the newest development is off the island to the east.

The majority of Ayutthaya's ancient remains are spread out across the western half of the island in a patchwork of parkland: two of the most evocative temples, **Wat Phra**

Mahathat and **Wat Ratburana**, stand near the modern centre, while a broad band runs down the middle of the parkland, containing the scant vestiges of the **royal palace and temple**, the most revered Buddha image at **Viharn**

The golden age of Ayutthaya

Ayutthaya takes its name from the Indian city of Ayodhya ("invincible"), legendary birthplace of Rama (see p.62). Founded in 1351 by U Thong, later **King Ramathibodi I**, it rose rapidly by exploiting the expanding trade routes between India and China, and by the mid-fifteenth century its empire covered most of what is now Thailand. Ayutthaya grew into a vast amphibious city built on a 140-kilometre network of canals (few of which survive); by 1685 a million people – roughly double the population of London at the time – lived on its waterways, mostly in houseboats.

By the seventeenth century, Ayutthaya's wealth had attracted **traders** of forty different nationalities, including Chinese, Portuguese, Dutch, English and French. Many lived in their own ghettos, with their own docks for the export of rice, spices, timber and hides. The kings of Ayutthaya deftly maintained their independence from outside powers, while embracing the benefits of contact: they employed foreign architects and navigators, and Japanese samurai as bodyguards; even their prime ministers were often outsiders, who could look after foreign trade without getting embroiled in court intrigues.

This 400-year **golden age** came to an abrupt end in 1767, when the Burmese sacked Ayutthaya, taking tens of thousands of prisoners. The ruined city was abandoned to the jungle, but its memory endured: the architects of the new capital on Ratanakosin island in Bangkok perpetuated Ayutthaya's layout in every possible way.

AYUTTHAYA

Phra Mongkol Bopit, and the two main **museums**. To the north of the island you'll find the best-preserved temple, **Wat Na Phra Mane**, while to the southeast lie the giant chedi of **Wat Yai Chai Mongkol** and **Wat Phanan Choeng**, still a vibrant place of worship.

Ayutthaya can easily be visited on a day-trip from Bangkok, though dedicated ruin-baggers might want to stay overnight (see p.243). The best way of **getting there** is by **train** – there are twenty a day, via Bang Pa-In (see p.231), concentrated in the early morning and evening (1hr 30min). To get to the centre of town from the station on the east bank of the Pasak, take the two-baht ferry from the jetty 100m west of the station; it's then a five-minute walk to the junction of U Thong and Chao Phrom roads.

Though frequent, **buses** to Naresuan Road in the centre of Ayutthaya are slower and much less convenient, as they depart from Bangkok's remote Northern Terminal (every 15min; 2hr–2hr 30min). It's also possible to get there by scenic **boat tour** from Bangkok via Bang Pa-In: the *Oriental Hotel* (℃236 0400), among others, runs swanky day-trips for around B1500 per person, and a plushly converted teak rice barge called the *Mekhala* (℃256 7168 or 256 7169) does exorbitantly priced overnight cruises.

The Ayutthaya tourist police and the helpful TAT tourist information office (daily 8.30am–4.30pm; ℃035/246076 or 246077; can be found next to the city hall on the west side of Si Sanphet Road, opposite the Chao Sam Phraya National Museum (Map 9, F6).

For **getting around** Ayutthaya's widespread sights, **bicycles** can be rented at the guesthouses for around B50 per day (*Old BJ Guesthouse* also has a moped for B300 a day), or it's easy enough to hop on a **tuk-tuk** – B4–5 for a short journey if you're sharing, B30 if you're on your own. If

AYUTTHAYA

you're short on time you could hire a tuk-tuk for a whistle-stop tour of the old city for around B150 an hour, either from the train station or from Chao Phrom market.

To get a feel for Ayutthaya's amphibious past, you can charter a **tour boat** from the pier outside the Chantharakasem Palace on U-Thong Road. A two-hour trip down the Pasak River and up the Chao Phraya (B450–500 for the boat) will take in Wat Phanan Choeng (see p.242), **Wat Phutthaisawan**, a fetchingly dilapidated complex founded by Ayutthaya's first king, Ramathibodi, and the recently restored **Wat Chai Watthanaram**, which was built by King Prasat Thong in 1630 to commemorate his victory over Cambodia, taking as its model the imposing symmetry of the Baphuon temple at Angkor.

WAT PHRA MAHATHAT

Map 9, H4. Daily 8.30am–4.30pm; B30.

Heading west out of the new town centre along Chao Phrom Road (which becomes Naresuan Road), the first ruins you'll come to, after about 1km, are a pair of temples on opposite sides of the road. The overgrown **Wat Phra Mahathat**, on the left, is the epitome of Ayutthaya's nostalgic atmosphere of faded majesty.

The name "Mahathat" (Great Relic) indicates that the temple was built to house remains of the Buddha himself: according to the royal chronicles – never renowned for historical accuracy – King Ramesuan (1388–95) was looking out of his palace one morning when ashes of the Buddha materialized out of thin air here. A gold casket containing the ashes was duly enshrined in a grand 38-metre-high prang. The prang later collapsed, but the reliquary was unearthed in the 1950s, along with a hoard of other treasures including a gorgeous marble fish which opened to reveal gold, amber, crystal and porcelain ornaments – all now on show in the Chao Sam Phraya National Museum (see p.239).

You can climb what remains of the prang to get a good view of the broad, grassy complex, with dozens of brick spires tilting at impossible angles and headless Buddhas scattered around like spare parts in a scrapyard – look out for the serene head of a stone Buddha which has become nestled in the embrace of a bodhi tree's roots.

WAT RATBURANA

Map 9, H4. Daily 8.30am–4.30pm; B30.

Across the road from Wat Phra Mahathat, the towering **Wat Ratburana** was built in 1424 by King Boromraja II to commemorate his elder brothers Ay and Yi, who managed to kill each other in an elephant-back duel over the succession to the throne, thus leaving it vacant for him. Four elegant Sri Lankan chedis lean outwards as if in deference to the main prang, on which some of the original stucco work can still be seen, including fine statues of garudas swooping down on nagas.

It's possible to go down steep steps inside the prang to the crypt, where on two levels you can make out fragmentary murals of the early Ayutthaya period. Several hundred Buddha images were buried down here, most of which were snatched by grave robbers, although some can be seen in the Chao Sam Phraya Museum. They're in the earliest style that can be said to be distinctly Ayutthayan – an unsmiling Khmer expression, but on an oval face and elongated body that show the strong influence of Sukhothai.

WAT PHRA SI SANPHET

Map 9, E4. Daily 8.30am–4.30pm; B30.

Further west you'll come to **Wat Phra Si Sanphet**, built in 1448 by King Boromatrailokanat as his private chapel.

Formerly the grandest of Ayutthaya's temples, and still one of the best preserved, it took its name from one of the largest standing metal images of the Buddha ever known, the **Phra Si Sanphet**, erected here in 1503. Towering 16m high and covered in 173kg of gold, it was smashed to pieces when the Burmese sacked the city, though Rama I rescued the fragments and placed them inside a chedi at Wat Po in Bangkok (see p.65). The three remaining grey chedis were built to house the ashes of three kings; their style is characteristic of the old capital, and they have now become the most hackneyed image of Ayutthaya.

> The Wang Luang (Royal Palace) to the north of Wat Phra Si Sanphet was destroyed by the Burmese in 1767 and then plundered for bricks to build Bangkok. The only way to form a picture of this huge complex is to consult the model in the Historical Study Centre (see p.239).

VIHARN PHRA MONGKOL BOPIT

Map 9, E5. Daily 8.30am–4.30pm; free.

Viharn Phra Mongkol Bopit, on the south side of Wat Phra Si Sanphet, attracts tourists and Thai pilgrims in about equal measure. The pristine hall – a replica of a typical Ayutthayan viharn with its characteristic chunky lotus-capped columns around the outside – was built in 1956, with help from the Burmese to atone for their flattening of the city two centuries earlier, in order to shelter the revered **Phra Mongkol Bopit**, one of the largest bronze Buddhas in Thailand. The powerfully plain image, with its flashing mother-of-pearl eyes, was cast in the fifteenth century, then sat exposed to the elements from the time of the Burmese invasion until its new home was built. During restoration, the hollow image was found to contain hundreds of

Buddha statuettes, some of which were later buried around the shrine to protect it.

CHAO SAM PHRAYA NATIONAL MUSEUM

Map 9, F6. Daily 8.30am–4.30pm; B30.

A ten-minute walk south of the viharn brings you to the largest of the town's three museums, the **Chao Sam Phraya National Museum**, where most of the movable remains of Ayutthaya's glory – those which weren't plundered by treasure hunters or taken to the National Museum in Bangkok – are exhibited. Apart from numerous Buddhas, it's bursting with **gold treasures** of all shapes and sizes – betel-nut sets and model chedis, a royal wimple in gold filigree, a model elephant dripping with gems and the original relic casket from Wat Mahathat.

A second gallery, behind the main hall, explores foreign influences on Thai art and is particularly good on the origins of the various styles of Buddha images. This room also contains skeletons and artefacts from the site of the Portuguese settlement founded in 1540 just south of the town on the banks of the Chao Phraya. The Portuguese were the first Western power to establish ties with Ayutthaya, when in 1511 they were granted commercial privileges in return for supplying arms.

HISTORICAL STUDY CENTRE

Map 9, G6. Daily 8.30am–4.30pm; B100.

The **Historical Study Centre**, five minutes' walk from the national museum along Rotchana Road, is the town's showpiece, with a hefty admission charge to go with it. The visitors' exhibition upstairs puts the ruins in context, dramatically presenting a wealth of background detail through videos, sound effects and reconstructions – temple murals and model ships, a peasant's wooden house and a small-scale model of the Royal Palace – to build up a broad social history of Ayutthaya.

The centre's **annexe** (same times, same ticket), 500m south of Wat Phanan Choeng on the road to Bang Pa-In, also merits a visit despite its remoteness. Built with Japanese money on the site of the old Japanese settlement, it tells the fascinating story of Ayutthaya's relations with foreign powers, using a similar array of multi-media effects, as well maps, paintings, and historic documents prised from museums around the world.

CHANTHARAKASEM PALACE

Map 9, J2. Daily 8.30am–4.30pm; B30.

In the northeast corner of the island, the museum of the **Chantharakasem Palace** was traditionally the home of the heir to the Ayutthayan throne. The Black Prince, Naresuan, built the first *wang na* (palace of the front) here in about 1577 so that he could guard the area of the city wall which was most vulnerable to enemy attack. Rama IV had the palace rebuilt in the mid-nineteenth century, and it now displays many of his possessions, including a throne platform overhung by a white *chat*, a ceremonial nine-tiered parasol which is a vital part of a king's insignia. The rest of the museum is a jumble of beautiful ceramics, Buddha images and random artefacts.

WAT NA PHRA MANE

Map 9, E2. No fixed times, but generally open daylight hours; free.

Wat Na Phra Mane, on the north bank of the Lopburi River opposite the Wang Luang, is Ayutthaya's most immediately rewarding temple, as its structures and decoration survived the ravages of the Burmese. The story goes that when the Burmese were on the brink of capturing Ayutthaya in 1760, a siege gun positioned here burst, mortally wounding their king and prompting their retreat; when they came back to devastate the city in 1767, they left the temple standing out of superstition.

The main **bot**, built in 1503, shows the distinctive features of Ayutthayan architecture: outside columns topped with lotus cups, and slits in the walls instead of windows to let the wind pass through. Inside, underneath a rich red and gold coffered ceiling representing the stars around the moon, sits a powerful six-metre-high Buddha in the disdainful, overdecorated royal style characteristic of the later Ayutthaya period.

In sharp contrast is the dark green **Phra Khan Thavaraj** Buddha which dominates the tiny viharn behind to the right. Seated in the "European position", with its robe delicately pleated and its feet up on a large lotus leaf, the gentle figure conveys a reassuring serenity. It's advertised as being from Sri Lanka, the source of Thai Buddhism, but is more likely to be a Mon image from Wat Phra Mane at Nakhon Pathom, dating from the seventh to ninth centuries.

WAT YAI CHAI MONGKOL

Map 9, L7. No fixed times, but generally open daylight hours; free.

To the southeast of the island, if you cross the suspension bridge over the Pasak River and the rail line, then turn right at the major roundabout, you'll pass through Ayutthaya's new business zone and some rustic suburbia before reaching the ancient but still functioning **Wat Yai Chai Mongkol**, nearly 2km from the bridge.

Surrounded by formal lawns and flower beds, the wat was established by King Ramathibodi in 1357 as a meditation site for monks returning from study in Sri Lanka. King Naresuan put up the celebrated **chedi** to mark the decisive victory over the Burmese at Suphanburi in 1593, when he himself had sent the enemy packing by slaying the Burmese crown prince in a duel. Built on a colossal scale to outshine the huge Burmese-built chedi of Wat Phu Khao Thong on the northwest side of Ayutthaya, the chedi has come to symbolize the prowess and devotion of Naresuan and, by implication, his descendants down to the present king.

By the entrance, a **reclining Buddha**, now gleamingly restored in toothpaste white, was also constructed by Naresuan; elsewhere in the grounds, the wat maintains its contemplative origins with some highly topical maxims pinned to the trees such as "Cut down the forest of passion not real trees."

WAT PHANAN CHOENG

Map 9, J8. No fixed times, but generally open daylight hours; free.

In Ayutthaya's most prosperous period the docks and main trading area were located near the confluence of the Chao Phraya and Pasak rivers, to the west of Wat Yai Chai Mongkol. This is where you'll find the oldest and liveliest working temple in town, **Wat Phanan Choeng** (and the annexe to the Historical Study Centre – see p.239).

If you can get here during a festival, especially Chinese New Year, you'll be in for an overpowering experience. The main viharn is filled with the sights, sounds and smells of an incredible variety of merit-making activities, as devotees burn huge pink Chinese incense candles, offer food and rattle fortune sticks. It's even possible to buy tiny golden statues of the Buddha to be placed in one of the hundreds of niches which line the walls, a form of votive offering peculiar to this temple.

The nineteen-metre-high Buddha, which almost fills the hall, has survived since 1324, shortly before the founding of the capital, and tears are said to have flowed from its eyes when Ayutthaya was sacked by the Burmese. However, the reason for the temple's popularity with the Chinese is to be found in the early eighteenth-century shrine by the pier, with its image of a beautiful Chinese princess who drowned herself here because of a king's infidelity: his remorse led him to build the shrine at the place where she had walked into the river.

ACCOMMODATION

Ayutthaya Guesthouse
Map 9, J4. 16/2 Chao Phrom Rd ℂ035/251468.
Friendly place on a quiet lane in the town centre, with decent rooms and an outdoor bar/restaurant. It's also a good source of local information. ①

Krung Sri River
Map 9, K6. 27/2 Moo 11, Rojana Rd ℂ035/244483-7, fax 243777.
Ayutthaya's newest and most upmarket accommodation is a grand affair, with swanky lobby and attractive pool, occupying a prime, but noisy, position at the eastern end of the Pridi Damrong Bridge. ⑧

Old BJ Guesthouse
Map 9, J4. NG16/7 Naresuan Rd ℂ035/251526.
Next door but one to the *Ayutthaya Guesthouse*, with much the same to offer, though it's a little more cramped. ①

Ruenderm (Ayutthaya Youth Hostel)
Map 9, K5. 48 Moo 2 Tambon Horattanachai, U Thong Rd (just north of Pridi Damrong Bridge) ℂ035/241978.
Large, simple rooms, with shared but plentiful cold-water bathrooms, in a shambolic riverside teak house scattered with antiques. ③

AYUTTHAYA: ACCOMMODATION

....

For details of the accommodation price codes used in these listings, see p.136.

....

EATING

There's a lamentable dearth of decent **places to eat** in Ayutthaya. Around the central ruins you'll come across a few slightly pricey air-conditioned restaurants for lunch. Otherwise, your best bet is the atmospheric riverside terrace at the *Ruenderm* youth hostel, which serves reasonable food in some weird combinations, amid gnarled wooden furniture and curios.

Nakhon Pathom

Nakhon Pathom (Map 1, F5) is probably Thailand's oldest town, and is thought to be the point at which Buddhism first entered the region over two thousand years ago. The modern city's star attraction is the enormous **Phra Pathom Chedi**, an imposing stupa that dominates the skyline from every direction.

The town is 56km west of Bangkok and easily reached from the capital by train or bus. **Trains** leave Bangkok's Hualampong Station ten times a day and take about 80 minutes; there are also three trains a day from Bangkok Noi (70min). Arriving at Nakhon Pathom train station, a five-minute walk south across the khlong and through the market will get you to the chedi. **Buses** leave Bangkok's Southern Bus Terminal every ten minutes and take about an hour. Try to avoid being dumped at the bus terminal, which is about 1km east of the town centre – most buses circle the chedi first, so get off there instead. Everything described below is within ten minutes' walk of the omnipresent chedi.

PHRA PATHOM CHEDI

Measuring a phenomenal 120m high, **Phra Pathom Chedi** stands as tall as St Paul's Cathedral in London, and is a popular place of pilgrimage for Thais from all parts of the kingdom.

Although the Buddha never actually came to Thailand, legend has it that he rested here after wandering the country, and the original 39-metre high Indian-style chedi may have been erected to commemorate this. Since then, the chedi has been rebuilt twice; its earliest fragments are entombed within the later layers, and its origin has become indistinguishable from folklore.

Approaching the chedi from the main (northern) staircase you're greeted by the eight-metre-high Buddha image known as **Phra Ruang Rojanarit,** standing in front of the north viharn. Each of the viharns – there's one at each of the cardinal points – has an inner and an outer chamber containing tableaux of the life of the Buddha.

Proceeding clockwise around the monument – as is the custom at all Buddhist chedis – you can weave between the outer promenade and the inner cloister by climbing through the red-lacquered Chinese **moon windows** that connect them. Many of the trees that dot the promenade have a religious significance, such as the bodhi tree (*ficus religiosa*) under which the Buddha was meditating when he achieved enlightenment.

The museums

There are two museums within the chedi compound and, confusingly, both call themselves **Phra Pathom Museum.** The newer, more formal setup is clearly signposted from the bottom of the chedi's south staircase (Wed–Sun 9am–noon & 1–4pm; B30). It displays a good collection of Dvaravati-era (sixth to eleventh centuries) artefacts excavated nearby, including Wheels of Law – an emblem introduced by Theravada Buddhists before naturalistic images were permitted – and Buddha statuary with the U-shaped robe and thick facial features characteristic of Dvaravati sculpture.

For a broader, more contemporary overview, hunt out the other magpie's nest of a collection, which is half way up the steps near the east viharn (Wed–Sun 9am–noon & 1–4pm; free). More a curiosity shop than a museum, the small room is an Aladdin's cave of Buddhist amulets, seashells, gold and silver needles, Chinese ceramics, Thai musical instruments, world coins and banknotes, gems and ancient statues.

PRACTICALITIES

Nakhon Pathom's sights only merit half a day, and at any rate **accommodation** here is no great shakes. If you have to stay the night, opt for the inexpensive *Mitrsampant Hotel* (℡034/242422; ②), opposite the west gate of the chedi compound at the Lang Phra/Rajdamnoen intersection, or for the more comfortable *Nakorn Inn Hotel* (℡034/251152, fax 254998; ⑥) on Rajvithee Road, or the *Whale Hotel* (℡034/251020, fax 253864; ⑤), on Soi 19, off Rajvithee Road.

....

If you're just stopping off for a few hours, leave your luggage in the controller's office at the train station.

....

For inexpensive Thai and Chinese dishes head for either *Thai Food* or *Hasang*, both located on Phraya Gong Road just south across the khlong from the train station, on the left. Night-time **food** stalls next to the *Muang Thong Hotel* specialize in noodle broth and chilli-hot curries, and during the day the market in front of the station serves up the usual takeaway goodies, including reputedly the tastiest *khao laam* (bamboo cylinders filled with steamed rice and coconut) in Thailand.

You can **change money** at the exchange booth (open banking hours only) which is one block south of the train station on the road to the chedi, beside the bridge over the khlong.

Damnoen Saduak floating markets

To get an idea of what shopping in Bangkok used to be like before all the canals were tarmacked over, make an early-morning trip to the **floating markets** (*talat khlong*) of **Damnoen Saduak** (Map 1, E7), 109km southwest of Bangkok. Vineyards and orchards here back onto a labyrinth of narrow canals thick with paddle boats overflowing with fresh fruit and vegetables: local women ply these waterways every morning between 6 and 11am, selling their produce to each other and to the residents of the weatherworn homes built on stilts along the banks. Many wear the deep-blue jacket and high-topped straw hat traditionally favoured by Thai farmers. It's all richly atmospheric, which naturally makes it a big draw for tour groups – but you can avoid the crowds if you leave before they arrive, at about 9am.

THE MARKETS

The target for most groups is the main **Talat Khlong Ton Kem**, 2km west of the tiny town centre at the intersection of Khlong Damnoen Saduak and Khlong Thong Lang. Many of the wooden houses here have been expanded and converted into warehouse-style souvenir shops and tourist restaurants, diverting trade away from the khlong vendors and into the hands of large commercial enterprises. But, for the moment at least, the traditional water trade continues, and the two bridges between Ton Kem and **Talat Khlong Hia Kui** (a little further south down Khlong Thong Lang) make rewarding and unobtrusive vantage points.

Touts invariably congregate at the Ton Kem pier to hassle you into taking a **boat trip** around the khlong network (asking an hourly rate of anything from between B50 per person to B300 for the whole boat) and while this may be worth it to get to the less accessible **Talat Khlong Khun Phitak** to the south, there are distinct disadvantages in being propelled between markets at top speed in a noisy motorized boat. For a less hectic and more sensitive look around, explore the walkways beside the canals.

PRACTICALITIES

One of the reasons why Damnoen Saduak hasn't yet been totally ruined is that it's a two-hour **bus** journey from Bangkok. To make the trip in a day you'll have to catch one of the earliest buses from Bangkok's Southern Bus Terminal: the first air-con buses leave at 6am and 6.30am and take two hours; the first non-air-con bus (#78) leaves at 6.20am and takes half an hour longer.

Damnoen Saduak's **bus terminal** is just north of Thanarat Bridge and Khlong Damnoen Saduak. Songthaews cover the 2km to Ton Kem, but walk if you've got the time: a walkway follows the canal, which you can get down to from Thanarat Bridge, or you can cross the bridge and take the road to the right (Sukhaphiban 1 Road, but unsignposted) through the orchards. The small **tourist information** office on the corner of this road keeps random hours and nobody there speaks much English.

The best way to see the markets is to **stay overnight** in Damnoen Saduak and get up before the buses and coach tours from Bangkok arrive – and, if possible, explore the khlongside walkways the evening before. The only **place to stay** in town is the *Little Bird Hotel*, also known as *Noknoi* (✆032/241315; ②), whose sign is clearly visible from the main road and Thanarat Bridge. Although it's a motel with a trade in "short-stay" customers (note the condom display in the lobby), the rooms are good value: enormous, clean and all with en-suite bathrooms.

Kanchanaburi and the River Kwai

Set in a landscape of limestone hills 121km northwest of Bangkok, **Kanchanaburi** (Map 1, C4) is most famous as the location of the Bridge over the River Kwai, but it has a lot more to offer, including fine riverine scenery and some moving relics from World War II, when the town served as a POW camp and base for construction work on the notorious Thailand–Burma Death Railway.

Trains from Bangkok Noi (2hr 40min) or Nakhon Pathom (1hr 25min) are the most scenic way to get there; they depart from Bangkok twice a day at approximately 7.50am and 1.45pm, stopping at Nakhon Pathom around 9.20am and 2.50pm. The non-stop air-conditioned **buses** from Bangkok's Southern Bus Terminal are faster (about 2hr 20min) and more frequent (every 15 mins). The speediest transport option is to take one of the **tourist mini-buses** from Bangkok's Khao San Road, which take two hours.

Kanchanaburi is best explored by **bicycle**, since the town measures about 5km from north to south and all the war sights are sandwiched between the River Kwai and the busy Saeng Chuto Road. Bikes can be rented for around B30–50 per day from A.S. Mixed Travel, Corner Shop, and the *Green Bamboo Restaurant,* all on Maenam Kwai Road, *Punnee Bar* on Ban Neua Road, or the shop opposite Aree Bakery on Pak Praek Road. Alternatively, you can use the **public songthaew** (minivan) service that runs from outside the Bata shoe shop on Saeng Chuto Road (one block north of the bus station), goes north via the Kanchanaburi War Cemetery and then up Maenam Kwai Road to the bridge. Songthaews leave about every fifteen minutes during daylight hours, take about fifteen minutes to the bridge and cost about B5. Failing that, there are plenty of **samlor** (cycle rickshaws) available for hire.

The TAT office (daily 8.30am–4.30pm; ©034/511200) is a few hundred metres south of the bus station on Saeng Chuto Road (Map 10, F6). Several banks on Saeng Chuto Road offer money changing facilities.

THE JEATH WAR MUSEUM

Map 10, E7. Daily 8am–6pm; B30.

The **JEATH War Museum** gives the clearest introduction to local wartime history, putting the notorious sights of the Death Railway in context and painting a vivid picture of the gruesome conditions suffered by the POWs who worked on the line. It includes many harrowing accounts of life in the camps, recorded in newspaper articles, paintings and photographs. JEATH is an acronym of six of the countries involved in the railway: Japan, England, Australia, America, Thailand and Holland. The museum is housed in a reconstructed Allied POW hut of thatched palm beside the river, about 200m from the TAT office or a fifteen-minute walk southwest of the bus station.

The Death Railway

Shortly after entering World War II in December 1941, Japan began looking for a supply route to connect its newly acquired territories that now stretched from Singapore to the Burma-India border. In spite of the almost impenetrable terrain, the River Kwai basin was chosen as the route for a new 415km-long **Thailand–Burma Railway**.

About 60,000 Allied POWs were shipped up from captured Southeast Asian territories to work on the link, their numbers later augmented by as many as 200,000 conscripted Asian labourers. Work began at both ends in June 1942. Three million cubic metres of rock were shifted and nine miles of bridges built with little else but picks and shovels, dynamite and pulleys. By the time the line was completed, fifteen months later, it had more than earned its nickname, the **Death Railway**: an estimated 16,000 POWs and 100,000 Asian labourers died while working on it.

Food rations were meagre for men forced into backbreaking eighteen-hour shifts, often followed by night-long marches to the next camp. Many suffered from beri-beri, many more died of dysentery-induced starvation, but the biggest killers were cholera and malaria, particularly during the monsoon. It is said that one man died for every sleeper laid on the track.

KANCHANABURI WAR CEMETERY (DON RAK)

Map 10, D3. Daily 8am–4pm; free.

Many of the Allied POWs who died during the construction of the Thailand–Burma Railway are buried in the **Kanchanaburi War Cemetery**, also known as **Don Rak**, opposite the train station on Saeng Chuto Road. The 6982 POW graves are laid out in straight lines amid immaculate lawns and flowering shrubs. Many of the identical stone memorial slabs state simply "A man who died for his country" – at the upcountry camps, bodies were thrown onto mass funeral pyres, making identification impossible. Others, inscribed with names, dates and regiments, indicate that the overwhelming majority of the dead were under 25 years old.

THE BRIDGE OVER THE RIVER KWAI

Map 10, A1.

For most people the plain steel arches of the **Bridge over the River Kwai** come as a disappointment: it lacks drama and looks nothing like as hard to construct as it does in David Lean's famous film of the same name. But it is the film, of course, that draws tour buses here by the dozen, and makes the bridge approach seethe with trinket-sellers and touts. To get here either take any songthaew heading north up Saeng Chuto Road, hire a samlor, or cycle – it's 5km from the bus station.

The fording of the Kwai Yai at this point was one of the first major obstacles in the construction of the Thailand–Burma Railway. Sections of a steel bridge were brought up from Java and reassembled by POWs using only pulleys and derricks. A temporary **wooden bridge** was built alongside it, taking its first train in February 1943; three months later the steel bridge was finished. Both bridges were severely damaged by Allied bombers in 1944 and 1945; only the stumps of the wooden bridge remain, but the steel bridge was repaired after the war and is still in use today. In fact the best way to see the bridge is by **taking the train over it** – see opposite for details.

The bridge forms the dramatic centrepiece of the annual *son et lumière* River Kwai Bridge Festival, held over ten nights from the end of November to commemorate the first Allied bombing of the bridge on November 28, 1944.

WORLD WAR II MUSEUM

Map 10, A2. Daily 8am–6pm; B30.

Not to be confused with the JEATH War Museum (see p.252), the **World War II Museum** is a privately owned collection of rather bizarre curiosities. The war section comprises a very odd mixture of memorabilia (a rusted bombshell, the carpet used by the local Japanese commander) and reconstructed tableaux featuring emaciated POWs. More light-hearted displays include stamp and banknote collections and a gallery of selected "Miss Thailand" portraits from 1934.

RIDING THE DEATH RAILWAY

The two-hour rail journey from Kanchanaburi to Nam Tok is one of Thailand's most scenic. Leaving Kanchanaburi via the Bridge over the River Kwai, the train chugs through the Kwai Noi valley, stopping frequently at pretty flower-decked country stations.

The most hair-raising section of track begins shortly after Tha Kilen at **Wang Sing**, also known as Arrow Hill, when the train squeezes through thirty-metre solid rock cuttings, dug at the cost of numerous POW lives. Six kilometres further, it slows to a crawl at the approach to the **Wang Po viaduct**, where a 300-metre trestle bridge clings to the cliff face as it curves with the Kwai Noi – almost every man who worked on this part of the railway died. Half an hour later, the train reaches its terminus at the small town of **Nam Tok**.

There are three **Kanchanaburi–Nam Tok trains** daily in both directions, so a day return is quite feasible; Kanchanaburi TAT has timetables. Many Kanchanaburi tour operators offer a day-trip that includes war sights and waterfalls as well as a ride on the railway. It is possible to do the **Bangkok–Kanchanaburi–Nam Tok round trip** in one day – bear in mind though, that this leaves no time for exploring, and that only third class, hard seats are available. The 7.50am train from Bangkok Noi arrives in Nam Tok at 1pm, then departs for Bangkok at 1.15pm, returning to the capital at 6.10pm.

On weekends and national holidays, the State Railway runs special day trips from Bangkok's Hualamphong Station along the Death Railway. The trips include short stops at Nakhon Pathom, the Bridge over the River Kwai and Nam Tok, the terminus of the line. Advance booking is essential, see p.37.

ACCOMMODATION

Jolly Frog Backpackers

Map 10, C3. Soi China, just off the southern end of Maenam Kwai Rd ©034/514579.

Large, popular complex of comfortable bamboo huts, some with bathroom, ranged around a riverside garden. ①–②

River Kwai Hotel (aka *Rama of River Kwai*)

Map 10, F4. 284/3–16 Saeng Chuto Rd ©034/511184, fax 511269.

The town's top hotel is nowhere near the river, but all rooms have air con, and there's a swimming pool. ⑦–⑧

Sam's House

Map 10, B2. Maenam Kwai Rd ©034/515956.

Comfortably furnished rafthouses, most with bathroom, prettily floating among riverine lotuses. Plus some air-con rooms on the riverbank. ①–④

Sugar Cane Guesthouse

Map 10, B3. 22 Soi Pakistan, off Maenam Kwai Rd ℰ034/624520.
Peaceful, family-run place with just twelve comfortable huts
(all with bathroom) prettily set round a riverside lawn. ②–③

**For details of the accommodation price codes used in
these listings, see p.136.**

EATING

Apple's Guesthouse Restaurant

Map 10, D3. c/o *A.S. Mixed Travel* at 293 Maenam Kwai Rd.
Exceptionally delicious, mid-priced menu, which includes
mouthwatering met and veggie *massaman* curries.

Northeastern Restaurant

Map 10, D5. Song Kwai Rd.
Typical inexpensive northeastern fare, including barbecued
chicken (*kai yang*) and spicy papaya salad (*somtam*).

Pae Karn

Map 10, E6. Song Kwai Rd.
The best of the touristy floating restaurants. Moderate prices.

River Kwai Park Fast Food Hall

Map 10, A2. 50m south of the bridge on Maenam Kwai Rd.
The cheapest place to eat in the vicinity of the bridge, this is a
collection of curry and noodle stalls where you buy coupons
for meals that cost just B25 or B30.

KANCHANABURI AND THE RIVER KWAI: EATING

CONTEXTS

The historical framework

Bangkok is a comparatively new capital, founded in 1782 after Ayutthaya, a short way upriver, had been razed by the Burmese, but it has established an overwhelming dominance in Thailand. Its history over the last two centuries directly mirrors that of the country as a whole, and the city has gathered to itself, in the National Museum and elsewhere, the major relics of Thailand's previous civilizations, principally from the eras of Ayutthaya and its precursor, Sukhothai.

Early history

The region's first distinctive civilization, **Dvaravati**, was established around two thousand years ago by an Austroasiatic-speaking people known as the Mon. One of its mainstays was Theravada Buddhism, which had been introduced to Thailand during the second or third century BC by Indian missionaries. From the discovery of monastery boundary stones (*sema*), clay votive tablets and Indian-influenced Buddhist sculpture, it's clear that the Dvaravati city states (including **Nakhon Pathom**) had their greatest flourishing between the sixth and ninth centuries AD. Meanwhile, in the eighth century, peninsular Thailand to the south of Dvaravati came under the control of the **Srivijaya** empire, a Mahayana Buddhist state centred on Sumatra which had strong ties with India.

From the ninth century onwards, however, both Dvaravati and Srivijaya Thailand succumbed to invading **Khmers** from Cambodia, who consolidated their position during the watershed reign of **Jayavarman II** (802–50). To establish his authority, Jayavarman II had himself initiated as a *chakravartin* or universal ruler, the living embodiment of the **devaraja**, the divine essence of kingship – a concept which was adopted by later Thai rulers. From their capital at **Angkor**,

Jayavarman's successors took control over northeastern, central and peninsular Thailand, thus mastering the most important trade routes between India and China. By the thirteenth century, however, the Khmers had overreached themselves and were in no position to resist the onslaught of a vibrant new force in Southeast Asia, the Thais.

The earliest Thais

The earliest traceable history of the **Thai people** picks them up in southern China around the fifth century AD, when they were squeezed by Chinese and Vietnamese expansionism into sparsely inhabited northeastern Laos. Their first significant entry into what is now Thailand seems to have happened in the north, where some time after the seventh century the Thais formed a state known as **Yonok**. Theravada Buddhism spread to Yonok via Dvaravati around the end of the tenth century, which served not only to unify the Thais themselves but also to link them to the wider community of Buddhists.

By the end of the twelfth century, they formed the majority of the population in Thailand, then under the control of the Khmer empire. The Khmers' main outpost, at Lopburi, was by this time regarded as the administrative capital of a land called **"Syam"** (possibly from the Sanskrit *syam*, meaning swarthy) – a mid-twelfth-century bas-relief at Angkor portraying the troops of Lopburi preceded by a large group of self-confident Syam Kuk mercenaries, shows that the Thais were becoming a force to be reckoned with.

Sukhothai

At some time around 1238, Thais in the upper Chao Phraya valley captured the main Khmer outpost in the region at **Sukhothai** and established a kingdom there. For the first forty years, it was merely a local power, but an attack by the ruler of the neighbouring principality of Mae

Sot brought a dynamic new leader to the fore: the king's nineteen-year-old son, Rama, defeated the opposing commander, earning himself the name **Ramkhamhaeng**, "Rama the Bold". When Ramkhamhaeng himself came to the throne around 1278, he seized control of much of the Chao Phraya valley, and over the next twenty years, more by diplomacy than military action, gained the submission of most of Thailand under a complex tribute system.

Although the empire of Sukhothai extended Thai control over a vast area, its greatest contribution to the Thais' development was at home, in cultural and political matters. A famous **inscription** by Ramkhamhaeng, now housed in the Bangkok National Museum, describes a prosperous era of benevolent rule: "In the time of King Ramkhamhaeng this land of Sukhothai is thriving. There is fish in the water and rice in the fields ... [The King] has hung a bell in the opening of the gate over there: if any commoner has a grievance which sickens his belly and gripes his heart ... he goes and strikes the bell ... [and King Ramkhamhaeng] questions the man, examines the case, and decides it justly for him."

Although this plainly smacks of self-promotion, it seems to contain at least a kernel of truth: in deliberate contrast to the Khmer god-kings (*devaraja*), Ramkhamhaeng styled himself as a **dhammaraja**, a king who ruled justly according to Theravada Buddhist doctrine and made himself accessible to his people. A further sign of the Thais' growing self-confidence was the invention of a new **script** to make their tonal language understood by the non-Thai inhabitants of the land.

The growth of Ayutthaya

After the death of Ramkhamhaeng around 1299, however, his empire quickly fell apart. By 1320 Sukhothai had regressed to being a kingdom of only local significance, though its mantle as the capital of a Thai empire was taken up shortly after to the south at **Ayutthaya**. Soon after founding the city in 1351, the ambitious king **Ramathibodi** united the principalities of the lower Chao Phraya valley, which had formed the western provinces of the Khmer empire. When he recruited his bureaucracy from the urban elite of Lopburi, Ramathibodi set the **style of government** at Ayutthaya, elements of which persisted into the Bangkok empire and up to the present day. The elaborate etiquette, language and rituals of Angkor were adopted, and, most importantly, the conception of the ruler as *devaraja*: when the king processed through the town, ordinary people were forbidden to look at him and had to be silent while he passed.

The site chosen by Ramathibodi was the best in the region for an international port and so began Ayutthaya's rise to prosperity, based on exploiting the upswing in **trade** in the middle of the fourteenth century along the routes between India and China. By 1540, the Kingdom of Ayutthaya had grown to cover most of the area of modern-day Thailand. Despite a 1568 invasion by the Burmese, which led to twenty years of foreign rule, Ayutthaya made a spectacular comeback, and in the seventeenth century its **foreign trade** boomed. In 1511 the Portuguese had become the first Western power to trade with Ayutthaya, and a treaty with Spain was concluded in 1598; relations with Holland and England were initiated in 1608 and 1612 respectively. European merchants flocked to Thailand, not only to buy Thai products, but also to gain access to Chinese and Japanese goods on sale there.

The Burmese invasion

In the mid-eighteenth century, however, the rumbling in the Burmese jungle to the north began to make itself heard again. After an unsuccessful siege in 1760, in February 1766 the Burmese descended upon the city for the last time. The Thais held out for over a year, during which they were afflicted by famine, epidemics and a terrible fire which destroyed ten thousand houses. Finally, in **April 1767**, the walls were breached and the city taken. The Burmese savagely razed everything to the ground and led off tens of thousands of prisoners to Burma, including most of the royal family. The city was abandoned to the jungle, and Thailand descended into banditry.

Taksin and Thonburi

Out of this lawless mess, however, emerged **Phraya Taksin**, a charismatic and brave general, who had been unfairly blamed for a failed counter-attack against the Burmese at Ayutthaya and had quietly slipped away from the besieged city. Taksin was crowned king in December 1768 at his new capital of **Thonburi**, on the opposite bank of the river from modern-day Bangkok. Within two years he had restored all of Ayutthaya's territories; more remarkably, by the end of the next decade Taksin had outdone his Ayutthayan predecessors by bringing Cambodia and much of Laos into a huge new empire.

However, by 1779 all was not well with the king. Taksin was becoming increasingly paranoid about plots against him, a delusion that drove him to imprison and torture even his wife and sons. At the same time he sank into religious excesses, demanding that the monkhood worship him as a god. By March 1782, public outrage at his sadism and dangerously irrational behaviour had reached such fervour that he was ousted in a coup.

Chao Phraya Chakri, Taksin's military commander, was invited to take power and had Taksin executed. In accordance with ancient etiquette, this had to be done without royal blood touching the earth: the mad king was duly wrapped in a black velvet sack and struck on the back of the neck with a sandalwood club. (Popular tradition has it that even this form of execution was too much: an unfortunate substitute got the velvet sack treatment, while Taksin was whisked away to a palace in the hills near Nakhon Si Thammarat, where he is said to have lived until 1825.)

The early Bangkok empire: Rama I

With the support of the Ayutthayan aristocracy, Chakri – reigning as **Rama I** (1782–1809) – set about consolidating the Thai kingdom. His first act was to move the capital across the river to what we know as **Bangkok**, on the more defensible east bank where the French had built a grand but short-lived fort in the 1660s. Borrowing from the layout of Ayutthaya, he built a new royal palace and impressive monasteries in the area of **Ratanakosin** – which remains the city's spiritual heart – within a defensive ring of two (later expanded to three) canals. In the palace temple, Wat Phra Kaeo, he enshrined the talismanic Emerald Buddha, which he had snatched during his campaigns in Laos. Initially, as at Ayutthaya, the city was largely amphibious: only the temples and royal palaces were built on dry land, while ordinary residences floated on thick bamboo rafts on the river and canals, and even shops and warehouses were moored to the river bank.

During Rama I's reign, trade with China revived, and the style of government was put on a more modern footing: while retaining many of the features of a *devaraja*, he shared more responsibility with his courtiers, as a first among equals.

Rama II and Rama III

The peaceful accession of his son as **Rama II** (1809–24) signalled the establishment of the **Chakri dynasty**, which is still in place today. This Second Reign was a quiet interlude, best remembered as a fertile period for Thai literature. The king, himself one of the great Thai poets, gathered round him a group of writers including the famous Sunthorn Phu, who produced scores of masterly love poems, travel accounts and narrative songs.

In contrast, **Rama III** (1824–51) actively discouraged literary development and was a vigorous defender of conservative values. To this end, he embarked on an extraordinary redevelopment of **Wat Po**, the oldest temple in Bangkok. Hundreds of educational inscriptions and mural paintings, on all manner of secular and religious subjects, were put on show, apparently to preserve traditional culture against the rapid change which the king saw corroding the country.

The danger posed by Western influence became more apparent in the Third Reign. As early as 1825, the Thais were sufficiently alarmed by **British colonialism** to strengthen Bangkok's defences by stretching a great iron chain across the mouth of the Chao Phraya River, to which every blacksmith in the area had to donate a certain number of links. In 1826 Rama III was obliged to sign the **Burney Treaty**, a limited trade agreement with the British by which the Thais won some political security in return for reducing their taxes on goods passing through Bangkok.

Mongkut

Rama IV, more commonly known as **Mongkut** (1851–68), had been a Buddhist monk for 27 years when he succeeded his brother. But far from leading a cloistered life, Mongkut had travelled widely throughout Thailand, had maintained scholarly contacts with French and American missionaries, and had taken an interest in Western learning, studying English, Latin and the sciences.

When his kingship faced its first major test, in the form of a threatening **British mission** in 1855 led by **Sir John Bowring**, Mongkut dealt with it confidently. Realizing that Thailand would be unable to resist the military might of the British, the king reduced import and export taxes,

MONGKUT

allowed British subjects to live and own land in Thailand and granted them freedom of trade. Furthermore, Mongkut quickly made it known that he would welcome diplomatic contacts from other Western countries: within a decade, agreements similar to the Bowring Treaty had been signed with France, the United States and a score of other nations.

Thus by skilful diplomacy the king avoided a close relationship with just one power, which could easily have led to Thailand's annexation. And as a result of the open-door policy, foreign trade boomed, financing the redevelopment of Bangkok's waterfront and, for the first time, the building of paved roads. However, Mongkut ran out of time for instituting the far-reaching domestic reforms which he saw were needed to drag Thailand into the modern world.

Chulalongkorn

Mongkut's son, **Chulalongkorn**, took the throne as Rama V (1868–1910) at the age of only fifteen, but he was well prepared by an excellent education which mixed traditional Thai and modern Western elements – provided by Mrs Anna Leonowens, subject of The King and I. When Chulalongkorn reached his majority after a five-year regency, he set to work on the reforms envisioned by his father.

One of his first acts was to scrap the custom by which subjects were required to prostrate themselves in the presence of the king. He constructed a new residential palace for the royal family in **Dusit**, north of Ratanakosin, and laid out that area's grand European-style boulevards. In the 1880s Chulalongkorn began to **restructure the government** to meet the country's needs, setting up a host of departments, for education, public health, the army and the like, and bringing in scores of foreign advisers to help with everything from foreign affairs to rail lines.

Throughout this period, however, the Western powers maintained their pressure on the region. The most serious threat to Thai sovereignty was the **Franco–Siamese Crisis** of 1893, which culminated in the French sending gunboats up the Chao Phraya River to Bangkok. Flouting numerous international laws, France claimed control over Laos and made other outrageous demands, which Chulalongkorn had no option but to concede. During the course of his reign the country was obliged to cede almost half of its territory, and forewent huge sums of tax revenue, in order to preserve its independence; but by Chulalongkorn's death in 1910, the frontiers were fixed as they are today.

The end of absolute monarchy

Chulalongkorn was succeeded by a flamboyant, British-educated prince, **Vajiravudh** (Rama VI, 1910–25). However, in 1912 a group of young army lieutenants, disillusioned by the absolute monarchy, plotted a **coup**. The conspirators were easily broken up, but this was something new in Thai history: the country was used to in-fighting among the royal family, but not to military intrigue by men from comparatively ordinary backgrounds. By the time the young and inexperienced **Prajadhipok** – seventy-sixth child of Chulalongkorn – was catapulted to the throne as Rama VII (1925–35), Vajiravudh's extravagance had created severe financial problems. The vigorous community of Western-educated intellectuals who had emerged in the lower echelons of the bureaucracy were becoming increasingly dissatisfied with monarchical government. The Great Depression, which ravaged the economy in the 1930s, came as the final shock to an already moribund system.

On June 24, 1932, a small group of middle-ranking officials, led by a lawyer, **Pridi Phanomyong**, and an army major, **Luang Phibunsongkhram** (Phibun), staged a **coup** with only a handful of troops. Prajadhipok weakly submitted to the conspirators, and 150 years of absolute monarchy in Bangkok came to a sudden end. The king was sidelined to a position of symbolic significance, and in 1935 he abdicated in favour of his ten-year-old nephew, **Ananda**, then a schoolboy living in Switzerland.

Up to World War II

The success of the 1932 coup was in large measure attributable to the army officers who gave the conspirators credibility, and it was they who were to dominate the constitutional governments that followed. Phibun` emerged as prime minister after the decisive elections of 1938, and encouraged a wave of nationalistic feeling with such measures as the official institution of the name Thailand in 1939 – Siam, it was argued, was a name bestowed by external forces, and the new title made it clear that the country belonged to the Thais rather than the economically dominant Chinese.

The Thais were dragged into **World War II** on December 8, 1941, when, almost at the same time as the assault on Pearl Harbor, the Japanese invaded the east coast of peninsular Thailand, with their sights set on Singapore to the south. The Thais at first resisted fiercely, but realizing that the position was hopeless, Phibun quickly ordered a ceasefire.

The Thai government concluded a military alliance with Japan and declared war against the United States and Great Britain in January 1942, probably in the belief that the Japanese would win. However, the Thai minister in Washington, Seni Pramoj, refused to deliver the declaration of war against the US and, in cooperation with the Americans, began organizing a resistance movement called **Seri Thai**. Pridi Phanomyong, now acting as regent to the young king, furtively coordinated the movement under the noses of the occupying Japanese, smuggling in American agents and housing them in a European prison camp in Bangkok.

By 1944 Japan's defeat looked likely, and in July Phibun, who had been most closely associated with them, was forced to resign by the National Assembly. Once the war was over, American support prevented the British from imposing heavy punishments on the country for its alliance with Japan.

Postwar upheavals

With the fading of the military, the election of January 1946 was for the first time contested by organized political parties, resulting in Pridi's becoming prime minister. A new constitution was drafted, and the outlook for democratic, civilian government seemed bright. Hopes were shattered, however, on June 9, 1946, when **King Ananda** was **found dead** in his bed, with a bullet wound in his forehead. Three palace servants were hurriedly tried and executed, but the murder has never been satisfactorily explained. Pridi resigned as prime minister, and in April 1948 Phibun, playing on the threat of communism, took over the premiership.

As communism developed its hold in the region with the takeover of China in 1949 and the French defeat in Indochina in 1954, the US increasingly viewed Thailand as a bulwark against the red menace. Between 1951 and 1957, when its annual state budget was only about $200 million a year, Thailand received a total $149 million in American economic aid and $222 million in military aid. This strengthened Phibun's dictatorship, while enabling leading military figures to divert American money and other funds into their own pockets.

Phibun narrowly won a general election in 1957, but only by blatant vote rigging and coercion. Although there's a strong tradition of foul play in Thai elections, this is remembered as the dirtiest ever: after vehement public outcry, **General Sarit**, the commander-in-chief of the army, overthrew the new government in September 1957.

Believing that Thailand would prosper best under a unifying authority, Sarit set about re-establishing the monarchy as the head of the social hierarchy and the source of legitimacy for the government. Ananda's successor, **Bhumibol** (Rama IX), was pushed into an active role, while Sarit ruthlessly silenced critics and pressed ahead with a plan for economic development, achieving a large measure of stability and prosperity.

The Vietnam War

Sarit died in 1963, whereupon the military succession passed to **General Thanom**. His most pressing problem was the **Vietnam War**. The Thais, with the backing of the US, quietly began to conduct military operations in Laos, to which North Vietnam and China responded by supporting anti-government insurgency in Thailand. The more the Thais felt threatened by the spread of communism, the more they looked to the Americans for help – by 1968 around 45,000 US military personnel were on Thai soil, which became the base for US bombing raids against North Vietnam and Laos.

The effects of the **American presence** were profound. The economy swelled with dollars, and hundreds of thousands of Thais became reliant on the Americans for a living, with a consequent proliferation of prostitution – centred on Bangkok's infamous Patpong district – and corruption. What's more, the sudden exposure to Western culture led many to question the traditional Thai values and the political status quo.

The democracy movement and civil unrest

Poor farmers in particular were becoming increasingly disillusioned with their lot, and many turned against the Bangkok government. At the end of 1964, the **Communist Party of Thailand** and other groups formed a **broad left coalition** which soon had the support of several thousand insurgents in remote areas of the northeast and the north. By 1967, a separate threat had arisen in southern Thailand, involving **Muslim dissidents** and the Chinese-dominated **Communist Party of Malaysia**, as well as local Thais.

Thanom was now facing a major security crisis, especially as the war in Vietnam was going badly. In November 1971 he imposed repressive military rule. In response, **student demonstrations** began in June 1973, and in October as many as 500,000 people turned out at Thammasat University in Bangkok to demand a new constitution. Clashes with the police ensued but elements in the army, backed by King Bhumibol, prevented Thanom from crushing the protest with troops. On October 14, 1973, Thanom was forced to resign and leave the country.

In a new climate of openness, **Kukrit Pramoj** formed a coalition of seventeen elected parties and secured a promise of US withdrawal from Thailand, but his government was riven with feuding. In **October 1976**, the students demonstrated again, protesting against the return of Thanom to Bangkok to become a monk at Wat Bowonniwet. This time there was no restraint: supported by elements of the military and the government, the police and reactionary students launched a massive assault on Thammasat University. On October 6, hundreds of students were brutally beaten, scores were lynched and some even burned alive; the military took control and suspended the constitution.

Premocracy

Soon after, the military-appointed prime minister, **Thanin Kraivichien**, forced dissidents to undergo anti-communist indoctrination, but his measures seem to have been too repressive even for the military, who forced him to resign in October 1977. General Kriangsak Chomanand took over, and began to break up the insurgency with shrewd offers of amnesty. He in turn was displaced in February 1980 by **General Prem Tinsulanonda**, backed by a broad parliamentary coalition.

Untainted by corruption, Prem achieved widespread support, including that of the monarchy. Overseeing a period of rapid economic growth, Prem maintained the premiership until 1988, with a unique mixture of dictatorship and democracy sometimes called **Premocracy**: although never standing for parliament himself, Prem was asked by the legislature after every election to become prime minister. He eventually stepped down because, he said, it was time for the country's leader to be chosen from among its elected representatives.

The 1992 demonstrations

The new prime minister was indeed an elected MP, **Chatichai Choonhavan**, a retired general with a long civilian career in public office. He pursued a vigorous policy of economic development, but this fostered widespread corruption, in which members of the government were often implicated. Following an economic downturn and Chatichai's attempts to downgrade the political role of the military, the armed forces staged a bloodless **coup** on February 23, 1991, led by Supreme Commander **Sunthorn** and General **Suchinda**, the army commander-in-chief, who became premier.

When Suchinda reneged on promises to make democratic amendments to the constitution, hundreds of thousands of ordinary Thais poured onto the streets around Bangkok's Democracy Monument in **mass demonstrations** between May 17 and 20, 1992. Hopelessly misjudging the mood of the country, Suchinda brutally crushed the protests, leaving hundreds dead or injured. Having justified the massacre on the grounds that he was protecting the king from communist agitators, Suchinda was forced to resign when King Bhumibol expressed his disapproval in a ticking-off that was broadcast on world television.

Chuan, Banharn and Chavalit

In the elections on September 13, 1992, the **Democrat Party**, led by **Chuan Leekpai**, a noted upholder of democracy and the rule of law, gained the largest number of parliamentary seats. Despite many successes through a period of continued economic growth, he was able to hold onto power only until July 1995, when he was forced to call new elections.

Chart Thai and its leader, **Banharn Silpa-archa** – nicknamed by the local press the "walking ATM", a reference to his reputation for buying votes – emerged victorious. Allegations of corruption soon mounted against Banharn and in the following year he was obliged to dissolve parliament.

In November 1996, **General Chavalit Yongchaiyudh**, leader of the **New Aspiration Party** (NAP), just won what was dubbed as the most corrupt election in Thai history, with an estimated 25 million baht spent on vote-buying in rural areas. The most significant positive event of his tenure was the approval of a **new constitution**. Drawn up by an independent drafting assembly, its main points included: direct elections to the senate, rather than appointment of senators by the prime minister; acceptance of the right of assembly as the basis of a democratic society and guarantees of individual rights and freedoms; greater public accountability; and increased popular participation in local administration. The eventual aim of the new charter was to end the traditional system of patronage, vested interests and vote-buying.

The economic crisis

At the start of Chavalit's premiership, the Thai economy was already on shaky ground. In February 1997 foreign-exchange dealers began to mount speculative **attacks on the baht**, alarmed at the size of Thailand's private foreign debt – 250 billion baht in the unproductive property sector alone, much of it accrued through the proliferation of prestigious skyscrapers in Bangkok. The government valiantly defended the pegged exchange rate, spending $23 billion of the country's formerly healthy foreign-exchange reserves, but at the beginning of July was forced to give up the ghost – the baht was floated and soon went into free-fall.

Blaming its traditional allies the Americans for neglecting their obligations, Thailand sought help from Japan; Tokyo suggested the **IMF**, who in August put together a **rescue package** for Thailand of $17 billion. Among the conditions of the package, the Thai government was to slash the national budget, control inflation and open up financial institutions to foreign ownership.

Chavalit's performance in the face of the crisis was viewed as inept, more concerned with personal interests and political game-playing than managing the economy properly. In November he resigned, to be succeeded by **Chuan Leekpai**, who took up what was widely seen as a poisoned chalice for his second term. He could at least call on the services of two respected technocrats, finance minister Tarrin Nimmanhaeminda and deputy prime minister Supachai Panichpakdi, to head his economic team, but the prospects looked bleak. Businesses unable to pay their debts were looking to lay off hundreds of thousands of employees (thousands of office workers, for example, were unemployed because of the suspension of 58 financial companies), the IMF was keeping the squeeze on the government to implement its austerity measures, and analysts were forecasting that there would be at least two more years of hardship before Thailand could get back on track.

Religion: Thai Buddhism

Over ninety percent of Thais consider themselves Theravada Buddhists, followers of the teachings of a holy man usually referred to as the Buddha (Enlightened One), though more precisely known as Gautama Buddha to distinguish him from three lesser-known Buddhas who preceded him, and from the fifth and final Buddha who is predicted to arrive in the year 4457 AD. Theravada Buddhism is one of the two main schools of Buddhism practised in Asia, and in Thailand it has absorbed an eclectic assortment of animist and Hindu elements into its beliefs as well. The other ten percent of Thailand's population comprises Mahayana Buddhists, Muslims, Hindus, Sikhs and Christians.

The Buddha: his life and beliefs

Buddhists believe that Gautama Buddha was the five-hun-dredth incarnation of a single being: the stories of these five hundred lives, collectively known as the **Jataka**, provide the inspiration for much Thai art.

In his last incarnation he was born in Nepal as **Prince Gautama Siddhartha** in either the sixth or seventh cen-tury BC. Astrologers predicted that Gautama was to become universally respected, either as a worldly king or as a spiritual saviour, depending on which way of life he pur-sued. Much preferring the former idea, the prince's father forbade the boy to leave the palace grounds, and took it upon himself to educate Gautama in all aspects of the high life. Most statues of the Buddha depict him with elongated earlobes, a reference to his pampered early life, when he would have worn heavy precious stones in his ears.

The prince married and became a father, but at the age of 29 he flouted his father's authority and sneaked out into the world beyond the palace. On this fateful trip he encountered successively an old man, a sick man, a corpse and a hermit, and was thus made aware for the first time that pain and suffering were intrinsic to human life. Contemplation seemed the only means of discovering why this should be so – and therefore Gautama decided to leave the palace and become a **Hindu ascetic**.

For six or seven years he wandered the countryside leading a life of self-denial and self-mortification, but failed to come any closer to the answer. Eventually concluding that the best course of action must be to follow a "Middle Way" – neither indulgent nor overly ascetic – Gautama sat down beneath the famous riverside bodhi tree at Bodh Gaya in India, facing the rising sun, to meditate until he achieved enlightenment. For 49 days he sat crosslegged in the "lotus position", contemplating the causes of suffering and wrestling with temptations that materialized to distract him, until at last he attained **enlightenment** and so become a Buddha.

The Buddha preached his **first sermon** in a deer park in India, where he characterized his *Dharma* (doctrine) as a wheel. Thais celebrate this event with a public holiday in July known as *Asanha Puja*. On another occasion 1250 people spontaneously gathered to hear the Buddha speak, an event remembered in Thailand as *Maha Puja* and marked by a public holiday in February. For the next forty-odd years the Buddha travelled the region, converting nonbelievers and performing miracles.

The Buddha "died" at the age of eighty on the banks of a river at Kusinari in India – an event often dated to 543 BC, which is why the Thai calendar is 543 years out of synch with the Western one. Lying on his side, propping up his head on his hand, the Buddha passed into **Nirvana** (giving rise to the classic pose, the Reclining Buddha), the unimaginable state of nothingness which knows no suffering and from which there is no reincarnation. Buddhists believe that the day the Buddha entered Nirvana was the same date on which he was born and he achieved enlight-

THE BUDDHA: HIS LIFE AND BELIEFS

enment, a triply significant day that Thais honour with the *Visakha Puja* festival in May.

Buddhist doctrine

After the Buddha entered Nirvana, his **doctrine** spread relatively quickly across India, and probably was first promulgated in Thailand around the third century BC. His teachings, the *Tripitaka*, were written down in the Pali language – a derivative of Sanskrit – in a form that became known as Theravada or "The Doctrine of the Elders".

As taught by the Buddha, **Theravada Buddhism** built on the Hindu theory of perpetual reincarnation in the pursuit of perfection, introducing the notion of life as a cycle of suffering which could only be transcended by enlightened beings able to free themselves from earthly ties and enter into the blissful state of Nirvana. For the well-behaved but unenlightened Buddhist, each reincarnation marks a move up a vague kind of ladder, with animals at the bottom, women figuring lower down than men, and monks coming at the top – a hierarchy complicated by the very pragmatic notion that the more comfortable your lifestyle the higher your spiritual status.

The Buddhist has no hope of enlightenment without acceptance of the **four noble truths**. In encapsulated form, these hold that desire is the root cause of all suffering and can be extinguished only by following the eightfold path or Middle Way. This **Middle Way** is essentially a highly moral mode of life that includes all the usual virtues like compassion, respect and moderation, and eschews vices such as self-indulgence and anti-social behaviour. But the key to it all is an acknowledgement that the physical world is impermanent and ever-changing, and that all things – including the self – are therefore not worth craving. Only by pursuing a condition of complete **detachment** can human beings transcend earthly suffering.

The monkhood

In Thailand it's the duty of the 200,000-strong **Sangha** (monkhood) to set an example to the Theravada Buddhist community by living a life as close to the Middle Way as possible and by preaching the *Dharma* to the people. A monk's life is governed by 227 strict rules that include celibacy and the rejection of all personal possessions except gifts.

Each day begins with an alms round in the neighbourhood so that the laity can donate food and thereby gain themselves merit (see p.282), and then is chiefly spent in meditation, chanting, teaching and study. Always the most respected members of any community, monks also act as teachers, counsellors and arbiters in local disputes. Although some Thai women do become nuns, they belong to no official order and aren't respected as much as the monks.

Monkhood doesn't have to be for life: a man may leave the *Sangha* three times without stigma and in fact every Thai male (including royalty) is expected to **enter the monkhood** for a short period at some point in his life, ideally between leaving school and marrying, as a rite of passage into adulthood. So ingrained into the social system is this practice that nearly all Thai companies grant their employees paid leave for their time as a monk. The most popular time for temporary ordination is the three-month Buddhist retreat period – **Pansa**, sometimes referred to as "Buddhist Lent" – which begins in July and lasts for the duration of the rainy season. **Ordination ceremonies** take place in almost every wat at this time and make spectacular scenes, with the shaven-headed novice usually clad entirely in white and carried about on friends' or relatives' shoulders. The boys' parents donate money, food and necessities such as washing powder and mosquito repellent, processing around the temple compound with their gifts, often joined by dancers or travelling players hired for the occasion.

Buddhist practice

In practice most Thai Buddhists aim only to be **reborn** higher up the incarnation scale rather than set their sights on the ultimate goal of Nirvana. The rank of the reincarnation is directly related to the good and bad actions performed in the previous life, which accumulate to determine one's **karma** or destiny – hence the Thai obsession with "merit-making".

Merit-making (*tham bun*) can be done in all sorts of ways, from giving a monk his breakfast to attending a Buddhist service or donating money to the neighbourhood temple, and most festivals are essentially communal merit-making opportunities. For a Thai man, temporary ordination is a very important way of accruing merit not only for himself but also for his mother and sisters – wealthier citizens might take things a step further by commissioning the casting of a Buddha statue or even paying for the building of a wat.

One of the more bizarre but common merit-making activities involves **releasing caged birds**: worshippers buy one or more tiny finches from vendors at wat compounds and, by liberating them from their cage, prove their Buddhist compassion towards all living things. The fact that the birds were free until netted earlier that morning doesn't seem to detract from the ritual at all. In riverside and seaside wats, birds are sometimes replaced by fish or even baby turtles.

Spirits and non-Buddhist deities

While regular Buddhist merit-making insures a Thai for the next life, there are certain **Hindu gods** and **animist spirits** that most Thais also cultivate for help with more immediate problems. Sophisticated Bangkokians and illiterate farmers alike will find no inconsistency in these apparently incompatible practices, and as often as not it's a Buddhist monk who is called in to exorcize a malevolent spirit. Even the Buddhist King Bhumibol employs Brahmin priests and astrologers to determine auspicious days and officiate at certain royal ceremonies and, like his royal predecessors of the Chakri dynasty, he also associates himself with the Hindu god Vishnu by assuming the title Rama, after the seventh avatar of Vishnu and hero of the Hindu epic the *Ramayana*.

If a Thai wants help in achieving a short-term goal, like passing an exam, becoming pregnant or winning the lottery, then he or she will quite likely turn to the **Hindu pantheon**, visiting an enshrined statue of either Brahma, Vishnu, Shiva, Indra or Ganesh, and making offerings of flowers, incense and maybe food. If the outcome is favourable, devotees will probably come back to show thanks, bringing more offerings and maybe even hiring a dance troupe to perform a celebratory *lakhon chatri* as well. Built in honour of Brahma, Bangkok's Erawan Shrine is the most famous place of Hindu-inspired worship in the country.

Whereas Hindu deities tend to be benevolent, **spirits** (or *phi*) are not nearly as reliable and need to be mollified more frequently. They come in hundreds of varieties, some more malign than others, and inhabit everything from trees, rivers and caves to public buildings and private homes – even taking over people if they feel like it. So that these *phi* don't pester human inhabitants, each building has a special **spirit house** in its vicinity, as a dwelling for spirits ousted by the building's construction.

Usually raised on a short column and designed to look like a wat or a traditional Thai house, these spirit houses are generally about the size of a dolls' house, but their ornamentation is supposed to reflect the status of the humans' building – thus if that building is enlarged or refurbished, then the spirit house should be improved accordingly. Daily offerings of incense, lighted candles and garlands of jasmine are placed inside the spirit house to keep the *phi* happy – a disgruntled spirit is a dangerous spirit, liable to cause sickness, accidents and even death.

SPIRITS AND NON-BUDDHIST DEITIES

Art and architecture

Aside from pockets of Hindu-inspired statuary and architecture, the vast majority of Thailand's cultural monuments take their inspiration from Theravada Buddhism, and so it is **temples** and **religious images** that constitute Bangkok's main sights. Few of these can be attributed to any individual artist, but with a little background information it becomes fairly easy to recognize the major artistic styles. Though Bangkok's temples nearly all date from the eighteenth century or later, many of them display features that originate from a much earlier time. The National Museum (see p.72) is a good place to see some of Thailand's more ancient Hindu and Buddhist statues, and a visit to the fourteenth-century ruins at Ayutthaya (see p.233), less than two hours from Bangkok, is also recommended.

The Wat

The **wat** or Buddhist temple complex has a great range of uses, as home to a monastic community, a place of public worship, a shrine for holy images and a shaded meeting place for townspeople and villagers. Wat architecture has evolved in ways as various as its functions, but there remain several essential components which have stayed constant for some fifteen centuries.

The most important wat building is the **bot** (sometimes known as the *ubosot*), a term most accurately translated as the "ordination hall". It usually stands at the heart of the compound and is the preserve of the monks: lay persons are rarely allowed inside, and it's generally kept locked when not in use. There's only one bot in any wat complex, and often the only way to distinguish it from other temple buildings is by the eight **sema** or boundary stones which always surround it.

Often almost identical to the bot, the **viharn** or assembly hall is for the lay congregation, and as a tourist this is the building you're most likely to enter, since it usually contains the wat's principal **Buddha image**, and sometimes two or three minor images as well. Large wats may have several viharns, while strict meditation wats, which don't deal with the laity, may not have one at all.

Thirdly, there's the **chedi** or stupa, a tower which was originally conceived as a monument to enshrine relics of the Buddha, but has since become a place to contain the ashes of royalty – and anyone else who can afford it.

Buddhist iconography

In the early days of Buddhism, image-making was considered inadequate to convey the faith's abstract philosophies, so the only approved iconography comprised doctrinal **symbols** such as the *Dharmachakra* (Wheel of Law, also known as Wheel of Doctrine or Wheel of Life). Gradually these symbols were displaced by **images of the Buddha**, construed chiefly as physical embodiments of the Buddha's teachings rather than as portraits of the man.

Of the four postures in which the Buddha is always depicted – sitting, standing, walking and reclining – the **seated Buddha**, which represents him in meditation, is the most common in Thailand. A popular variation shows the Buddha seated on a coiled serpent, protected by the serpent's hood – a reference to the story about the Buddha meditating during the rainy season, when a serpent offered to raise him off the wet ground and shelter him from the storms. The **reclining** pose symbolizes the Buddha entering Nirvana at his death, while the **standing** and **walking** images both represent his descent from Tavatimsa heaven.

Hindu iconography

Hindu images tend to be a lot livelier than Buddhist ones, partly because there is a panoply of gods to choose from, and partly because these gods have mischievous personalities and reappear in all sorts of bizarre incarnations.

Vishnu has always been especially popular: his role of "Preserver" has him embodying the status quo, representing both stability and the notion of altruistic love. He is most often depicted as the deity, but frequently crops up in other human and animal incarnations. There are ten of these manifestations (or avatars) in all, of which **Rama** (number seven) is by far the most popular in Thailand. The epitome of ideal manhood, Rama is the super-hero of the epic story the *Ramayana* (see p.62) and appears in storytelling reliefs and murals in every Hindu temple in Thailand; in painted portraits you can usually recognize him by his green face. Manifestation number eight is **Krishna**, more widely known than Rama in the West, but slightly less common in Thailand. Krishna is usually characterized as a flirtatious, flute-playing, blue-skinned cowherd and is a crucial moral figure in the *Mahabarata*. Confusingly, Vishnu's ninth avatar is the **Buddha** – a manifestation adopted many centuries ago to minimize defection to the Buddhist faith.

When represented as the **deity**, Vishnu is generally shown sporting a crown and four arms, his hands holding a conch shell (whose music wards off demons), a discus (used as a weapon), a club (symbolizing the power of nature and time), and a lotus (symbol of joyful flowering and renewal). The god is often depicted astride a **garuda**, a half-man, half-bird.

Statues and representations of **Brahma** (the Creator) are very rare. Confusingly, he too has four arms, but you should recognize him by the fact that he holds no objects, has four faces (sometimes painted red), and is generally borne by a goose-like creature called a *hamsa*.

Shiva (the Destroyer) is the most volatile member of the pantheon. He stands for extreme behaviour, for beginnings and endings, and for fertility, and is a symbol of great energy and power. His godlike form typically has four, eight or ten arms, sometimes holding a trident (representing creation, protection and destruction) and a drum (to beat the rhythm of creation). In abstract form, he is represented by a **lingam** or phallic pillar.

Close associates of Shiva include **Parvati**, his wife, and **Ganesh**, his elephant-headed son. Depictions of Ganesh abound, both as statues and, because he is the god of knowledge and overcomer of obstacles (in the path of learning), as the symbol of the Fine Arts Department – which crops up on all entrance tickets to museums and historical parks.

Lesser mythological figures include the **yaksha** giants who ward off evil spirits (like the enormous freestanding ones guarding Bangkok's Wat Phra Kaeo); the graceful half-woman, half-bird **kinnari**; and the ubiquitous **naga**, or serpent king of the underworld, often depicted with seven heads.

The schools

For Thailand's architects and sculptors, the act of creation was an act of merit and a representation of unchanging truths, rather than an act of expression, and thus Thai art history is characterized by broad schools rather than individual names. In the 1920s art historians and academics began to classify these schools along the lines of the country's historical periods.

Dvaravati (sixth–eleventh centuries)

Centred around Nakhon Pathom, U Thong, Lopburi and Haripunjaya (modern-day Lamphun), the Dvaravati state was populated by Theravada Buddhists who were strongly influenced by Indian culture.

In an effort to combat the defects inherent in the poor-quality limestone at their disposal, Dvaravati-era **sculptors** made their Buddhas quite stocky, cleverly dressing the figures in a sheet-like drape that dropped down to ankle level from each raised wrist, forming a U-shaped hemline – a style which they used when casting in bronze as well. Nonetheless many **statues** have cracked, leaving them headless or limbless. Where the faces have survived, Dvaravati statues display some of the most naturalistic features ever produced in Thailand, distinguished by their thick lips, flattened noses and wide cheekbones.

Srivijaya (eighth–thirteenth centuries)

While Dvaravati's Theravada Buddhists were influencing the central plains, southern Thailand was paying allegiance to the Mahayana Buddhists of the **Srivijayan** empire. Mahayanists believe that those who have achieved enlightenment should postpone their entry into Nirvana in order to help others along the way. These stay-behinds, revered like saints both during and after life, are called **bodhisattva**, and statues of them were the mainstay of Srivijayan art.

The finest Srivijayan *bodhisattva* statues were cast in bronze and show such grace and sinuosity that they rank among the finest sculpture ever produced in the country. Many are lavishly adorned, and some were even bedecked in real jewels when first made. By far the most popular *bodhisattva* subject was **Avalokitesvara**, worshipped as compassion incarnate and generally shown with four or more arms and clad in an animal skin. Bangkok's National Museum holds a beautiful example.

Khmer and Lopburi (tenth–fourteenth centuries)

By the end of the ninth century the **Khmers** of Cambodia were starting to expand from their capital at Angkor into the Dvaravati states, bringing with them the Hindu faith and the cult of the god-king (*devaraja*). As lasting testaments to the sacred power of their kings, the

Khmers built hundreds of imposing stone sanctuaries across their newly acquired territory.

Each magnificent castle-temple – known in Khmer as a **prasat** – was constructed primarily as a shrine for a *shiva lingam*, the phallic representation of the god Shiva. Almost every surface of the sanctuary was adorned with intricate **carvings**, usually gouged from sandstone, depicting Hindu deities, incarnations and stories, especially episodes from the *Ramayana* (see p.62).

During the Khmer period the former Theravada Buddhist principality of **Lopburi** produced a distinctive style of Buddha statue. Broad-faced and muscular, the classic Lopburi Buddha wears a diadem or ornamental headband – a nod to the Khmers' ideological fusion of earthly and heavenly power – and the *ushnisha* (the sign of enlightenment) becomes distinctly conical rather than a mere bump on the head.

Sukhothai (thirteenth–fifteenth centuries)

Two Thai generals established the first real Thai kingdom in **Sukhothai** in 1238, and over the next two hundred years the artists of this realm produced some of Thailand's most refined art. Sukhothai's artistic reputation rests above all on its **sculpture**. More sinuous even than the Srivijayan images, Sukhothai Buddhas tend towards elegant androgyny, with slim oval faces and slender curvaceous bodies usually clad in a plain, skintight robe that fastens with a tassle close to the navel. Fine examples include the Phra Buddha Chinnarat image at Bangkok's Wat Benchamabophit, and the enormous Phra Sri Sakyamuni, in Bangkok's Wat Suthat. Sukhothai sculptors were the first to represent the walking Buddha, a supremely graceful figure with his right leg poised to move forwards.

Sukhothai era architects also devised a new type of chedi, as elegant in its way as the images their sculptor colleagues

THE SCHOOLS

were producing. This was the **lotus-bud chedi**, a slender tower topped with a tapered finial that was to become a hallmark of the Sukhothai era.

Ancient Sukhothai is also renowned for the skill of its potters, who produced a **ceramic ware** known as Sawankhalok, after the name of one of the nearby kiln towns. It is distinguished by its grey-green celadon glazes and by the fish and chrysanthemum motifs used to decorate bowls and plates.

Ayutthaya (fourteenth–eighteenth centuries)

From 1351 Thailand's central plains came under the thrall of a new power centred on **Ayutthaya,** and over the next four centuries, the Ayutthayan rulers commissioned some four hundred grand wats as symbols of their wealth and power. Though essentially Theravada Buddhists, the kings also adopted some Hindu and Brahmin beliefs from the Khmers – most significantly the concept of *devaraja* or god-kingship, whereby the monarch became a mediator between the people and the Hindu gods.

Retaining the concentric layout of the typical Khmer **temple complex**, Ayutthayan builders refined and elongated the prang into a **corncob-shaped tower**, rounding it off at the top and introducing vertical incisions around its circumference. The most famous example is Bangkok's Wat Arun, which though built during the subsequent Ratanakosin period (see p.291) is a classic Ayutthayan structure.

Ayutthaya's architects also adapted the Sri Lankan **chedi** so favoured by their Sukhothai predecessors, stretching the bell-shaped base and tapering it into a very graceful conical spire, as at Wat Sri Sanphet in Ayutthaya. The **viharns** of this era are characterized by walls pierced by slit-like windows, designed to foster a mysterious atmosphere by limiting the amount of light inside the building.

From Sukhothai's Buddha **sculptures** the Ayutthayans copied the soft oval face, adding an earthlier demeanour to the features and imbuing them with a hauteur in tune with the *devaraja* ideology. Like the Lopburi images, early Ayutthayan statues wear crowns to associate kingship with Buddhahood; as the court became ever more lavish, so these figures became increasingly adorned, until – as in the monumental bronze at Wat Na Phra Mane – they appeared in earrings, armlets, anklets, bandoliers and coronets. The artists justified these luscious portraits of the Buddha – who was, after all, supposed to have given up worldly possessions – by pointing to an episode when the Buddha transformed himself into a well-dressed nobleman to gain the ear of a proud emperor, whereupon he scolded the man into entering the monkhood.

Ratanakosin (eighteenth century to the present)

When **Bangkok** emerged as Ayutthaya's successor in 1782, the new capital's founder was determined to revive the old city's grandeur, and the **Ratanakosin** (or Bangkok) period began by aping what the Ayutthayans had done. Since then neither wat architecture nor religious sculpture has evolved much further.

The first **Ratanakosin building** was the bot of Bangkok's Wat Phra Kaeo, built to enshrine the Emerald Buddha. Designed to a typical Ayutthayan plan, it's coated in glittering mirrors and gold leaf, with roofs ranged in multiple tiers and tiled in green and orange. To this day, most newly built bots and viharns follow a more economical version of this paradigm, whitewashing the outside walls but decorating the pediment in gilded ornaments and mosaics of coloured glass. The result is that modern wats are often almost indistinguishable from each other, though Bangkok does have a few exceptions, including Wat Benchamabophit, which uses marble cladding for its walls

THE SCHOOLS

and incorporates Victorian-style stained-glass windows, and Wat Rajapobhit, which is covered all over in Chinese ceramics.

Early Ratanakosin sculptors produced adorned **Buddha images** very much in the Ayutthayan vein, sometimes adding real jewels to the figures, and more modern images are notable for their ugliness rather than for any radical departure from type. The obsession with size, first apparent in the Sukhothai period, has plumbed new depths, with graceless concrete statues up to 60m high becoming the norm (as in Bangkok's Wat Indraviharn), a monumentalism made worse by the routine application of browns and dull yellows. Most small images are cast from or patterned on older models, mostly Sukhothai or Ayutthayan in origin.

Books

The following books should be available in the UK, US or, more likely, in Bangkok. Publishers' details for books are given in the form "UK publisher/US publisher" where they differ. "O/p" means out of print – consult a library or specialist secondhand bookseller.

Travel

Charles Nicholl, *Borderlines* (Picador/Viking Penguin). Thrilling real-life adventures and dangerous romance in Thailand's "Golden Triangle".

James O'Reilly and Larry Habegger (eds), *Travelers' Tales: Thailand* (Travelers' Tales). This chunky volume of lively contemporary writings about Thailand makes perfect background reading for any trip to Bangkok.

Alistair Shearer, *Thailand: the Lotus Kingdom* (o/p in UK and US). Amusing and well-researched contemporary travelogue.

William Warren, *Bangkok's Waterways: An Explorer's Handbook* (Asia Books). Attractively produced survey of the capital's riverine sights, spiced with cultural and historical snippets.

Culture and society

Vatcharin Bhumichitr, *The Taste of Thailand* (Pavilion/Collier). Lovely, glossy introduction to Thailand's food, including 150 recipes adapted for Western kitchens.

Michael Carrithers, *The Buddha* (Oxford University Press). Clear, accessible account of the life of the Buddha, and the development and significance of his thought.

Sanitsuda Ekachai, *Behind the Smile* (Thai Development Support Committee). Collected articles of a *Bangkok Post* journalist highlighting the effect of Thailand's sudden economic growth on the country's rural poor.

TRAVEL, CULTURE AND SOCIETY

293

Marlane Guelden, *Thailand: Into the Spirit World* (Times Editions). Richly photographed coffee-table book focusing on the role of magic and spirits in Thai life, from tattoos and amulets to the ghosts of the violently dead.

William J. Klausner, *Reflections on Thai Culture* (Siam Society, Bangkok). Humorous accounts of an anthropologist living in Thailand since 1955.

Trilok Chandra Majupuria, *Erawan Shrine and Brahma Worship in Thailand* (Tecpress, Bangkok). The most concise introduction to the complexities of Thai religion.

Cleo Odzer, *Patpong Sisters* (Arcade Publishing). An American anthropologist's funny and touching account of her life with the bar girls of Bangkok's notorious red-light district.

Pasuk Phongpaichit and Sungsidh Piriyarangsan, *Corruption and Democracy in Thailand* (Political Economy Centre, Faculty of Economics, Chulalongkorn University). Fascinating academic study, revealing the nuts and bolts of corruption in Thailand and its links with all levels of political life.

Denis Segaller, *Thai Ways* and *More Thai Ways* (Asia Books, Bangkok). Two intriguing anthologies of pieces on Thai customs written by an English resident of Bangkok.

Thanh-Dam Truong, *Sex, Money and Morality: Prostitution and Tourism in South-East Asia* (Zed Books, o/p in US). Hard-hitting analysis of the marketing of Thailand as sex-tourism capital of Asia.

Steve van Beek, *The Arts of Thailand* (Thames and Hudson). Lavishly produced introduction to the history of Thai architecture, sculpture and painting, with superb photographs by Luca Invernizzi Tettoni.

William Warren, *Living in Thailand* (Thames and Hudson). Luscious coffee-table volume of traditional houses and furnishings; seductively photographed by Luca Invernizzi Tettoni.

History

Michael Smithies, *Old Bangkok* (Oxford University Press). Brief, anecdotal history of the capital's early development, emphasizing what remains to be seen of bygone Bangkok.

John Stewart, *To the River Kwai: Two Journeys – 1943, 1979* (Bloomsbury). A survivor of the horrific World War II POW camps along the River Kwai returns to the region.

William Warren, *Jim Thompson: the Legendary American of Thailand* (Jim Thompson Thai Silk Co, Bangkok). The engrossing biography of the ex-OSS agent, art collector and Thai silk magnate.

Joseph J. Wright Jr, *The Balancing Act: A History of Modern Thailand* (Asia Books). Highly readable analysis of the Thai political scene from the end of the absolute monarchy in 1932 until the February 1991 coup.

Fiction

Botan, *Letters from Thailand* (DK Books). Probably the best introduction to the Chinese community in Bangkok, presented in the form of letters written over a twenty-year period by a Chinese emigrant to his mother.

Alex Garland *The Beach* (Penguin/Riverhead). Gripping and hugely enjoyable thriller about a young Brit who gets involved with a group of travellers living a utopian existence on an uninhabited Thai island.

Khammaan Khonkhai, *The Teachers of Mad Dog Swamp* (Silkworm Books). The engaging story of a young teacher who encounters opposition to his progressive ideas when he is posted to a remote village school in the northeast.

Chart Korpjitti, *The Judgement* (Thai Modern Classics). Sobering modern-day tragedy about a good-hearted Thai villager who is

FICTION

295

ostracized by his hypocritical neighbours. Winner of the SEAwrite award in 1982.

Rama I, *Thai Ramayana* (Chalermnit). Slightly stilted prose translation of King Rama I's version of the epic Hindu narrative.

Nikom Rayawa, *High Banks, Heavy Logs* (Penguin). Gentle tale of a philosophizing woodcarver and his traditional elephant-logging community, which won the SEAwrite award.

Khamsing Srinawk, *The Politician and Other Stories* (Oxford University Press). A collection of brilliantly satiric short stories, which capture the vulnerability of Thailand's peasant farmers as they try to come to grips with the modern world.

Language

Thai belongs to one of the oldest families of languages in the world, Austro-Thai, and is radically different from many of the other tongues of Southeast Asia. Being tonal, Thai is difficult for Westerners to master, but by building up from a small core of set phrases, you'll quickly pick up enough to get by. Most Thais who deal with tourists speak some English, but you'll impress and get better treatment if you at least make an effort to speak a few words.

Thai script is even more of a problem to Westerners, with 44 consonants to represent 21 consonant sounds and 32 vowels to deal with 48 different vowel sounds. However, street signs in Bangkok are nearly always written in Roman script as well as Thai, and in other circumstances you're better off asking than trying to unscramble the swirling mess of symbols, signs and accents.

For the basics, the most useful **language book** on the market is *Thai: A Rough Guide Phrasebook*, which covers the essential phrases and expressions in both Thai script and phonetic equivalents, as well as dipping into grammar and providing a menu reader and fuller vocabulary in dictionary format (English–Thai and Thai–English). Among pocket dictionaries available in Bangkok, G.H. Allison's *Mini English–Thai and Thai–English Dictionary* (Chalermnit) has the edge over *Robertson's Practical English–Thai Dictionary* (Asia Books), although it's more difficult to find. The best **teach-yourself course** is the expensive *Linguaphone Thai*, which includes six cassettes.

Pronunciation

Mastering **tones** is probably the most difficult part of learning Thai. Five different tones are used – low, middle, high, falling, and rising – by which the meaning of a single syllable can be altered in five different ways. Thus, using four of the five tones, you can make a sentence just from just one syllable: *mái mài mâi mãi* – "New wood burns, doesn't it?" As well as the natural difficulty in becoming attuned to speaking and listening to these different tones, Western efforts are complicated by our tendency to denote the overall meaning of a sentence by modulating our tones – for example, turning a statement into a question through a shift of stress and tone. Listen to native Thai speakers and you'll soon begin to pick up the different approach to tone.

The pitch of each tone is gauged in relation to your vocal range when speaking, but they should all lie within a narrow band, separated by gaps just big enough to differentiate them. The **low tones** (syllables marked `), **middle tones** (unmarked syllables), and **high tones** (syllables marked ´) should each be pronounced evenly and with no inflection. The **falling tone** (syllables marked ^) is spoken with an obvious drop in pitch, as if you were sharply emphasizing a word in English. The **rising tone** (marked ~) is pronounced as if you were asking an exaggerated question in English.

As well as the unfamiliar tones, you'll find that, despite the best efforts of the transliterators, there is no precise English equivalent to many **vowel and consonant sounds** in the Thai language. The lists that follow give a rough idea of pronunciation.

VOWELS

a as in dad.

aa has no precise equivalent, but is pronounced as it looks, with the vowel elongated.

ae as in there.

ai as in buy.

ao as in now.

aw as in awe.

e as in pen.

eu as in sir, but heavily nasalized.
i as in tip.
ii as in feet.
o as in knock.
oe as in hurt, but more closed.
oh as in toe.
u as in loot.
uay "u" plus "ay" as in pay.
uu as in pool.

CONSONANTS

r as in rip, but with the tongue flapped quickly against the palate – in everyday speech, it's often pronounced like "l".
kh as in keep.
ph as in put.
th as in time.
k is unaspirated and unvoiced, and closer to "g".
p is also unaspirated and unvoiced, and closer to "b".
t is also unaspirated and unvoiced, and closer to "d".

Thai words and phrases

GREETINGS AND BASIC PHRASES

Whenever you speak to a stranger in Thailand, you should end your sentence in *khráp* if you're a man, *khâ* if you're a woman – these untranslatable politening syllables will gain good will, and should always be used after *sawàt dii* (hello/goodbye) and *khàwp khun* (thank you). *Khráp* and *khâ* are also often used to answer "yes" to a question, though the most common way is to repeat the verb of the question (precede it with *mâi* for "no"). *Châi* (yes) and *mâi châi* (no) are less frequently used than their English equivalents.

Hello	*sawàt dii*
Where are you going? (not always meant literally, but used as a general greeting)	*pai nãi?*
I'm out having fun/I'm travelling (answer to pai nãi, almost indefinable pleasantry)	*pai thîaw*
Goodbye	*sawàt dii/la kàwn*
Good luck/cheers	*chôk dii*
Excuse me	*khãw thâwt*
Thank you	*khàwp khun*
It's nothing/it doesn't matter/ no problem	*mâi pen rai*
How are you?	*sabai dii reũ?*
I'm fine	*sabai dii*
What's your name?	*khun chêu arai ?*
My name is . . .	*phõm (men)/diichãn (women) chêu . . .*
I come from . . .	*phõm/diichãn maa jàak . . .*
I don't understand	*mâi khâo jai*
Do you speak English?	*khun phûut phasãa angkrìt dâi mãi?*
Do you have . . . ?	*mii . . . mãi?*
Is there . . . ?	*. . . mii mãi?*
Is . . . possible?	*. . . dâi mãi?*
Can you help me?	*chûay phõm/diichãn dâi mãi?*

(I) want . . .	ao . . .
(I) would like to . . .	yàak jà . . .
(I) like . . .	châwp . . .
What is this called in Thai?	nîi phasăa thai rîak wâa arai?

GETTING AROUND

Where is the . . . ?	. . . yùu thîi năi?
How far?	klai thâo rai?
I would like to go to . . .	yàak jà pai . . .
Where have you been?	pai năi maa?
Where is this bus going?	rót nîi pai năi?
When will the bus leave?	rót jà àwk mêua rai?
What time does the bus arrive in . . . ?	rót theŭng . . . kìi mohng?
Stop here	jàwt thîi nîi
here	thîi nîi
over there	thîi nâan/thîi nôhn
right	khwăa
left	sái
straight	trong
near/far	klâi/klai
street	thanŏn
train station	sathăanii rót fai
bus station	sathăanii rót meh
airport	sanăam bin
ticket	tŭa
hotel	rohng raem
post office	praisanii

restaurant	*raan ahãan*
shop	*raan*
market	*talàat*
hospital	*rohng pha-yaabaan*
motorbike	*rót mohtoesai*
taxi	*rót táksîi*
boat	*reua*

ACCOMMODATION AND SHOPPING

How much is . . . ?	*. . . thão rai/kìi bàat?*
How much is a room here per night?	*hâwng thîi nîi kheun lá thão rai?*
Do you have a cheaper room?	*mii hâwng thùuk kwàa mãi?*
Can I/we look at the room?	*duu hâwng dâi mãi?*
I/We'll stay two nights	*jà yùu sãwng kheun*
Can you reduce the price?	*lót raakhaa dâi mãi?*
cheap/expensive	*thùuk/phaeng*
air-con room	*hãwng ae*
ordinary room	*hãwng thammadaa*
telephone	*thohrásàp*
laundry	*sák phâa*
blanket	*phâa hòm*
fan	*phát lom*

GENERAL ADJECTIVES

alone	*khon diaw*
another	*ìik . . . nèung*
bad	*mâi dii*
big	*yài*

clean	*sa-àat*
closed	*pìt*
cold (object)	*yen*
cold (person or weather)	*nǎo*
delicious	*aròi*
difficult	*yâak*
dirty	*sokaprok*
easy	*ngâi*
fun	*sanùk*
hot (temperature)	*ráwn*
hot (spicy)	*pèt*
hungry	*hiǔ khâo*
ill	*mâi sabai*
open	*pòet*
pretty	*sǔay*
small	*lek*
thirsty	*hiǔ nám*
tired	*nèu-ai*
very	*mâak*

GENERAL NOUNS

Nouns have no plurals or genders, and don't require an article.

bathroom/toilet	*hǎwng nám*
boyfriend or girlfriend	*faen*
food	*ahǎan*
foreigner	*fàràng*
friend	*phêuan*
money	*ngoen*
water	*nám*

GENERAL VERBS

Thai verbs do not conjugate at all, and also often double up as nouns and adjectives, which means that foreigners' most un-idiomatic attempts to construct sentences are often readily understood.

come	*maa*
do	*tham*
eat	*kin/thaan khâo*
give	*hâi*
go	*pai*
sit	*nâng*
sleep	*nawn làp*
take	*ao*
walk	*doen pai*

NUMBERS

zero	*suũn*
one	*nèung*
two	*sãwng*
three	*sãam*
four	*sìi*
five	*hâa*
six	*hòk*
seven	*jèt*
eight	*pàet*
nine	*kâo*
ten	*sìp*
eleven	*sìp èt*
twelve, thirteen, etc	*sìp sãwng, sìp sãam . . .*
twenty	*yîi sìp/yiip*
twenty-one	*yîi sìp èt*
twenty-two, twenty-three, etc	*yîi sìp sãwng, yîi sìp sãam . . .*

thirty, forty, etc	*sāam sìp, sìi sìp . . .*
one hundred, two hundred, etc	*nèung rói, sāwng rói . . .*
one thousand	*nèung phan*
ten thousand	*nèung mèun*

A Thai glossary

Avalokitesvara Bodhisattava representing compassion.

Avatar Earthly manifestation of a deity.

Ban Village or house.

Bencharong Polychromatic ceramics made in China for the Thai market.

Bodhisattva In Mahayana Buddhism, an enlightened being.

Bot Main sanctuary of a Buddhist temple.

Brahma One of the Hindu trinity: "the Creator".

Chedi Reliquary tower in Buddhist temple.

Chofa Finial on temple roof.

Dharma The teachings or doctrine of the Buddha.

Dharmachakra Buddhist Wheel of Law.

Erawan Mythical three-headed elephant; Indra's vehicle.

Farang A foreigner; a corruption of the word français.

Ganesh Hindu elephant-headed deity.

Garuda Mythical Hindu creature – half-man half-bird; Vishnu's vehicle.

Hanuman Monkey god.

Indra Hindu king of the gods.

Jataka Stories of the five hundred lives of the Buddha.

Khlong Canal.

Khon Classical dance-drama.

Kinnari Mythical creature – half-woman, half-bird.

Lakhon Classical dance-drama.

Lak muang City pillar; revered home for the city's guardian spirit.

Meru/Sineru Mythical mountain in Hindu and Buddhist cosmologies.

Mondop Small, square temple building to house minor images.

Muay Thai Thai boxing.

Mudra Symbolic gesture of the Buddha.

Mut mee Tie-dyed cotton or silk.

Naga Mythical dragon-headed serpent in Buddhism and Hinduism.

Nirvana Final liberation from the cycle of rebirths; state of non-being.

Pali Language of ancient India.

Phra Honorific term for a person – literally "excellent".

Prang Central tower in a Khmer temple.

Prasat Khmer temple complex or central shrine.

Rama Human manifestation of Hindu deity Vishnu.

Ramayana Hindu epic of good versus evil.

Ravana Rama's adversary in the Ramayana.

Rot ae/rot tua Air-conditioned bus.

Rot thammada Ordinary bus.

Sanskrit Sacred language of Hinduism, also used in Buddhism.

Sanuk Fun.

Sema Boundary stone to mark consecrated ground.

Shiva One of the Hindu trinity – "The Destroyer".

Shiva lingam Phallic representation of Shiva.

Soi Alley or side-road.

Songkhran Thai New Year.

Songthaew Pick-up used as public transport.

Takraw Game played with a rattan ball.

Talat; Talat nam; Talat yen Market; Floating market; Night market.

Tha Pier.

Thanon Road.

Theravada Main school of Buddhist thought in Thailand.

Tripitaka Buddhist scriptures.

Tuk-tuk Motorized three-wheeled taxi.

Uma Shiva's consort.

Ushnisha Cranial protuberance on Buddha images.

Viharn Temple assembly hall for the laity.

Vishnu One of the Hindu trinity – "The Preserver".

Wai Thai greeting expressed by a prayer-like gesture with the hands.

Wat Temple.

Yaksha Mythical giant.

Yantra Magical combination of numbers and letters.

INDEX

Z

Stay in touch with us!

ROUGHNEWS is Rough Guides' free
newsletter.
In three issues a year we give you
news, travel issues, music reviews,
readers' letters and the latest
dispatches from authors on the road.

I would like to receive ROUGHNEWS: please put me on your free mailing list.

NAME . . . .

ADDRESS . . . .

Please clip or photocopy and send to: Rough Guides, 62-70 Shorts Gardens,
London WC2H 9AB, England

or Rough Guides, 375 Hudson Street, New York, NY 10014, USA.

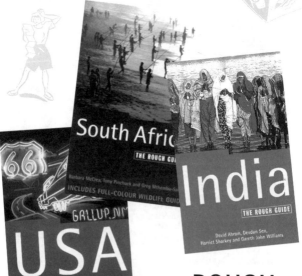

Wherever you're headed, **Rough Guides** tell you what's happening – the history, the people, the politics, the best beaches, nightlife and entertainment on your budget

GUIDES

100 destinations worldwide
...to Zimbabwe.

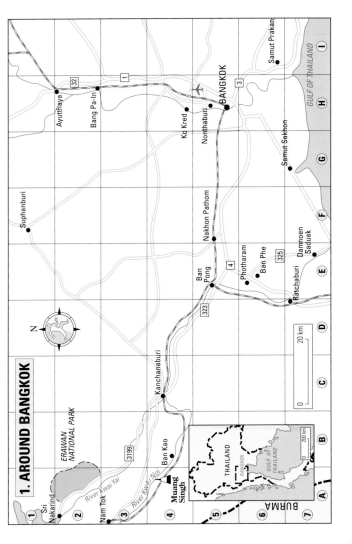

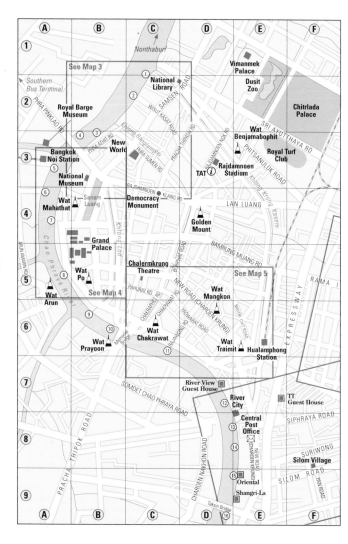

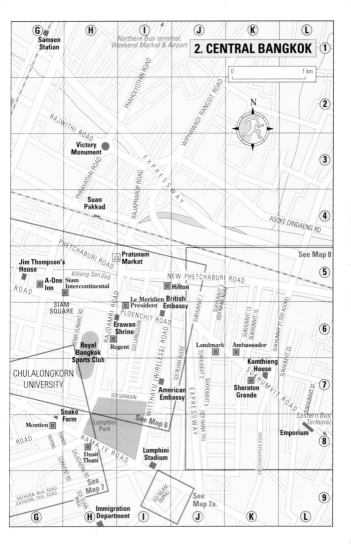

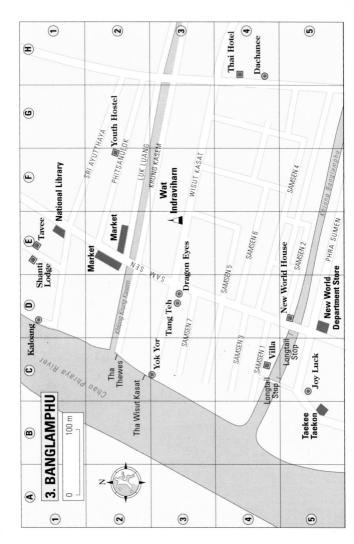

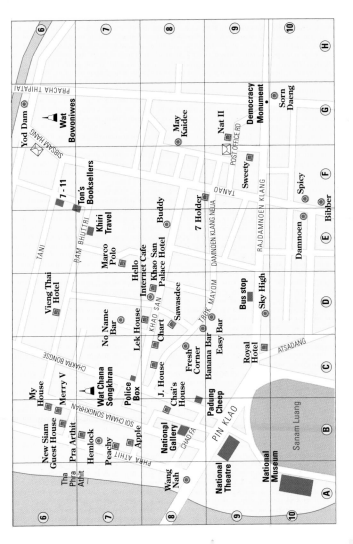

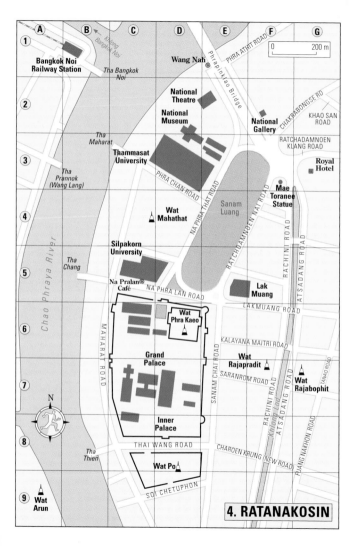

4. RATANAKOSIN

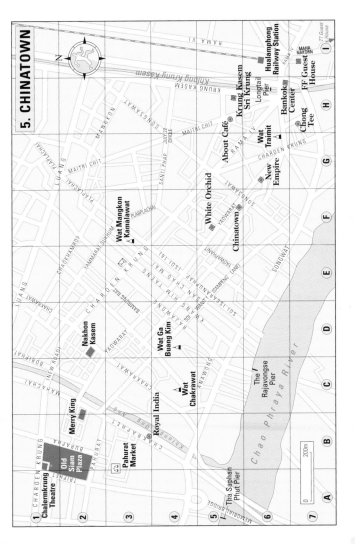

5. CHINATOWN

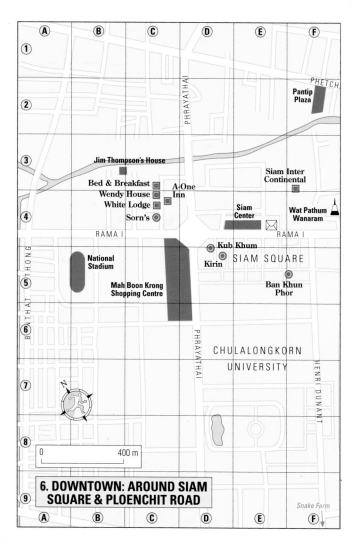

6. DOWNTOWN: AROUND SIAM SQUARE & PLOENCHIT ROAD

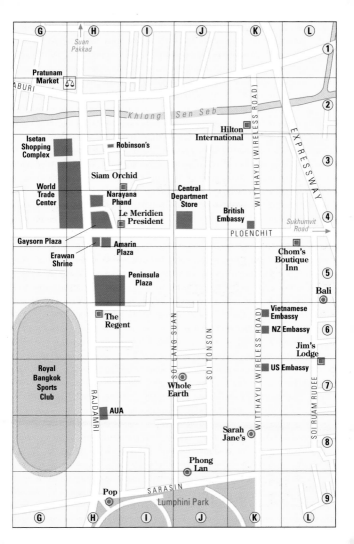

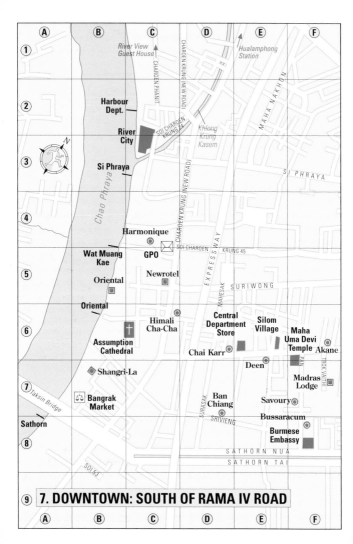

7. DOWNTOWN: SOUTH OF RAMA IV ROAD

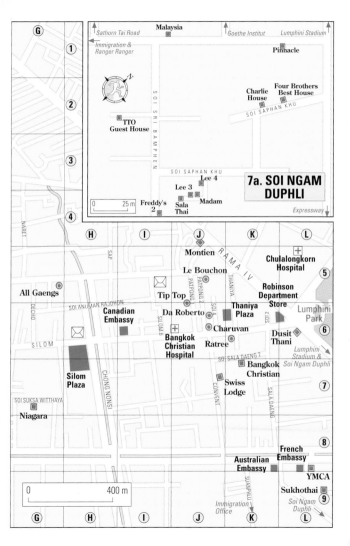

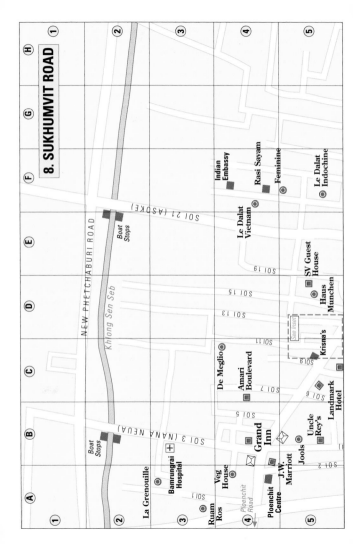

8. SUKHUMVIT ROAD

Boat Stops

La Grenouille

Bamrungrai Hospital

Veg House

Ruam Ros

Ploenchit Centre

Ploenchit Road

NEW-PHETCHABURI ROAD

Khlong Sen Seb

SOI 3 (NANA NEUA)

Boat Stops

De Meglio

Amari Boulevard

Grand Inn

J.W. Marriott

Jools

Uncle Rey's

Landmark Hotel

SOI 1

SOI 5

SOI 7

SOI 9

SOI 11

SOI 13

SOI 15

SOI 17

SOI 19

SOI 21 (ASOKE)

SOI 2

Krisna's

Haus Munchen

SV Guest House

Le Dalat Vietnam

Indian Embassy

Rasi Sayam

Feminine

Le Dalat Indochine

See inset

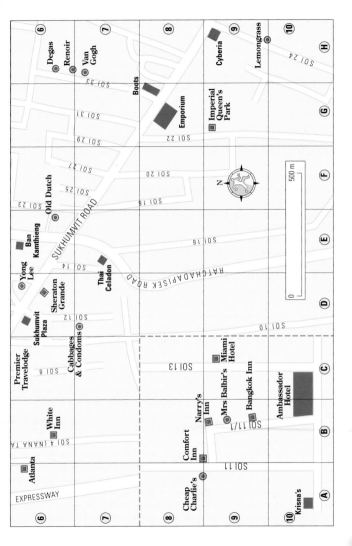

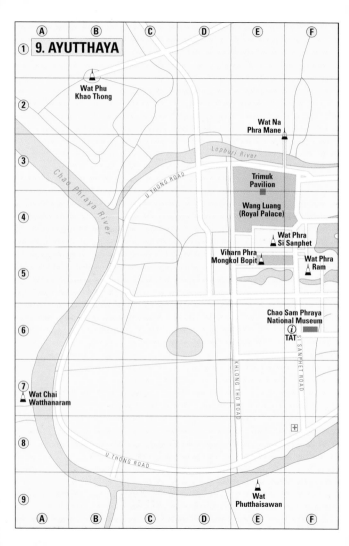

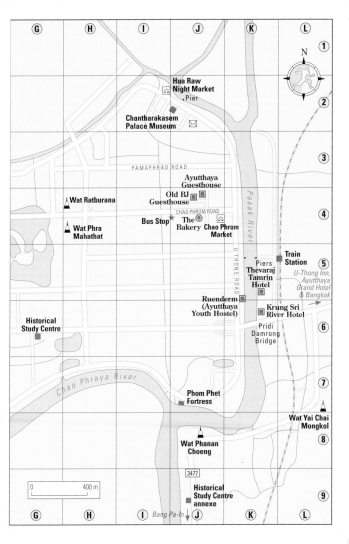

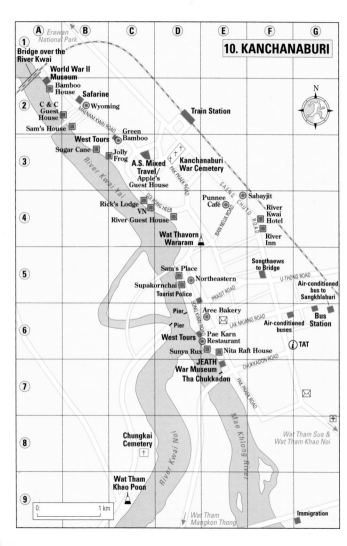